The mind is the source of all confusion

Buddha

#MentalHealthBook

How I am dealing with depression

1. English Edition, 2021

Author

Mario Dieringer

Translation from German to English

Geoff Hollingsworth

Cover, Illustrations & Graphics

Rautie, http://www.rautie.de

KDP-ISBN: 9798708509727

Content

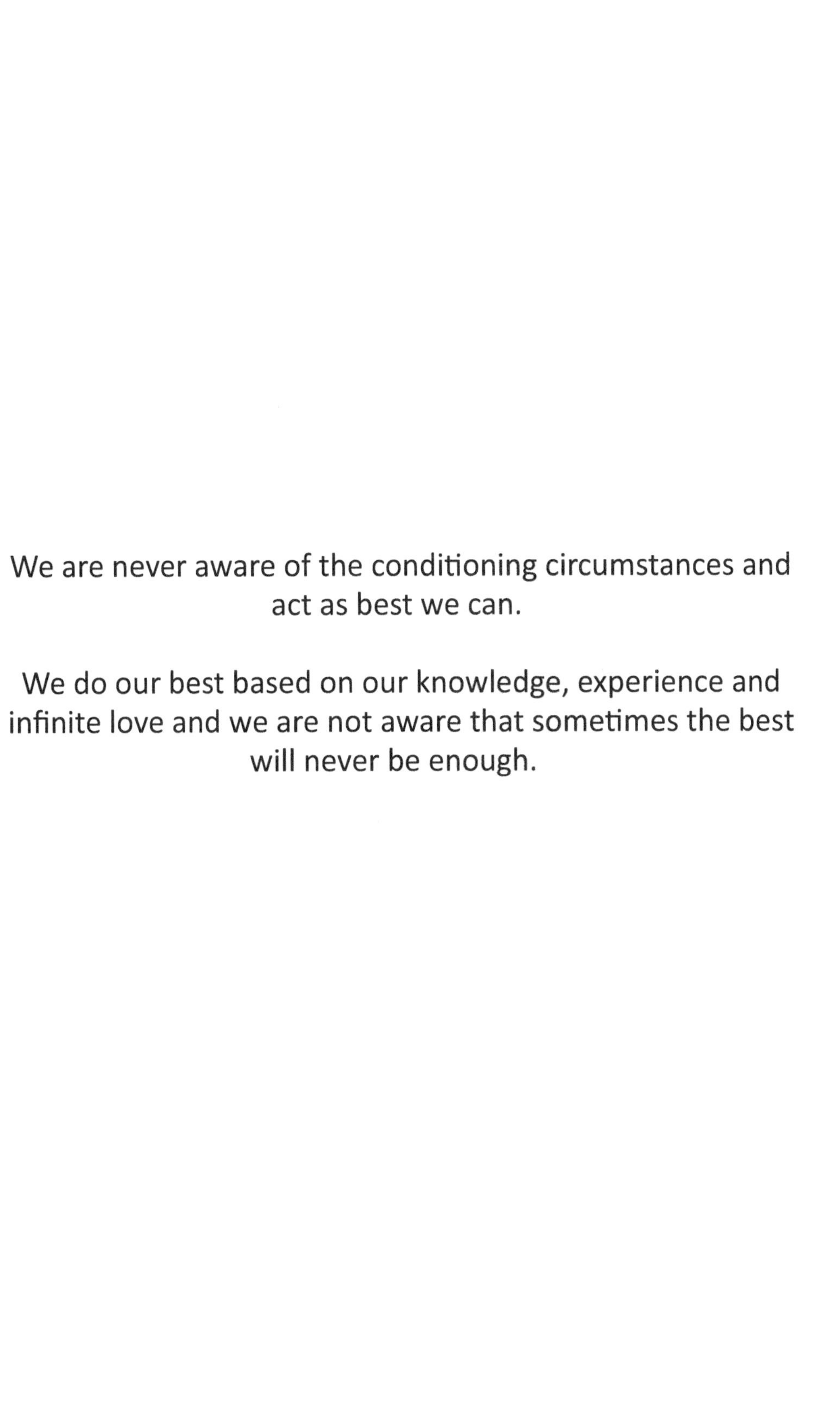

We are never aware of the conditioning circumstances and act as best we can.

We do our best based on our knowledge, experience and infinite love and we are not aware that sometimes the best will never be enough.

To whom I dedicate this book?

Every 40 seconds, somewhere on our planet, a person takes his or her own life. In Germany there is a successful suicide every hour. The number of unsuccessful suicide attempts is unknown but is alarmingly high. Suicide is the second most common cause of death among young people under the age of 25.

This book is dedicated to all those whose lives are affected by depression, fear and worry. I have written it for people with suicidal thoughts and I address myself to those who have attempted suicide or are planning one.

The following chapters are also aimed at the "healthy" general public. Almost everyone of us knows someone with depression. Many of us have experienced a suicide among our close or wider circle of family, friends, acquaintances and work colleagues. This often leads to trauma and a lifelong burden.

This book is addressed to journalists who still talk about suicide, turn victims into perpetrators and do not believe that positive courses of treatment are inspiring. In many cases, there is the Papageno effect, i.e., the imitation of treatment and the attempts for a way out, when people read or hear that full recovery is common. Especially when they can identify with the main character of the story.
Some people commit suicide because after reading a sensationalist article with precise instructions for the suicide of a prominent person, they feel they no longer stand a chance. If even a celebrity, with his millions in his bank account, fame, fans and a big villa, hasn't seen a way out, then the reader, who is suffering from depression and other mental illnesses, might think, 'What is to become of me?'. It can come to the Werther effect and the identification with the deceased.

I address everyone who deals with this subject or shows interest in it. All groups of people who want to be prepared just in case the day comes that leads to depression and more.

This book is for readers who dare to take a deeper look into another reality of life in order to gain new perspectives that can turn their everyday life upside down in a positive way.

And it is for those who now assume they are holding a sad book in their hands which is as dry as old bones and deals with death instead of life and which is like chewing gum, bleak and boring.

Short and sweet:
This book is for you, for us and a little bit for me, too.

P.S. My thoughts are not directed at terminally ill people who are faced with the decision whether they should die from their terminal illness or whether they will bring about a self-determined end in full possession of their mental faculties. I pay my deepest respect to this group of people.

Prologue

I have a vision: TREES of MEMORY.
Since March 2018 I have been hiking around the world planting Trees of Memory for suicide victims. Before that I sank into depression, survived a suicide attempt by being resuscitated and a short time later I lost my partner because he took his own life after an argument. From one moment to the next I was trapped in the depths of hell. At that point I no longer believed that I would get out of it alive.

This book describes a child's journey into the mental underworld, right down to being on the verge of death. It is my journey back into the light, into a life and into the future of an adult whose inner child has never given up dreaming. Now I have happily dedicated myself to my future dream. It is not always simple, but is healing.

This book is very personal and contains information and descriptions that would be far too private for most people to share with the world. I have made a conscious decision to publish my experiences, facts, dates, circumstances and personal interpretations. Only in this way is it possible to understand how my depressions arose and how they have developed over the years. This is the only way for readers and those affected to come closer to my suicide attempt and to gain the necessary understanding. I am convinced that it takes every single chapter to understand how I managed to find my way out of the deadly impasse and back into a life full of joy, fulfilment and exciting future prospects.

My hope is that readers will find themselves again in this book and learn to understand what makes them tick.
I would be extremely happy if you could find a sentence, a section or a chapter on the following pages that explains your life perspective and helps to change it in some positive way. I would be blessed if this book could free just one person from depression or suicidal tendencies. Perhaps it will help to save those affected in the future.

I am not a doctor. I interpret life. I follow my own world view, which saved me. I have not reinvented the wheel and I live the vision of my reality. My journalistic knowledge shows that no one is alone with their ideas, desires, longings and experiences. Sometimes we just don't understand it. We are never alone.

P.S.
All names appearing in the book, except for those that have given me permission to do so, have been changed by me to protect their personality.

Do not praise the evening before the morning

When you wake up in the morning, you don't know that the coming hours will change your whole life and nothing will be left of what your being and your presence is all about.

When I woke up on Easter Monday, 2016, at around 12 noon with a thick head, my whole body cried out for food and coffee. My friend Hans was out and his fridge was empty. So I went out to the Kollwitz-Platz in Berlin's Prenzlauer Berg to have a hearty lunch.

I was in the city since Good Friday and had been partying all the time at various parties, because I wanted to get out of Frankfurt and the bad situation there, so as not to go crazy. I had had a fight with my boy friend Jose before. It was not the first time. But this weekend all the pent-up fears and annoyances of our two and a half year relationship exploded. I was tired of being emotionally abused by him. I was tired of having the world explained to me by someone who had never travelled it. But the worst thing and the real reason for our argument was that Jose refused to have suitable therapy for his depression even though he had all the options. He was having treatment and told his therapist nothing but lies, fairy tales and excuses. When he came home from a session, he laughed himself silly because he had been pulling the psychologist's leg, as he had been doing for weeks, but he had reinvented it again and again, but always the same. It made me sick because I was afraid for him and I had worked my arse off so he could start therapy as soon as possible. I had even given him my own psychotherapy sessions.

Jose came from a family where severe depression was passed on from grandparents. His mother had two attempts at suicide behind her. She lived for decades on antidepressants that kept her alive. For many years, care was taken in the apartment to ensure that nothing was accessible with which she could take her own life. This family background did not matter to Jose. His standard comments were "Oh honey, I don't want to get that old" and "I've had suicidal thoughts since I was 16 years old. Everything has always gone well so far," and

these robbed me of sleep and scared me to death. The elevator in his mind went once again many floors down into hell, because he had stopped his antidepressants from now on.
It was not the first time, but the third time in a few months.

In those days and weeks, the man I had fallen in love with no longer existed. Not only the human warmth, the relaxed laughter, the hopeful future or the beautiful togetherness were missing, but all respect. I went elsewhere for compassion and the confrontation with my fears, because he had neither one nor the other. This was not the man I wanted to grow old with. This was not the life partner whose eyes allowed me a deep look into his desires, which I knew very well and could understand. That was no longer the man who stopped the whole world with a single embrace and gave me a stillness and peace like I had never experienced before in my life. There was only the guy who put me in the greatest fear because I could no longer be sure that I would meet him alive in the evening. I was really scared to death for him. I couldn't stand all this anymore. I deserved a bright future, just like any other person, and I didn't want to be terrorised any more. I told him, "You have four days to decide on in-patient therapy or our relationship is at an end," and I went to Berlin, where I had always travelled for many years at Easter.
My trip was accompanied by a torrent of wild texts. I warned him several times that he should stop. In the end I had to turn off my mobile phone to find my peace.

When I turned it on again at 1 pm, three days later, at Kollwitz-Platz, 120 mostly voice messages, reached me. It took over an hour to listen to everything. Jose cried, he laughed, he scolded, he raved, he was desperate, he wanted to come to Berlin. He insisted on marrying me, he made up his mind to move into an apartment with me, he pretended to do everything if only I would come back to him. There was not a single message in which he told me that he was going to the hospital. He told me that "you" would say that I had left because I wanted to dump him from the ouset. By "you" he meant his ex-boyfriend, a Catholic priest and dean, with whom he had had a seven-year relationship. He told me about conversations with his ex, where he was at that time and from whose toilet he sent me numerous messages. I was the devil incarnate to this professionally lost and morally degenerate hypocrite. It was me that Jose had met one day and for whom he had ended this hidden relationship full of disappointments, lies and psychological violence. You can imagine that this guy did not speak well of me and hated me like the devil hates holy water. Nevertheless, in his desperation, Jose went to him hoping for help and comfort. Jose's mood went up and down, back and forth, he cursed me, he pleaded desperately, he talked about things I couldn't relate to, and his voice became quieter and quieter. His last message was: "This is the last kiss for you" followed by a kiss and crying.

I listened and cried my eyes out. I tried to call him, but no one answered the phone. I wrote one text after another and explained myself again and again. I reminded him that I would come to his place tonight after all, and that we would then talk to each other in peace. I kept pressing the status message of my outgoing text messages. Finally, a message brought relief: Sent, Received and most importantly, Read.
Crying, I collapsed on a bench and thanked the good Lord a million times that everything was well again. I assured Jose, as we had agreed, I would come to him in the evening directly from the train so that we could talk.
I still don't know who read my messages. Jose had been dead for two days at that point. Suicide.

What I suffered psychologically and physically as a result can hardly be put into words. I was and still am called a murderer, I had lost the other half of my life. Many times I believed that I could only escape the emotional hell in which I was trapped by my own suicide. Again and again I heard that they wanted to help me and the only thing I felt in response and yelled in my mind was: "You can't do this!

For six months I cried day and night until one Thursday morning in the shower a journey back to the light began. A mental trip, far into the darkness of the past, towards my own suicide in December 2014, which I had only just escaped by resuscitation.
An expedition out into an incredibly intoxicating present and away into a future that knows only one goal: To hike round the world, to plant trees in remembrance of suicide victims and to give comfort and strength to the bereaved, no matter how.
A voyage of discovery that is intended to encourage people affected by suicidal thoughts and proves that there is always a future, even if you are no longer able to see it.
A journey that should show that it is always worthwhile to believe in yourself, to trust the great movement in which all our lives are involved, to hope constantly and to fight for your ideals, goals and dreams.

I would like to take you along on this adventure. If you suffer from depression and sometimes think of death, I may give you hope and courage. With my own history and my experiences I strive to rekindle in you the will to live and to be well.

I invite you into my mentally challenging and exciting life.

Welcome to Trees of Memory.

The value of the human being

When I was asked this question in September 2016 at a seminar that was supposed to help me find my salvation, it seemed quite strange to me. At my next thought I was quite horrified. I had no answer.

The person opposite did not let up. The more he asked, the more uncertain I became. How do you measure this? According to which parameters can I calculate my worth? What do I base such a calculation on? An hourly wage? The projects I had successfully implemented to date?All the things I had messed up? My unfinished tasks? The years of my life so far multiplied by my annual gross income? The number of sex partners? The size of my circle of friends? What about my friendship? Does it have a value that can be measured? I have already heard: "You are priceless". What does that mean? How much would you pay for me? Twenty Euros, but only with a happy ending? I don't have an answer because I don't know whether yours truly has a measurable value or is not at all important.

"I ask you again: What are you worth? What are you worth to me, as a friend, as a colleague, as a spouse, as an affair, as a neighbour, as a human being? Do you have a value for me that cannot be replaced or do I get something like you on every street corner? Are you a great guy, worth a million Euros? Or are you not worth the dirt on my shoes?" The workshop leader stared at me questioningly. My heart was beating desperately, my brain was pulsating, my face flickered sometimes deathly pale, then deep red. My voice failed. My eye pressure increased because I started to hold back the tears. My fist clenched in my trouser pocket. My anger began to boil and gradually turned to hatred. Finally I made a quick about turn, left the room with the loudest door slam in my life, went to the toilet and cried my eyes out.

My horrible thoughts were just going round and round. Stopping them was no longer possible with willpower alone. I took two sedatives, breathed deeply and got myself back into the workshop. For months my life was spent taking pills to get me through the days and nights without killing myself.
The more I thought about my worth, the more desperate I became the gloomier was my state of mind. Something that I could not use at all. Not now, not after only 8 months had passed since Jose had taken his own life. What was I worth to Jose? Nothing - not even so much that he felt the need to try therapy. No, I was not worth anything to him. Less than that. So little that life itself no longer had any meaning. So insignificant that death was more valuable than his lifetime, happiness or a relationship with me. No, to want to be dead was a clear statement. At the same time his suicide had other multiple truths. Being dead rather than undergoing treatment was one of them. In general, and regardless of all the people around him, not wanting to do

anything anymore, no matter how his parents, daughter and siblings would cope, was another.

The question was not answered. What am I worth? I would have preferred to have stopped functioning. No wonder, when you just realise that you are worth nothing, and have been for a lifetime. What a realisation.

The workshop continued and with it, witty, diffuse shreds of consciousness trickeld in. Here a thought and there a revelation experience. The days and weeks went by and from the question 'What are you worth', a myriad of thoughts developed from which I continue to draw strength. I was no longer forced to be valued like a piece of gold. The definition succeeds if its not subject to a currency. The question 'What are you worth' is pointless.

"WHAT AM I WORTH TO MYSELF" is the evaluation I need to pay attention to. It is part of the source of being and the oil that lubricates the personal ability to function. Our thoughts, meanings and actions come from it.
.
I remember my fellow patients in the psychosomatic hospital in Frankfurt. We all had a value deficit. The perceived worthlessness was not a fact, but a symptom of our psychological impairments. This insight is important in order to progress. Nevertheless, this idea is not nice and it hurts. Nobody wants to hear that he/she has mental deficits, whether the trait is an illness or not.

I should not anticipate my story. I try to speak for myself and tell my life's story as I have experienced it. It is one perspective among many. It is my truth that has shaped me and that has forced emotions and meanings upon me that I could gladly do without.

I strive to use this personal reality of life to give a little hope to people who suffer from depression and are plagued by suicidal thoughts. I am not a psychologist or a learned philosopher. I am experimenting with home made psychology and often fail. But in the last three years on my hikes all over Germany, I have found answers that have brought me back to a fulfilled life and have made me well.

Sometimes I still find myself in this phase, in which the heart begins to ask questions because the head no longer provides answers. I must say that these are the most precious moments that provide me with solutions by posing questions. The lightness I feel is rarely interrupted by fear and worry. If this is the case, I know the background to it and can take action against it. I have learned to listen to my heart and make unpopular decisions. Of course I cannot say if this is the wisdom of last resort. Probably not. But in the here and now it helps me. The multiple levels of knowledge that crept in have saved my life. They pumped me full of energy, with which I live my everyday life and the project TREES of MEMORY, the hike around the world to plant trees in remembrance of suicide victims, with a love that was foreign to me until then. I want to speak about it and explain the meaning that seems to be hidden behind almost everything and everyone. I would like to try to give a ray of hope to those affected and to give thoughts to those who have lost someone, which help them to overcome grief.

.

People who are affected, possibly you, could copy me. Unfortunately, the one-size-fits-all approach does not work. Your experiences are not mine. But it is conceivable that the thoughts and insights conveyed here will support you in understanding or interpreting your life in a new way. There is a possibility that you can reduce your depressions, even get rid of them, if you allow the change and keep open the alternative solution of "what if it is true". This is certainly not comfortable. I am aware of this. It will be easier if you start by not judging what you read. These are my experiences, lessons learned and conclusions based on my personal story. The end resilt is for me as logical as a mathematical calculation. But 2+3 does not always have to add up to 5. In your world it may be that seven is the only logical result. You will feel it. I wish with all my heart, that you will be able to diminish, better still, completely remove the uncertainty, the paralyzing pain of the mind, the nights of horror, the deep-seated grief and the depressing hopelessness.

I have the need to support you in this. Now, at this moment, with this book, later with a chat on Facebook or on a hike together, no matter in which country.
Get in touch with me whenever you have a need. I look forward to our exchange.

How it all began

My grandparents had already showed me what I would be worth when I was not yet even born. No sooner had my mother, who was quite young at the time, confessed that she had got herself pregnant by an Italian work colleague, than the already gloomy Swabian nightmare darkened. In no time at all, the fun-loving and incredibly good-looking young woman found herself on her way into exile in Munich-Wolfratshausen, as in a „Nacht und Nebelaktion" (reminiscent of the war years when someone undesirable dissappeared, never to be seen again). The family shame was removed, although the grandmother was pregnant at the same time and I could have grown up with my aunt. Why they did not support their own daughter will remain a mystery to me forever. A few years before, it was called racial defilement. There was no reason for joy for my mother, because at the end of her journey she found herself in a convent. Far away from home and even further from her great love, nuns were to keep an eye on her and many other underage pregnant girls who found a place there to give birth.

So under the rule of the Catholic Cross, in a rigid system typical of the 1960s in Germany, I grew in my mother's womb. In the end, my 3500 grams spread over 51 cm in the early, bitterly cold morning of 19th December , 1966, caused the amniotic sac to burst and little Mario saw the light of day. I don't know if my mother didn't think deep down inside that I was responsible for all her misfortune that was to come and of which she had no idea at that time. You could not have blamed her. Had I not developed in her womb, she could have stayed at home. Perhaps she would have run away one day with her great love Francesco Giovanni Mauro, my father, and established an extended family in safe Italy. I imagine that she hated me for having stolen her life. Only she knows the truth.

The older I got, a kind of certainty became clearer to me. Actually, I should ask her. But this is not a conversation you have with your mother. Especially not when the relationship with her is lousy and our phone calls, which we made every four to six weeks, were only due to the fact that she is my mother and that's the way it is done. I regret the coldness of heart that resonates in these words. I wish with all my heart nothing more than to have a mother or a family that sticks together. A mum, a dad and brothers and sisters for whom nothing can replace the sanctity of the family. Well, just a normal family, a little bit Italian too.

But is it possible that the events of those years and the anger I assume towards me prevented a deep love and to this day simply exclude it? Any speculation about it, whether from me or a psychologist, will remain what it is: an assumption, a possibility, another viewpoint amongst many.

If I asked my mother, there would be a clear answer: No, of course not. You are my son. When things became unpleasant, my mother has always lied. She didn't care whether it was obvious or not. Her reasoning, which I heard many thousands of times during the first 18 years of my life, was always the same: "Oh you know, I want to be left alone".
That's how she lived. Always anxious to experience as little annoyance as possible.

She did not fight, but gave up her whole life. She chose to sit it out and did not realise what a price she was paying for it. Her life is nothing but a big lie. She has learned nothing from it. She has fought for no values, herself or me.

What I am writing here is speculation. But it is my felt truth that has been confirmed so often. Of course I am aware of how weak and how unwise my mother was sometimes. She did not know how to help herself. Fear paralysed her. At no time did she want to leave her comfort zone. Not even when she was pregnant with me.
I wonder if you don't have dreams at 15? Aren't you obsessed with ideals? Don't you want to do better than your parents? I always had visions and it was not a great skill in this case to fulfill them more positively than the parents had.

I set no limits to my daydreams. Thank God, because those without dreams of the future often have little strength and will to live. I was to experience this bitterly when 48 years later Jose answered my question "What do you dream of and what do you want to do?" I assumed at the time that he was overwhelmed by the question. But no, Jose truly had no dreams or visions.

That connected him with my mother in spirit. She had no goal, no bucket list, and if she did, she wanted only love. I have wished for that as well for as long as I can remember. I did not get it from her.

My existence is an eyesore in an Aryan family's wish story. I feel that I was given an unexpressed and accusing responsibility for the shitty life of my mother. Thank God I can't be blamed for that. My baptism was a faux pas. The name Mario a rebellion. The only one in her life. Still I have to be grateful to her. My heart is Italian and the feelings are as dramatic as the path of life. The thinking is as wild and romantic as my conception.

Well, if what I heard is true, my father was a real big shot and shone out with big cars at a young age. But not only that. He was probably the only guy I ever heard of who had a record player in his car. What a cool sod. Probably my mother wasn't the only one he laid, in the back of the car. Somewhere there was a turntable, which surely put an end to every record with all the romping around. In any case, I'm not surprised that I get goose bumps and tears in my eyes when listening to ancient, scratched recordings of Italian bards. I used to be the fastest sperm of thousands, cheered on by a record groove, finding its way through every twist and turn into my mum and from there directly into the wintery, freezing cold Wolfratshausen near Munich.

To be born in a convent leaves traces. I have always had an existing aversion against crucified people. This is probably because the slap on my naked arse caused the first violent trauma. What was the first thing I saw when I opened my eyes in the convent and blinked uncertainly into my new life on earth? A dead man nailed to a wooden cross, covered in blood. And immediately afterwards I saw him again. Hanging in silver on the neck of a nun, who saw me as the fruit of original sin, rubbed me roughly and slapped me so that I cried. Tears meant that I had to catch my breath. Breath made life possible. Ergo, is it pain that makes life?

Let me think. A dead man on the cross, slaps on the bare arse and suffering that shows itself in the form of tears. A dead person, slaps and tears - all of these should regularly determine my path. But first I landed on the naked bosom of a teenager and stared at a golden shamrock with a chain, which she had received from my father for her 16th birthday. She gave me the pendant decades later and today I have it in a box, ready to find its new heir. I already know which pretty neck it should decorate one day. I hope that by then she will be aware of the importance of the gift.

Anyway, there I was, crying on the breasts of a woman who probably hated me for nine months and now had to accept that I had burst into her life as a bundle of joy. I was probably the prettiest child in the house. I only say: Italian, record player, amore.

Even if my dark-skinned looks and the big brown saucer eyes have made many a nun's heart beat with excitement and rapture, my irrevocable existence has not helped to turn an old Nazi into a loving grandfather. Even my grandmother, who was pregnant at the same time as my mother, did not stand by her daughter. There were no women who knew about the value of love and showed solidarity. I was and I still am the bastard to this day and that's how I was always treated by my grandparents. They did not know love. You don't really believe that I ever received a call from my grandmother congratulating me on my birthday? Not a single one. For nine years I didn't know that I had grandparents. In fact, they made sure that my mother had to stay with me in the convent for the first 24 months. Yes, even worse. My mother wasn't of age and so her parents decided on her behalf. Grandpa and Grandma were of the opinion that their sinful daughter should stay with the nuns and that the brat would best be put up for adoption. No sooner said than done and it didn't take long until the gentlemen from the youth welfare office showed up to bring me, the little dark-skinned child, to a family that would almost certainly have had a thing for me. In an adoptive family I would have certainly got what I was denied in my family: love. I wish with all my heart that I had been adopted.

You can guess it already: I was not released into a better childhood. According to unconfirmed hearsay my mother in her desperation attacked the officials with a knife. If the story really is true, I still don't understand why a child is left to a young person who tends to violence. I had to stay, and the office obviously didn't give a damn what became of me or under what circumstances I should grow up. The youth welfare department had guardianship until I was 18 years old. I only found out when I received the letter from the office that the guardianship ended on my 18th birthday. 15 years later I took a look at my file. It stated that all visits to my family to check on the welfare of the child had been extremely positive. When were they there? Did they see me or was I lying in my room, supposedly sleeping sweetly, beaten black and blue again under my cute sky-blue blanket, which, in the room decorated in cowboy and Indian wallpaper, lovingly watched over me, to make sure I didn't make a sound? If I did, there would be a torture pole! We know where rebellion ends. Dead on a cross. It's better to keep your mouth shut. In my youth, no one from the authorities ever showed up. Not once.

When I was 18 years old, the home for underage mothers was closed and we were invited to a last get-together. Over the years, my mother had received wonderful letters from the Mother Superior at Easter and Christmas. That is why I insisted that we go there. At first she did not want to, but finally she agreed. I had hoped that friends from back then would come. Unfortunately that was not the case. These petty and bourgeois times and their conditions are hardly imaginable by today's standards. Who were those women who were there? Who was the Rainer who lay in a crib with me and of whom there is a photo in the small brown photo album that my sister took, who has nothing to do with that time.

It was a special day for me. I saw where I was born and there was an experience that leaves me speechless to this day. On the way into the building my mother noticed that she had forgotten something in the car. She went back to get it. Driven by curiosity, I left for the convent. I remember a rather austere entrance hall and Mother Superior who appeared before me apparently out of nowhere. I did not know what to say. How do you greet a nun? She stood there, without a word, with a smile. I reached out my hand to introduce myself. She came before me, laughed and said, "Such a handsome young man. You are Mario, the son of our dear Marga." Well, that hit home. I still sit there and grin. It brings tears to my eyes. Then my mother came in and I could see that she was noticeably happy. Nevertheless, a certain restrain dominated the day. You can't blame her for that. After all, the convent management, together with the grandparents, did everything to ensure that she was never allowed to see my father again. The whole day my mother was rather reserved and looked around nervously the whole time. I had hoped that friends would be there. But she never met anyone. At some point during the extremely emotional speech of the Mother Superior, she asked me very unexpectedly to stand up in front of everyone. I was with the first children who saw the light of day in these sacred halls. The convent run home lasted 18 years and then times changed and underage mothers were no longer such a shame. When I think about it now, I'm not sure if my mother would have been happy to meet someone from the past. It's possible that there are secrets I'm not supposed to know about, but I do know about them, if they're true.

I have always hoped that the rumours were not true and that it was a perverted and infamous lie told by my stepfather, because he told them all his life to demonstrate his omnipotence.

The old geezer

The old geezer is my stepfather. He was ten years older than my mother. He was a friend of the family, although to this day I do not know how it came about and how they knew each other. He was a builder who easily drank a crate of beer every day while at work. I experienced it. I was with him twice at the building site doing a holiday job. Back then they all drank from seven o'clock in the morning. Some fathers, whose children were in my year at school, and the old geezer's work colleagues were themselves heavy drinkers and regarded as alcoholics. During the day he worked blind drunk and before, during and afterwards, drove his car. When he arrived home, he started drinking wine from the cellar. He usually made himself a spritzer and drank a bottle of wine before falling into bed. Every day he came back from his job more or less drunk. Sometimes he continued drinking with his colleagues after work in the local inns, the "Löwen" or the "Rössle". Not infrequently he would come staggering down the street singing. When he was blind drunk, he would screw mum, who usually put up with it. And when the little one, ie me, bawled, he was hit until he finally shut up.

Looking back, I ask myself why am I gay? With such a fat monster, stinking of beer and violence, surely no loving feelings could arise in relation to men? If homosexuality is not a change in the genes, I can only explain it as a deep-seated longing for love on my father's part. But fathers and old men do not fall into my prey. No matter how, it is good as it is and there is no need for me to question that. I have never suffered from it. I already knew as a young boy without ever being able to explain it that I would never have children. I do not miss it. Wife, child, house etc. would not have suited my lifestyle anyway. I never cared who loves whom. It does not matter if it is a man, a woman, a transsexual or an asexual. It is completely the same who is on top or underneath. And it's nobody's business who is having sex with who, based on desire or anything else. Love is the same in all cases. It is the only thing that counts in the lives of two people who like each other. Those who are happy and skipping through their days with a light heart, and follow what they feel, always do the right thing. In this respect I am carefree and satisfied.

Back to the topic. The question is, how the old geezer became a friend of the family and how it happened that my mother was sold off and forced to marry. That's exactly how it was. My mother was taken off to the convent in the darkness and silence of the night. During the next two years my mother was told that my biological father had cleared off and - typical for an Italian – he had left. In fact, my father was drafted into the military. As was customary abroad, a letter arrived saying: 'You military, Monday at six in the morning, otherwise prison - subito'. Yes, that's how it was. My father was forced to leave the country immediately to report to the barracks. That's why he had suddenly gone and couldn't say goodbye, especially since my grandparents had made all contact impossible. Mobile phones and co. did not exist at that time. My father wrote five letters to my mother and five letters to my grandfather. I have these letters with me and I have no idea why grandparents keep letters that prove that they belong to the lowest riffraff in society. They lied to their own daughter for years and made her believe that the creator of the brat had run away. And I have no idea why one day these letters were handed over to the unloved child with a grin. Grandpa and Grandma, you not only betrayed and sold your daughter, you tormented her emotionally. I would never have forgiven you for that, not for a moment.

My mother was brought back from the convent again secretly, when she was 18 years old. Betrayed, sold and married to a guy whose only emotional relationship was with his beer bottles and his daughter, who was born later. His flesh and blood, who thought the old geezer was okay after all. I would also say she had taken from me the whole inheritance without any thought or morals.

Dieringer is the family name of the old geezer. He did not adopt me. The name was forced upon me only so that people wouldn't gossip. In a village of 3000 souls you certainly don't know each other. In this shitty dump everyone knew that I was the Dago, of Italian descent, and I was even called Dago by teachers until the last year. I screamed out to defend my honour, referring to my mother's black hair. I fought regularly. Unfortunately it didn't help anything. I did not suspect that I would be the last of the 3000 inhabitants who would be bluntly told the truth twelve years later.

The neighbours had influenced my mother. They understood that it could not go on like this. My mother never understood that. Why did she never tell me this? Why didn't she ever take the weight off her heart and tell me the news much earlier, which would have been a relief, that I am not a Dieringer ? Because she wanted to have her peace and quiet and not have stress from the old geezer? It didn't cause her much trouble that the child of her great love was beaten almost to unconsciousness and hospitalised on a regular basis. And it was not only him who was beating me. My mother was so overwhelmed with her life, with her fate, with the violence the old geezer had done to her, that she obviously didn't know what to do other than beat my bare arse with a ladel, a belt or a carpet beater. This happened at some point every week. And I wasn't the only one who it happened to. The screams of Uwe, a neighbour's son who, like his whole family, had a mental disability, filled the entire street when he was beaten black and blue with the leather belt. No one ever cared. He was mistreated for hours by his mother and father. I could be thankful that my mother did not have much energy and at least, when she did not beat me, was reasonable. The old geezer hit me so hard that I buckled immediately when his fist, accelerated by his 120 kilos, hit me.

I was only seven years old, at a time when the class teacher used a bamboo cane to give 10 to 20 lashes to the fingertips of the outstretched hand, if you were not good or chatted in class. The teacher of religion, an old maid, whom one had to address as Miss, at 65 years of age, gave a hefty clip around the ears if you dared to talk during the school assembly or skive off, which I often did because I used the lesson to do my homework and I found the dear God really shit and useless after all he had done to me so far.
Our class was sent out to collect chestnuts for the art class the next day. So I met up with my classmates in the village where there were three old chestnut trees. We were children, the day was warm and we forgot the time. When I got home at five o'clock, there was a note on the table: I am looking for Mario. Immediately I knew that all hell would break loose if my mother was not at home in the next 10 minutes. Promptly the old geezer came home. As a child, I learned early on from my parents: If father and mother beat you senseless, then you learn to read their faces in time, if you want to survive.

At the age of seven, when his punch hit me in the face for the ninth time, I knew that his unpredictability had surprised me again, just because I had forgotten the time. "Where's your mother?" he yelled at me, steering the dirty builders' VW bus, in which he had beaten me, around the next curve with his left hand. From his lips the saliva splashed against the glass pane. I had long since lost the strength to protect myself from the next blow. "I don't know," I whispered, although I was screaming in my head. The crack of the nose and the explosion of pain when his right fist crashed into my face with full force, for the tenth time, made the blood splashing against the windshield a small matter. I was not sure if I would survive to see my next birthday. "Where is your mother?" I heard him scream again. I said no more. It was of no use. He steered the bus back into our street. There are still a good 500 meters to the house. "Tell me where your mother is," he screeched again. Without waiting for an answer, he struck again. I was lucky that I turned my head to the right at that moment. Through the mist of my tear-stained eyes I followed my blood trail on the side window. My head was rammed against the glass by his fist. But that was nothing compared to the almost broken nose earlier. I screamed like a pig on a spit and his fist repeatedly broke through my feeble shielding and hit me right in the face. I can still taste the blood on my tongue and see the stars dancing before my eyes. My mother could not be found, especially not where the chestnut trees were. She was nowhere. He raced through the village, screaming, spitting on the windshield and beating me. The intervals between the blows in my face got bigger, but it didn't stop. After about 30 minutes I had got over the worst. I didn't notice how we drove into our driveway. He pulled me out of the bus by the collar of my red plaid shirt and dragged me through the garage. Without letting go for a second, he dragged me through the house, flung open the door to my room and threw me onto the bed opposite. "I don't want to hear from you, and if your mother doesn't show up soon, I'll kick your arse." There was nothing that could stop him except the return of my mother.

That happened five minutes later. I could hear him screaming. "Where have you been?" he wanted to know. "Looking for Mario," she yelled back and the two of them raged through the apartment like madmen. Ten minutes later she was standing in my room in a rage with a carpet beater in her hand and beat me as if she had lost her mind, because it was my fault that she had got into trouble again.

Similar scenes were repeated regularly and there were times when they hit me every week. This went on until I was 13 years old, then it suddenly stopped. I think it was because I threatened to hit my mother back and broke the carpet beater into several pieces.

At 14 I could at least do what I wanted. I was left alone and no one was interested in what I was doing or where I was. At that time I entered the first music club that was not set up by the Catholic Youth Society in our village. Together with older friends from the volleyball club, where I had played for years, I went to the legendary Tropy in Albstadt-Ebingen, which was to be my Saturday evening home for over 15 years. In the following years I moved to Stuttgart to the Baghwan-Disco, the Ostgut in Berlin, the Kitkat-Club and the Lofthouse in Frankfurt. These became the places of my psychotherapy. Music with Oomph. Close your eyes and whirl on the dance floor for 6 hours at a time until physical exhaustion drove you into the taxi. I still do that, but much less often.

Years later, when I was 35 years old, once again in the place where I had spent my childhood, I visited the street where I had previously lived, the neighbours

told me, ashamed and with bowed heads, that they knew what was going on. But what should they have done? Then as now, they didn't care about the neighbours and it was nobody's business how others raised their children. Everyone wanted to live in peace and have a nice chat over
the garden fence. No one wanted to risk a bad atmosphere just because a child was being hit. I was grateful to them anyway, because they were my friends' parents. I was allowed to be there, eat there, spend the night, was
not only tolerated but also welcomed. I don't think that, as someone who was not involved, you can understand what this did to me and what all this has produced in me to this day. 53 partly shitty years, in which the question of how someone could do such a thing to an innocent child went round and round in my mind and affected my days and nights. I never received an answer. Denying and playing it down is my mother's strategy, and that of my half-sister, who never experienced her father in this way.
When I was about 18 years old, my mother suffered a heart attack. She was lying unconscious in the hallway on a Saturday morning. I had called the family doctor and he and I had to do CPR for 35 minutes until the ambulance came. Then it took another 30 minutes before her condition allowed her to be transported to the hospital. She was operated on, fitted with a pacemaker and suffered no permanent damage. She regularly uses this experience as a reason why she does not want to remember unpleasant things. Strangely enough, everything that was good is recalled very well and is told regularly.

Just like the story when I gave her the cleaning agent Ata for her birthday when I was about eight years old. The old geezer told us never to give useless presents. He always wanted to have some energy tonic for the heart. I thought that a cleaning agent would definitely be useful. Anyway, my mother never remembers if it doesn't suit her purposes.

I remember very well how she tried to run away. My earliest and only memory as a toddler is that my mother pulled me out of my child's bed in the middle of the night. She put on a petroleum-black jacket with a lily pattern or something like that and left the house with me, running and running. The old geezer is after us and I don't know if it was with kind words or violence that we were brought back into the house. As far as I remember, there were no further escape attempts. She often said she would leave him when the children were 18 years old. These were nothing more than empty words and empty promises. It was much more comfortable to stay at home. Besides, at least the old geezer had some money. As an unskilled seamstress, she could not earn a significant income. Since the house was built after their marriage, she was entitled to half. She could have left at any time. But she did not.

My age and my mother made sure again and again during my childhood that I had nothing to expect from them. Later, they assumed that they could buy me. But that did not work. I regarded the car they gave me as compensation. I did not care what they thought. There was no reason why I should be grateful. Not one. I suppose that I was the only child in Germany who dreamed that the threat to put me into a home, if I didn't do as I was told, would one day hopefully become a reality.

With every verbal put down in every discussion and with all their actions, they made me believe that I was worth nothing. I kept hearing, "You can't do anything and you have no talent for this or that". I was the personified failure and I was even too stupid to take the rubbish down or mow the lawn in such a way that anyone would be satisfied with it. There were no prospects in my life. The old geezer's rule applied. What he said was true. If I dared to go my own way, I was punished severely. The truth was in his fist.

Deep inside I kept dreaming and believing that I would certainly be useful for something and that I could certainly do something particularly well. I just had to find and prove what. One day, yes one day, I would punch the old geezer in the mouth, or better, I would defend myself with a knife if he dared to touch me again. That was my firm plan. It was never going to come to that.

I firmly believe in cause and effect and I am convinced that there is karma. Every single day of my childhood I begged God to finally get rid of this scumbag. He did not do that. I left my parents' house for good when I was 19 or 20 and never went back, with two or three exceptions. I never spoke a word to him again. He wasn't even 60 years old and had been a diabetic for a long time. He used to say, the doctors were all idiots and their advice was rejected. He got a diabetic toe that had to be amputated. Early retirement followed. He gradually became blind. This led to one operation after another. He told us the doctors were nothing more than quacks and his eyesight was on their conscience. The last time I saw him, he was sitting in front of the television at a distance of 10 cm watching a football match. It was a pathetic sight. He didn't even look round at me or exchange a word with me out of politeness. Nevertheless, I had no sympathy at that time, on the contrary. He had long since retired and my mother was always there. She cooked, she washed, she had lived in the former children's room for a long time and now and then she had a boyfriend. She put the food in the freezer, because he could defrost and warm it up almost blind when she met her lovers. Then he had his first stroke and ended up in bed. He needed nursing care. And who, incredibly, was still there? My mother. Probably she didn't want to give up her widow's pension. I know her. This was not an act of compassion or late love. The old geezer, however, made sure that neither my mother, nor I, would ever get anything from his inheritance. He gave everything to my sister. He granted my mother a right of residence until the day she got a new partner, then she would have to leave the house.

This fact, and the behaviour of my sister, are the reasons why I don't want anything more to do with her. To take part in this lousy game out of lust for money and to work against my own mother, I find so incomprehensibly indecent and unprincipled that I lack any word and understanding for it. It is not about money for me, but it would have been at that time some compensation to have at least got something from the house. I would have sold the house immediately and left everything to who ever I wanted. I didn't want to have anything more to do with it.

The old geezer had been lying in the bedroom for years, in need of nursing care and could hardly get out of bed. Then came the second stroke and he was even worse. He is said to have cried once because he could no longer see his grandchildren. And my mother told me that he thanked her once, just before he died. She cried when she spoke about it. The day came when he suffocated miserably. I don't know when that was, because no one told me about it and I happened to hear about it on the street while I was passing through, three villages away.

My dear Aunt Helga, whom I liked very much, also died during this period. Even this news was not given to me. Nobody from our huge family ever contacted me. When I confronted my sister, she lied, saying that she had a detective look for me professionally because she had no address. I lived in Frankfurt at the time and had been working as a journalist for many years and had my own website for almost a decade. In those days, as today, there are only two Mario Dieringers worldwide. One is an Austrian and the other is writing this book. I am still stunned how phoney, devious and fundamentally bad this family is. The anger that resonates in these lines is not good and I am ashamed of it. It should be over and done with. But it is not.

I couldn't beat up the old geezer and I didn't have to stab him with a knife. That's good. Karma works and in this case it was faster than I would have thought possible. Naturally, the fact that so often I wished him dead, followed by hell, would not fill my karma account with positivity. Today I see many factors differently. As a child I could not do that. With the fear of death in your heart you just want it all to stop. I had the feeling that only his passing away could save me. I did not know that my own salvation was possible. I lacked a lot of knowledge.
To move to Berlin was to seek refuge. I was allowed to be alive in the capital. The old geezer did not play a role anymore. At least I thought so. Today I'm sure that this guy sits deep in my soul and yells at me every now and then, pointing out my shortcomings. There are days when I think I'm too stupid to shit myself. My panic attacks are directly related to him. The feeling that something life-threatening is about to happen pursues me every now and then, though rarely throughout the day. In such moments I can hardly breathe and my bowels literally explode. I start to shake as if I have Parkinson's disease in its final stages. Sometimes my voice fails and I can't get on with my work. I swallow,but you can't swallow fear. The swallowing reflex stops. This leads to further panic. Then he is back and beats me up. He is omnipresent and I am not able to feel any pride. I feel like a good-for-nothing. Sometimes I ask myself why I should endure it. I do not have to put up with it. I could get out of the way. Besides suicide, there are ways to leave the panic attacks behind. I know that. But still the dark clouds hang over me and the thunder of his words do not always make my life worth living or continuing with.

Through him and my mother I have lost my ego. It was small. It was not finished and already it was torn out of my life. It was replaced by an infinite emptiness, which was covered with grief, anger, pain, doubt and disappointment. I did not endure this for long and turned away from my inner being and searched outside for what had been so brutally torn from me. To protect myself, I built a wall. A protective wall of adventure, trivialities, travel, big apartments, drugs, sex and countless acquaintances. This wall did not allow anything to get to me from outside. At the same time it made sure that my inside could no longer look out. It was difficult, to impossible, to build a fulfilling reality, which I could feel on the inside, let alone get it to the outside, and this would play an important part in my life's path. This produced additional depression, which culminated many years later in an attempted suicide. This was accompanied by the feeling of being the loneliest person in the world.

Now, years later, in which numerous problems have been solved and I am a different person, the threatening emptiness is gone. But I still feel like an orphaned human child, even when I am in the arms of a man who says he loves me. Will that ever change?

Suicide attempt, aged 9

I was not even ten years old and already broken. My daydreams about life and travelling to all the countries of the world made the days bearable. The hope that things would be better in the distant future kept me from doing stupid things. But there were moments, plenty of them, when I lost the will to live. Especially when I realised that none of the hard work I was given changed the outcome or led to any significant success.

The low point was reached in the summer of 1975. At the age of nine, I no longer had any prospects and I counted the weeks of my life by the number of punches I was given. Once again I'd had a handful of beatings. The old geezer had come home drunk and during the subsequent work in the garden, which he sweetened with litres of wine spritzer, I could not do anything right or good enough. Later in the evening he threw a full mustard jar at my mother and the doors were being slammed until late at night. The two of them screamed at the top of their voices and under the threat of violence we all remained in front of the TV. The atmosphere was as poisonous as ever and given the circumstances, lousy. When the two of them nagged and screamed at each other, I jumped up from the sofa and roared and cried. "Can't you stop yelling at each other for once!" I just couldn't take it anymore. Furious, the old geezer jumped up from the sofa and beat me until I was lying in the corner of the living room and didn't make a sound.

The following day I went to school with my dark purple glitter turtleneck sweater. Classes ended every day at shortly after twelve. At that time my mother worked as a seamstress in a basement only a few metres away from our house, together with a few other women. When I came home from school, I picked her up and there was a quick lunch. Afterwards she went back to work. When she was gone that day, I took a piece of paper and wrote a farewell letter in pencil, in scrawly handwriting "I can't do it anymore and you're to blame". I put the note under the pillow. Afterwards I rode my little orange child's bicycle through the village. There was a quarry there. At that time such places were freely accessible and nobody had to be protected. That was our adventure playground, which I often visited with friends. We climbed up the steep face and played hide and seek. When we were not in the quarry, we walked for miles, armed with flashlights, inside the large pipes into which the village stream flowed, the Starzel.

I knew the crumbly rock face inside out and it was clear that from high up I could jump off the steep edge of the quarry into the bottom. I would fall at least 30 meters, thud, break my neck and be dead. I had hidden my bike between the bushes. I did not want to be found right away. I set off on the ascent, which I had already done countless times before. My heart beat louder than any jackhammer. I wanted to be dead, but not to die. I wanted to jump, but not be in pain. Actually, I just wanted to get away. To get out of this family, actually it wasn't a family. In the weeks before, I had often spoken tearfully about wanting to go to a boarding school. Of course, that didn't happen. We were poor. How could a bricklayer and an unskilled seamstress afford boarding school? An elitist educational institution for a dreamer who couldn't even do decent maths and was too stupid to understand the simplest things? I had no future.

There I sat. High up, my short legs dangling over the edge, and the longer I stared into the depths and carefully slipped millimetre by millimetre over the edge, the greater my fear became. No visions of my past life occured, I felt nothing, I didn't even have any tears.Crying means breathing and air is life. No, I did not want to live anymore. But what would happen then? I was not able to think about it, because I was simply too young for philosophical questions. I didn't want to be beaten anymore. I begged for parents who would laugh with me and greet me with a hug. I dreamed of pillow fights, love, and just for a single moment the feeling of deeply rooted intimacy. I longed for a look that told me: "I am always here for you. Trust me." I have never seen that expression, not even today. Not from my parents, my sister, no one in the family.

My fear was too great. What if they found out that I was trying to end my young life so cruelly? Would I go to hell ? Would it really be worse in eternal purgatory than here on earth? For hours I sat high up with dangling legs and watched the little stones that I threw into the depths. I finally pulled myself up. Standing and jumping would be less problematic than pushing myself into the abyss while sitting.
I felt as if I had been standing there for an eternity, fighting against the dizziness. So many questions came up during those moments. What if I did not die, but was paralysed? I did not succeed in overcoming the immense fear of dying. In no time at all I climbed down the rocks, grabbed the bicycle and dashed home like lightning. It was late. The old geezer and my mother would soon be home. Under no circumstances could the farewell letter be found. I was standing in the bathroom, rubbing the sweat off my body, when a few minutes later, almost at the same time, both parents came home.

The old geezer had a strange idea that evening and surprised us once again with a meal that he ate constantly. I still choke when I recollect the sight. Smoked pig's ears and a pig's tail were to be eaten with hot mustard and fresh bread. You chew on the hairy cartilage. I then disappeared into my room, faked a stomach ache and preferred to stay hungry.

My real dad

By the way, there were beautiful days in my childhood and youth. Not many. Two, to be exact. Two days that were forever etched in my memory, because after that there was only one day left that was allowed to be added the hit list of best-of days. I can clearly remember each one. Hours full of jumping, dancing and a heart that threatened to burst with joy. A brain that was somewhat overloaded with all that endorphin. What do you do with so much happiness?

What do you do when your mother, urged by your neighbours, tells you that the old geezer is just your stepfather? When it comes out, in one fell swoop, that the teachers and children, who called me a Dago and often beat me up, were right after all?

It was in April 1980, sitting on the edge of the bed with the introductory words "I have something to tell you", that I learned my biological father was Italian. "Your biological father is Italian and his name is Franco..." The world stood still for a tiny moment under a huge rainbow. It still stands still when I take an imaginary travel back in time, like now, at this moment. Everything made sense. Suddenly it was clear why my mother had no contact for many years with her parents and why I met my grandparents only later in life.

At that moment an indescribable lightness and joy moved into my life. Hooray, I had nothing in common with the drunken thug. We do not share genes. I am nothing like him in anything. I will never be like him. Hallelujah. I keep telling myself that, over and over again. Hallelujah, Hallelujah, Hallelujah. I'm not a Dieringer and only carry this hated name. Immediately the differences were so obvious. The question "Why is he doing this to me?" made sense, at least in part. Nevertheless, making me pay for being brought into the marriage was a crime.
There I sat frozen in bliss. No sooner had my mother finished with the story, a thousand questions went through my mind, I was incapable of asking even a single one, other than I knew immediately I was going to look for my father. No matter what the cost. I had to find my father. He is my family, my flesh and blood. I am his.

This mother-son conversation held another surprise. My stepfather was privy to this information and approved of me being told. I am still surprised about this. But the danger would obviously have been too great that one day I would give him a thrashing, had I been told by someone else. I try to feel inside how it was for me at that time and I can't find the words to describe it. Infinite relief describes it best. How it gripped me emotionally can be seen from the fact that on the TV show "Missing", in which people search for their lost relatives, I usually cry my eyes out, because I know exactly what is going on in the child who after decades finally gets to know his father. I know the merciless feeling of not knowing who is responsible for your own appearance, character and much more. I know about the excitement when the time of getting to know each other has finally come.

Two days after this conversation I was back from school early. I had a few hours to rummage through every file in the entire house. I had to be careful, because the old geezer always noticed when you were in cupboards that were none of your business. I still wonder what he had to hide in his meaningless, boring and frustrating life. Then I found a single but important document. It was almost like finding the Holy Grail. A letter from the court and it was about my family name. It stated that my biological father, Giovanni Francesco Mauro, was not in Germany and had no right in law to paternity. In contrast to my birth certificate, on which my father is not registered, here his name was written in thick, bold letters and even his address in Italy. "My God, I have him," flashed through my mind. I felt breathless and my heart nearly stopped. I wrote down the address and rummaged a bit more. There was nothing else to find that mattered.

Bologna! First I had to get my school atlas and see where it was. Wow, it was a big city in the north of Italy. Immediately I sat down at my desk and wrote a long and emotional letter. I had to tell him everything. I wrote about my miserable life and all the anger came out. I didn't want my parents to know that I was going to search and they were not allowed to know anything about this letter. How could I do it so that they would not know? I certainly didn't feel like having a discussion about it, let alone being stopped from doing it

There was no way round it, I had to meet Papa. My heart immediately called him Papa. The worry that he might also be a drug-addicted thug did not arise. That was impossible. I want to see Papa. No matter what it cost.

The next day I had a conversation with the teacher responsibile for student support. I always liked him. He was easygoing, nice and not such an idiot as our class, maths, biology and physics teacher, who was characterless and emotionless. It was the first time that I told someone, in tears, about all the things that had happened in the previous years. Afterwards he took me in his arms for a very long time and promised to help. I should give him the letter which he would send to Italy with his name and phone number as the sender. Days, weeks and a month went by in which nothing happened. I felt an endless sadness rising in me because I didn't have a plan what to do if he didn't answer. What will I do if I do not find him? That just could not happen. Six weeks later, just before the summer break, I was invited to the teacher's room. A terrible moment, because you always think that there is trouble. Not so in this case. My teacher smiled at me and handed me a letter. "You've got a reply."

I think just then my heart stopped beating. I only saw the Italian stamp stuck on a blue envelope. The M is for Mario and Mauro had a nice flourish. Immediately I tore it open and started reading in the presence of the teacher. I was afraid to read that my father didn't want to know anything about me. Then I read for the first time the sentence that he would be very happy to see me. He was happy and grateful that I had contacted him and hoped that me and my mother were well. "I can hardly wait to see you," he wrote. I would like to call my uncle Walter, who lived only 30 km away from me and discuss everything with him. The two had already talked on the phone and agreed that my father would come to Germany to see me at Pentecost 1984. Pentecost? That was three weeks later. From that moment on I was busy. I gathered my best friends together and we made up a story that we were all going camping together. In the evening I got permission to go. It was no problem.

I can't remember why or how, but for some reason I told my mother all about it. I don't know if she was happy about it. But then the wish was overpowering that she had to see her great love again. So many things had happened and for years she had only been told lies and I think it was important for both of them to know the truth. A plan had to be made, because my mother could not leave the house just like that. From that day on she started to go for a walk. Every evening a walk through the forest. Until Pentecost.

I think I took the bus to the village where my uncle lived and that's where I first met my Italian branch of the family. My aunt opened the door, grinned at me and just said, "Look at him. Definitely a Mauro". And she was right. We all look extremely similar and if 100 people were gathered in one place, we could be recognized and fished out.

The coming hours should be informative. It was exciting because I knew that Papa was on his way. No one could say when he would arrive. There were no mobile phones. It was evening and still we waited. I was afraid that something might have happened. Night fell and I was already asleep when the door bell rang. I was too young, I was too sleepy. I didn't know what to say and just then I was the most shy, scared and speechless shadow of myself. What would happen if he found me stupid?

He did not find me stupid, on the contrary. Two hours later, he gave me a fat gold chain as a gift, which I have worn for 38 years and never taken off. They were the most ground breaking and important days of my life. Many hours in which my love developed. The best part of all was that I recognised myself. I had no resemblance whatsoever to my stepfather. Everyone always said: "You look like your mother with her black hair and dark skin." But no. They all had no idea. I don't look like my mother at all. I only inherited the "young genes" and the good skin. I am 100% the image of my father. We were like identical twins. Even the chest hair is identical. And when I meet people in Italy today, who knew my father, they often throw their hand in front of their mouth and call out in amazement: "Come tuo Papa" - just like your Papa.

Papa had brought my little sister Sabrina with him, who suddenly had a big brother who was the spitting image of her. And then there was this spectacularly beautiful woman named Angela, her mother and my father's wife. Angela is still incredibly attractive today and I love her, like my sister, with all my heart. I think it is understandable that in these initial moments my attention was focused on my father, especially because only he could speak German.

Two days after our first meeting, the time had come. Towards evening we all got up and travelled in the Italian cars into the woods to the agreed meeting point in my home town, so that my mother could meet Franco, her great love. Even Angela was there. I always wonder what it was like for her and whether she was afraid. I should ask her.

We did not have forever. There was only a short greeting and then the two of them disappeared in the forest and strolled around. I can't imagine what must have been going on in those two. To hear all the lies and to know what happened. There I stood with my uncle Walter and Angela. Sabrina stayed at home. For Angela it was certainly a difficult situation and I have great respect for her. In general I like Angela very much.

She was the one who made sure that I got to know my father. There were only rumours that Franco could have a son, but nobody knew for sure, because my Papa never talked about it and his mother hated my mother. So even in Italy everything was done to sweep me under the carpet. When asked about it by Angela, Papa always denied having a son. I cannot blame him for that. He thought that my mother no longer wanted him.

Now imagine the situation: Angela is at home, a full-blooded Italian woman, blessed with a loud, piercing voice with which she could, if necessary, call together half the town. And then she suddenly gets a visit from a former neighbour of Franco's. She has a letter with her and doesn't want it sent back to Germany. She took it because she knew where Franco lived today. I hope she got her place in paradise or a big karma boost in return.

Angela opens the letter, cannot read it, but sees the photo I had enclosed. A blind man could have seen who the father of the boy was.

When my Papa came home from work in the evening and drove his motorcycle into the street where they lived, Angela stood waiting on the balcony and waving the letter, yelled loudly. A hail of indignation and insults rained down on my poor Papa and the whole street, oh no, all of Bologna knew. What I would give to have witnessed this spectacle. It was Angela who told him that it would be mean not to meet me. She made sure that the whole family set off for Germany to meet his lost son. Thanks Angela. You are the angel of my life.

Finally, it was Pentecost Monday. It was time to say goodbye. My heart was full of sadness. My new family went back to Bologna. There remained a young man who was both happy and utterly sad. I would have loved to have packed my bags immediately and gone with him. Today I regret very much that I did not dare to do many things back then. Who knows what my life would have been like. In the following weeks my mother cried a lot and it took a long time until she found her way back into her shitty life. Sorry, but there is no other way to describe the situation. Of course I stayed in close contact with my Papa and we talked on the phone regularly. All my pocket money was spent in the phone box from which I always called him. When Angela or Sabrina were on the phone I could only say: "Ciao, Sono Mario. Come stai? Dove il mio Papa? The phone box swallowed five Marks for that sentence. I had to save for every phone call because I only got 15 Marks a week. That wasn't a great amount. As a result I didn't buy any more LPs, but invested my money in the telephone calls with Papa.

The next time I met Papa, Angela and my sister Sabrina again was a few months later at the school's country house in South Tyrol. It was arranged in great secrecy with the teachers that Papa could come and collect me in South Tyrol and I could go with him to Bologna for the day. What a palaver that was! All my classmates knew about it. I was really excited for days and then the moment came. Papa drove into the driveway with his huge swankyVolvo 765. Everyone was standing on the balcony because I had been standing by the window for hours to see when they would finally come.

I ran through the boarding house, Rasterhof, and yelled "You're here, I'll be off..."

The car door opened and first Angela's long legs appeared. Then my sister, who was still small at the time.

My family had a surprise with them. Angela's little sister Ivana, who was my age, had come along. She had a long black mane, my size, obviously Angela's sister, and beautiful. I was electrified and immediately shocked. She was the most beautiful girl I had ever met. There were 15 other spontaneously in love, pubescent, horny boys standing on the balcony watching Mario, who floated to the car in slow motion, grinning like a Cheshire cat. What a moment! It was the stage performance of my life. We went straight to Bologna, where first I had to put on a completely new outfit. I could not be shown off wearing the gear from the Swabian Alps. That was when I discovered my love for Bologna, which still lasts today. I would so much like to live there. Maybe I will one day.

Back in Germany the months passed and it would be Easter 1985 before we would meet again. Papa wrote me letters regularly and sent me a bit of money every now and then. In the meantime the old geezer knew. My contact with Papa was surprisingly OK for him. Maybe he hoped that he would get rid of me. I can't explain it any other way, because I can't believe it was due to feelings of responsibility, compassion or any form of love.

I took the train to Bologna at Easter 1985. Together with my Italian grandmother, who was visiting Germany at that time. It was the only time we had a close relationship. She accepted the situation, but she was not a loving grandmother. She and my Nazi grandparents were tarred with the same brush. Grandma Mauro hated my mother and didn't want her as a daughter-in-law any more than my father would ever become a member of my German family. But my Nazi grandparents were not quite so racist, as I was to discover surprisingly one day.

Dad's brother Igor would have been allowed to marry my mother if he had been my father. He is the only one in the family who is blond and you would not have seen that he was Italian. My grandpa told me that himself. If this wasn't my own story, I would assume that the writer had run away with his imagination. But that's how it happened and these many details are important to understand the bigger picture.

All this answered the question of what I was worth. Suddenly I had a value. I was someone. I am the son of Franco. I am the spitting image of my father and I am loved and treated with respect by all my relatives in Bologna. I didn't know it until that moment. In Germany none of my relatives cared about me, except my step-aunt Gertrud and her husband Hans, whom I both like. I was often with them. With uncle Hans I played table tennis and stuffed him with cigarettes for the whole week. They were always there for me. Unfortunately I could never tell them what was going on behind closed doors. If my aunt had asked the old geezer about it, I would not have been happy with my life. Apart from that, not one of the entire German family ever cared about me. They were all nice, but nobody was interested in how I was doing and how I was treated. None of the aunts and uncles on my mother's side ever stood up for me. They still do not care. Nor were they there after Jose's suicide. Even my own suicide attempt did not provoke any reaction. There are enough of my cousins who are in touch with me on Facebook. One has witnessed the whole disaster. No help was given. In Italy, however, Angela's relatives always want to see me and her mother has become my Nonna, my Italian grandma. They all ask me to write. What a pity that my Italian is so bad and that we always have a language barrier. But that will change in the near future. In three weeks I will have an Italian room mate from Naples. So I have someone to study and practice with.

In Papa's family there are also people who don't think its worth getting to know me or having any contact with me. One of his brothers and sister avoid all contact with me. The sister attacks me as if I were a grave robber. I saw her again after 30 years and I was very much looking forward to meeting her. She treated me like dirt. The same way she treats my sister and Angela has never been treated so shabbily and shitty by anyone in the past thirty years except by this characterless despot. I still cannot believe how someone can be so hostile. We have not seen each other for decades. I have done nothing to her. I never wanted anything. I am not party to the family inheritance dispute. Nevertheless, I had to be insulted and made to feel like an enemy. Today I see it more calmly. Karma was watching and the day will come when she will learn a lot. I have hardly any contact with my family and uncles, only with my cousins Oliver and Vittorio, to whom I write regularly.

1985 was the year I met my Papa. It was Pentecost again and during the school holidays I really wanted to go to Italy. On Whit Saturday in 1985 it was as if a train hit me at full speed and tore me into a thousand pieces when the phone rang and my uncle's mother-in-law was on the phone. She had taken on the sad task of telling me that my father had had a car accident and had died at the scene of the accident. It was the second time in my life that the world came to a standstill. I no longer felt myself. I did not hear a word. Every thought got stuck where it was in that second of nothingness. The next thing I remember is that I was just screaming and could not stop crying.

We managed to get a train ticket to Italy quite quickly and luckily I was able to go to Bologna the same day - alone. The old geezer drove me to the train station in Stuttgart. I sat in the car and just cried the whole trip. And then he did something that I will never forget and I still don't know how anyone can be so unbelievably perverse, vicious and a blatant liar like this abysmally hideous person. He began to tell me a story that has been deeply etched in my memory.

He told me about my mother and that he got a lot of opposition when he wanted to marry her. Her father, my beloved grandfather, would have offered him 20,000 Marks not to marry her. But the old geezer, the hero and do-gooder, did not let himself be put off by this and married her anyway, even though there were plenty of strange stories about my mother. My mother was said to have spent some time in a wheelchair because she suddenly couldn't walk anymore. He told me about how my mother had had something in a field with some guy. She was found lying there unconscious in a cornfield. When she woke up, she was paralysed. Somehow I still have 100 questions in my mind when I think about the situation at that time. Her suffering came to an end one day when the doorbell rang. Suddenly she got up just like that to open the door... and Jesus said: "You can walk again, Halleluja". If I hadn't been 15 years old, had rarely drunk alcohol and didn't even know what drugs were, I would not have believed it.

I have asked myself often enough over the past almost 40 years whether I really experienced this or whether my brain did something strange to me during those dramatic hours. But it is not a figment of my imagination. This is what happened. I never told my mother about it. I never asked her, because I would not get an answer anyway. I don't like to ask because then I might be told things that I don't even want to know. But of course I ask myself, what was all that about? Is there a deeper meaning? A story? What did my mother do? Was she a loose woman and allow the guys get to her and was she considered a slut? I don't know. I don't care. I'm easy to have too and I obviously enjoy it. But my private parts and my past belong to me. If she had fun, that's okay. Who am I to judge that. If something bad had happened, I would want to know about it but certainly not make a judgement.

But why did the old geezer tell me such stories in the hours after Papa's death? What did he want to achieve with it? I have no answer to this day. I see many events today in a different light. But all I can think of about this story is that the old geezer was a perverted and shitty heap of filth. How could he dare to tell such shit during those awful hours? Whether there is any truth in it or not, it doesn't matter. Why?

Papa was dead and when I arrived in Italy, the funeral had been over hours ago. In those days you could have a funeral within 24 hours. At the train station I met my grandmother and my brothers and sisters who set off again. Not being able to say goodbye has become a trauma for me. I lost the only person who ever loved me for myself. Two or three days later I left again and went back to Stuttgart. At that time I was a broken young man who had lost everything he believed in. I had no more hope. I was disillusioned. It was especially dramatic because shortly before his death Papa asked me if I would like to go to Italy to live with the whole family. I told him that I would finish school first. I had two more years to go until I got my school diploma. I couldn't speak Italian and to go into life without finishing at school, even if I could have worked in his company, a transport company, would not have been good. With a heavy heart I declined his offer. But I had a goal: the day after I got my exams I wanted to pack my bags and become Italian and be with my family. I wished so much that I had left everything and gone. But the universe always has a plan and nothing just happens. Every day, every action, for better or for worse, has a reason. Everything is always good for something. It just takes time to realise this and sometimes it takes a long time to come full circle.

Back home, my grandfather wanted to know what had happened. I told him and what answer did I get from the old Nazi: "Be glad he's dead, at least you'll inherit his company now!"

There I sat on the bench in the living room and had to listen to my Papa being nothing more than a lazy bastard anyway, and the value they attributed to him was based on a possible inheritance. He wanted to know exactly how many lorries Papa owned, which motorcycle and which car, etc. Of course I didn't inherit anything and if I had, I wouldn't have accepted it, because Sabrina and Angela needed every lira.
No matter how much Angela complains about Papa under certain conditions, he is still her great love. She never remarried.
Love can do everything, if you let it, except one thing: be replaced.

Forgiveness

Growing up under mentally extreme conditions, with fear and violence as central roles, and when gruesome strokes of fate rob you of all hope, then depression develops, which gradually changes the brain's chemistry. It has been proven that extremely unpleasant and lasting feelings, that turn into depression, transform the brain chemistry. No, this is not a joke, but corresponds to reality.

The emergence and exchange of messenger substances, such as noradrenalin and serotonin, experience a massive dysfunction. If they are not available in sufficient quantities, the metabolism between messenger substances and nerve cells changes. Biochemical processes for the transmission and processing of stimuli are thus massively disturbed and therefore the use of antidepressants is necessary and helpful. But this is a complex issue and you cannot just fill up with serotonin and then everything is fine again. It would be nice. At the same time I will not join the chorus that brands antidepressants as devil's stuff, especially on the internet.

These drugs have saved my life. I had good doctors and a bit of luck that the right drug was found for me straight away. I have no complaints or side effects.

The function and complexity of the brain is largely unknown. The number of different depressions and different degrees and effects is considerable. Many patients have the feeling of being guinea pigs and expect that after three conversations the physicians know exactly how their biochemistry ticks and what is wrong with them. This is stupid, especially since the doctor cannot take a brain sample to analyse it.

Depressive changes bring about a series of actions. Among other things, they ensure that we are not always aware of the effects of our actions or that there are blatant malfunctions. It is in these dysfunctions that the causes of suicidal thoughts and the suicide itself can be found. Modern medicine still faces a huge unknown with millions of records and at least as many realities. For those affected, depressive disorders lead to behavioural changes and the establishment of beliefs that often, possibly even mostly, shape them for the rest of their lives.

A belief works if we remember and at the same moment experience a feeling associated with it. We almost automatically perform an action that is sometimes bad and sometimes alarming, but rarely appropriate or good. Unless we are dealing with a positive experience. Therefore, we constantly experience how our personal life story shapes us. Every day we draw a comparison between the past and the present, and based on our emotions associated with memory, we make a decision for the near or distant future.

In my case this resulted in the immortality of the old geezer, who like an evil spirit wielded the sceptre over my being and my actions. Although I knew that he always had a say in everything and I begged to be left in peace, I could not break away from my stepfather. If there were a spell to get rid of unfortunate beliefs, none of us would have to suffer from trauma. So what was to happen if experiences and memories continued to tell me that I was not good enough and that fear was regulating my existence?

Jose's suicide has unfortunately made this situation worse. His death has renewed and consolidated the belief that was beaten into me. "I'm not good enough and I'm worth nothing." I was not even sufficiently appreciated for him to want to go on living. Having me at his side was exchanged for the uncertainty of death. I was unable to see how this opposite thought could become the alternative.
The thought that neither one nor the other could play a role, but that the illness of depression could make a value-free decision, did not occur to me. I had the misfortune to provide the trigger for an event that had been in the air for many years and would certainly have come one day. My begging him to go to the hospital, my threats, my love, no matter what, nothing could help Jose to see in us, or in me, a reason worth living for. At the end of the day, it remained what it had always been for me: you are worth nothing.

In recent years, many people have suggested that I forgive my old geezer, then the dear soul would have his rest. Especially religiously motivated people advised this. Regardless of the fact that I am not like that with the church and its teachings, I was frustrated because forgiveness was not possible for me. Letting it go turned out to be more difficult than anything else. My stepfather finally robbed me of part of my soul. He took away my dignity, stole my ego. Especially during childhood I wanted him dead rather than alive. I lived in the illusion that his death would bring me salvation. Then he died, and it was worse than ever before, because I was deprived of the possibility of simply hitting him in the face "one day".

His death did not release me from anger and did not bring out any mitigating feelings. The idea that he had accumulated so much bad karma that he was miserable, too young and died after years of suffering, did not change anything. On the contrary. Deep inside I, the little boy, still had the dream that one day the old geezer would turn to me with loving words, take me in his arms, tell me that he loved me, that he was sorry and that he was proud of me. Deep inside of me there was something that still wanted to believe in this possibility. As is well known, hope dies last.

It died loudly and dramatically after I learned of his passing. What should I do now? To permanently feel anger and rage and to be remotely controlled at the same time is no life. I no longer wanted to give him power, but how could I do that? From forgiveness comes healing, they say. Understanding should be the first step to inner transformation, write yogis and little Buddhas. The forgiveness of his mistakes and injustice had yet to be resolved. After what he had done to me? He is the root of all evil that drove me to suicide, which I barely survived. Forgiveness should be a great virtue and the grace of absolution the key to inner peace. What devilish thing must I take to silence the pain of my heart and the longing of a child's soul for eternal love? At regular intervals of my greatest inner despair and unrestrained anger I thought give this thing to me and I will take it, no matter what it costs.

In December 2016 I was invited to attend a discussion evening at a funeral director's in Frankfurt. A woman from Offenbach, who followed me on Facebook, had drawn my attention to it. A pastor had invited me to talk about his son's suicide on a railway line. People who were interested could also tell their story. That sounded exciting and I saw the opportunity to talk about TREES of MEMORY. Under certain circumstances the funeral director was interested in the project and I hoped he would in the future bring it to the attention of bereaved relatives. In the evening about 20 bereaved people gathered together. We sat in an open circle. Whoever wanted to could tell their story. All in all it was a difficult evening. So many terrible misfortunes. So many broken souls and hearts. The pastor spoke about two suicides in his childhood, sometime in the 50s. Both were buried in the middle of the path to the church entrance, so that the entire congregation had to trample over this final resting place of sinners for decades to get into the church. This is deeply etched in my memory and I often talk about it in my lectures. It is only one of many symbols of the inhuman way our churches dealt with the subject of suicide. Towards the end of the evening the man of God made a suggestion. He wanted to help us experience an encounter with the deceased. In the here and now we should get the chance to have a last conversation. Whoever wanted to could take part. I wanted to. I was curious, but at the same time it scared me. What would Jose say? I was afraid of a "You're to blame".

We all closed our eyes and breathed deeply into a state of relaxation that led us on a path across imaginary meadows and through forests. At some point I came to a river. It was spanned by an old arched bridge from the early Middle Ages. It was built of large blocks of natural stone. Slowly I walked on the bridge to its centre. On the right and on the left, at hip height, there were heavy, mossy stone slabs. The other bank could not be seen because a dense fog blocked the view. Hesitantly I walked into the dense grey and my fingers slipped over the damp moss growing on the stones. Arriving in the middle, the fog suddenly lifted. On the other side stood a group of people whom I did not recognise at first glance. But then I saw Jose breaking away from the crowd and slowly coming towards me. I was totally irritated because behind him I saw my beloved great-grandmother waving to me with her great laugh. She was exactly as I remembered her. This fun-loving woman whose love and dignity was not passed on to my grandma. She bought me my first aftershave: Russian Leather. I can still smell it when I close my eyes and travel into the past. Next to her stood my aunt Helga, who died shortly before or after the old geezer. She had inherited the laughter of her great-grandmother. Helga was my favourite aunt. I liked her and was allowed to be her best man. It hit me hard that I had never heard about her death and that nobody in the family had informed me. I found it just as terrible that she had never been told how ill she was. They let her die without her having been able to prepare for it. She had believed that everything would be okay. It was impossible for her to say goodbye. At least that's what I was told. Now my great-grandmother and Helga stood next to each other and shone. If I close my eyes at this very moment while writing, I can see them again and feel a wonderful lightness emanating from the two of them.

Next to them was my biological father, who transmitted such a vivid feeling of love to me that I was almost unable to pay attention to Jose. I sent him a "I miss you so much" and the look on his face told me not to worry.

There were three or four other people present that I could not recognise. As Jose stood in front of me, we hugged each other. He said nothing. I was not able to express anything verbally. No conversation, no apology, no blaming, no accusation, no "I'm okay now". We stood there and held each other tightly in our arms. Jose seemed sad and I still don't know how to sort it all out. He was always clumsy and non communicative. But this situation had nothing redeeming for him or for me. Nor did he seem tormented or like someone who has been released briefly from purgatory. The situation was characterised by quiet, value-free and intense sadness.

When I embraced him, my gaze flitted again and again to the group of people. Great-grandmother, with her snow-white hair was beside herself and pushed Helga in the ribs with her elbow, as if to say: "Look who's here".
Suddenly I see a guy in the second or third row straining and stretching and almost jumping up and down. He seemed as if he wanted to point out: "Look, I'm here too". At first I didn't even notice him. I had no idea who he was. But he was so insistent. I could not take my eyes off him. Damn, who is that, I asked myself again and again. I couldn't place him. All of a sudden I recognised him and my heart almost stopped. It was my stepfather. Unlike the other people, he was young. I guess between 20 and 30 years old.

Admittedly not unattractive at all. He was slim, sober and so different. When we looked into each other's eyes, he stopped jumping up and down. He didn't let me out of his sight and radiated an unaccustomed calm. Then he smiled. For heaven's sake, now I'm crying again just because I remember. He smiled at me with a love I never thought possible. He smiled and sent me the most loving look ever. And then he nodded at me almost respectfully and I clearly felt: "I am proud of you. Keep up the good work, don't let yourself be distracted." I felt paralysed. Stunned, I looked at Jose, who gave me another hug, grinned and then went back to the group without a word. My eyes wandered to my Papa, my great-grandmother, Aunt Helga and the other people I couldn't place. My stepfather didn't let me out of his sight as I was returning back, saying goodbye. I waved and the grey of the fog surrounded me again. Then I followed the way back into the forest and a short time later arrived back in the funeral parlour, in the midst of the other relatives.

No one spoke or said a word. Not one of them related what had just happened. A few minutes later, the circle broke up. It all happened very quickly. I tried to talk to the pastor again because of TREES of MEMORY. Unfortunately I never heard from him or the funeral director's again.

My stepfather, Georg Dieringer, brought me the inner peace that enabled me to forgive him. Even though I have never forgotten what happened and sometimes the anger and pain still come over me when I speak or write about the events of that time. Nevertheless I have forgiven him. Georg was merely the product of a tyrannical and selfish mother who made his life so difficult that he decided before his death not to end up in the family grave under any circumstances. She had mentally enslaved and abused him all her life. Not a single day went by when he did not drive by her first after leaving work. "First to Grandma" was the message constantly. When he came home, he was frustrated, drained and exhausted because he had to work in the garden or house. And he was thirsty.

Georg was the product of a generation influenced by war, privation, terror, fear and hunger, terrorised by the Nazis even in the most remote areas. His father was seriously injured in Russia. A bullet went into his head. He survived that. I remember how fascinated I was as a child when the part of his temple where the bone hadn't knit back together moved when he spoke. He had suffered no further physical damage, except that he could no longer sleep without sleeping pills. I walked hand in hand with him across the meadows and he sent me to steal plums for the first time. I loved my grandpa and was very sad when he died of hepatitis when I was 14 years old. As was custom in our Swabian country, being the oldest grandson, I had to carry the cross before the funeral procession and the coffin. That was indeed bad, but at the same time I could show him my respect once again. I was forced to pay the same tribute to my other grandfather as well, the Nazi grandfather, although I did not want to and I made that clear. I had to take part in carrying the coffin of the guy who said only one sentence to me after the accidental death of my biological father: "Be glad! At least you'll inherit something now". Decades later, my blood still boils.

Georg grew up during the war and in the post-war period, which was full of deprivation. He told me again and again that it was so cold in winter that his eyelashes froze and he couldn't open his eyes early in the morning. He would have liked to have become a lawyer. Instead, he always had to work in the potato field. At the age of 15, he started a bricklayer's apprenticeship. His life was not good all in all. But forgiveness and apology aside. I will never in my life understand how you can pass on to your children the most horrible behaviour which you yourself had suffered from. I will never understand how someone can use brute force against a child who is 100 kg lighter and does nothing but dream. It is incomprehensible why you don't have the desire to be a better father or mother than your own tyrannical parents.

If I had become a father, I would have sworn with my life to be a dad for whom you can feel nothing but love and who is available to everyone for messing about and having fun. I would have tried to do everything possible to give the children a worthy start in life. I would have supported their dreams. I would never have used violence. Never.

I obviously don't have to be able to understand everything in order to forgive Georg. What I do understand is the fact that people who do violence to others and have a very obnocious nature, have their own dramatic history and development behind them. What Georg did to me arose out of suffering. He acted out of his misery and passed his pain on to me. If I wanted to break out of this cycle of inflicting pain, I had to dissolve the suffering. For decades I was not able to escape this cycle. I could not extinguish his suffering nor my suffering, not yet.

But his smile behind the bridge has put an end to the suffering, made forgiveness possible and made space for healing. This has been instrumental in opening the door to a sort of transformation and change. Forgiveness is derived from the Greek word "amnestia" and means "not remembering". The disappearance of the dark thoughts have made space for something new again. It is no longer the harmful attitudes that materialise, but the positive things I have experienced through healing and forgiveness. Far Eastern philosophies and religions say that through forgiveness the prana, the life force, the life energy and the breath can flow again. When the blockages that hinder the flow of prana are dissolved, we become a new person. I must say that I feel something along these lines. To forgive does not mean to forget. It is more like looking at the past with different eyes. Now and then I need the memory. That helps me to understand the reasons for my actions.

Although I have been able to prove the opposite to the belief "I am not worth anything" now and again in the course of my life, it has not completely disappeared. To prove that I am capable of doing something, I always try to do it "higher, bigger and more", and this is what drives me. It is indeed exhausting, but it has made sure that I had, and have, a big, colourful life. I still experience the most incredible events. I almost have to be grateful for it. What would happen, if I did not follow this drive which causes illness? I think a great boredom would determine my existence.

But there is definitely a thank you for the fact that Georg has given me peace, without which I would not be where I am today.

Out of "Why" becomes "What"

In front of each person hangs a more or less opaque curtain that shields him from the observers in the arena of his life. As with all of us, encounters are judged directly by me, even if they were of short duration. He is a joker, busybody, egoist, liar, empathic, criminal, she is very nice, super sexy, extremely eloquent, has integrity. Whatever I have seen and perceived leads to an evaluative judgement.

When I take the curtain down and step on to their stage, I get closer to this person and lift the separation between us a little. We are now both in the spotlight. The understanding for him becomes a completely different one. Sitting in the audience can never be compared to performing on stage.

Everything I see from the new perspective can be traced back to an event. Behind every "What" there is a "Why" - both separated by a certain number of intermediate steps and yet inseparably connected.

The Why develops and leads to a What. The beatings in my childhood as a Why led to a What, the depression. The depressions are the Why for my suicide attempt, the What. The "I am worth nothing" is the Why for my business and the achievement of diverse goals is the What.

The Why is always there and is like a fat root ball deep in the earth. The Why supplies us with nutrients or it poisons us. As bad as it may sound, every perpetrator of even the most heinous act is usually a victim of a Why. No one is born as an evil monster. No killer is born as such. Every attack against me, you or your loved ones has its origin in a Why, which we usually do not see, do not know and never question. I sat down and asked myself why this or that person is the way he or she is. Only rarely do I know the Why, as with my stepfather. Mostly I do not know it or only in fragments, like with my mother. Often I do not question it I don't even want to know the Why when someone behaves like an arsehole towards me. But it would be much easier for each of us if we did know.

Everybody deals with his Why differently, but most of us are controlled by emotions and memories from our subconscious. My Why for TREES of MEMORY is one big, howling, deeply hurt Why, born out of the circumstances after the suicide of Jose and my own attempted suicide. My What, TREES of MEMORY, is the answer and is meant to protect me and others who were affected. The violence that has been done to me in the past is nothing more than pure helplessness, desperation and envy. At some point in the lives of these people there was a terrible Why, which turned an innocent child into a beating and violent tempered monster.

It is important to know my personal Why if I want to understand what makes me tick. It helps me discover how I can behave in a way which doesn't overburden me. It supports me by freeing me from depression. It is the most important element when it comes to suicidal behaviour. The Why does not take away the responsibility for my actions. Especially not when I am aware of it and have become aware of connections. But it takes away the guilt that was intended to be placed on me. It was not my responsibility that Jose refused treatment. The Why behind a person becomes the forgiveness, which I am able to give, when cause and effect reframe the picture. The old Why becomes a new reason that will one day produce a powerful What.

There are two or three people to whom I owe forgiveness. That is not easy. How am I supposed to forgive someone who makes me suffer all my life, even though all the cards are on the table and an "apology" would make it more bearable for both of us. Her pride will accompany her to the grave. My questions: "Why can't you admit for once in your life that what you did was terrible? Why aren't you able to love like any normal mother would?" will remain unanswered, even if I ask them another 100 times. She can't give me an answer. She does not deal with her Whys. The reasons for this are hidden. The fact is that it is not due to an inability on her part. The answer lies rather in a mixture of "I have finished with this" and selfish indifference. Yesterday was her birthday. We haven't had contact for years. In spirit I congratulated her and wished her another 30 years. I can forgive her. She is the way she is. She is a victim of her parents and her own circumstances. But that does not excuse her steadfast refusal to want to be a mother. Since I have worked through my anger about this, I can live very well with never seeing or speaking to her again. It was her own decision. For 50 years I had waited. The coming decades are mine. That suits me best.

The forgiveness towards my stepfather gave me a sigh of relief and removed all the negative beliefs he forced on me. I became freer and happier. It took a while, because absolving someone without getting anything back initially hurt my ego. It brings anxiety.

But forgiveness hurts the ego - I know that. Such absolution may hurt for a long time. But one day you wake up and realise that it has all been sorted.

I'm a real begrudging bastard when I've been hurt. I can forgive a lot meanwhile. I have learned to. I have developed new beliefs from it. It has made me free and healthier. But I am still Italian: I will never forget. And that's that.

My childhood dream

I have kept from you so far the other two happiest days in my life. After my training as a textile finisher, which was only a means to an end, I continued to pursue the goal of getting the dream job par excellence. Since childhood I wanted to become a policeman. My uncle Rüdiger was one. If there was a role model in the family, it was him. I looked up to him. He was always a cool guy. There was a catch to the plan. My grades were terribly bad. How was I going to manage it? I needed a miracle. Still, I could always see myself as a policeman in my dreams. There was no reason not to believe that I would not succeed. I never let myself be talked out of it. Whenever I was told that nothing would come of it I thought, "You'll see".

After finishing secondary school, which I did with a grade of 3.8, more good than bad, I got an apprenticeship as a textile finisher in Bisingen, where my mother had grown up. Mr. Bux, my trainer, who was about to retire and who was one of the old school, said that he would be able to sort it for me. He was strict, but fair. Even today I think he was the fairest and best boss I ever had. One who never ran anyone into the ground or took advantage of anyone. Someone who treated all the workers of the company with equal respect. He even managed to take away my fear of chemistry, physics and mathematics. For years, I had always scraped through with a grade 5 in these subjects.
I had the same teacher in these subjects. He was our class teacher and an idiot. He didn't really care about students and their talents. He was a washout as a teacher, not capable of imparting knowledge to children. As a result, shortly after the first year, I didn't feel like it anymore. Unfortunately, we had him until the final year.

During my three-year training I became a model student who had a lot of fun with chemistry and physics. This was clearly due to the great teachers at the Kerschensteiner vocational college in Stuttgart, where I studied for months. Suddenly I was able to break down endless formulas and sail through the periodic table blindly from back to front. Together with my classmate Norbert I was the best in class and I received a commendation in every report. In the end I finished my training with 1,5. There was a report from the company and Mr. Bux which certified that I was the best trainee ever. I am still very proud of that. Sometimes I still find it hard to believe that the dreaded company boss personally gave me such recognition. So I was able to do something after all, somehow. It was the first time I could believe in myself. I felt that something was dormant inside me that wanted to come out to show what I could do.

With these first-class grades, I could apply to the police without any problems and lo and behold, I immediately received an invitation and was allowed to travel to Biberach a few weeks later for the entrance exam. I passed. Even the sports part. I don't know how I did it, because in the speed test, for example, my paper flew off the table and it took me forever to pick it up and get to the next task. Also all the logic questions completely overwhelmed me, i.e. which number is missing in which row or when and where you should draw which points in a triangle. But at the end of the day I was congratulated for passing the test. I vividly remember how I drove home from the exam and had to stop because as I was sitting in the car I was crying my eyes out, I was so incredibly happy.

That was the second happiest day in my life after the announcement that my stepfather is not my father. My childhood dream had come true. Just like that. My unshakeable belief was rewarded. This was the first time that I made my inner self, my vision, my dream connect with reality in the outer world. I was the creator of my life, just because I believed in it, even though so many things worked against it. I learned then that my own power will always surround me and never leave me.

Many years later I would doubt that, which almost cost me my life. Today I am sure of it again and I know that everything exists within me that I wish for and therefore does not have to remain a stupid dream.

When I came home in the evening and told my parents, it was the first time that I had done something right and good. Now I was a policeman and soon a civil servant. Set up for life.. The old geezer actually bragged about it. He wasn't interested in the fact that I had received a training certificate from my previous employer, which certified that I had been the best trainee ever. But now that I was with the state, and as a future civil servant would be provided for life, I was suddenly the hero for him. But still, there was no hug from him. I was introduced with pride by my family. Certainly my stepfather often thought that it had been good that he had shown me regularly who was the boss and who set the rules. And so something did become of me after all. Actually it was his achievement that I became one of the boys in blue.

He would probably have let me paint in oil one day and hang the picture in the living room if I, the useless brat, hadn't realised that this dream job was pretty big shit. When I realised that I would be considered an arsehole by the nation for the rest of my life because 99.95% of the time policemen only bring bad news, my future was gone. I realised that I would never really progress, because I couldn't become a detective inspector with a secondary school certificate, no matter how good I was. Even though I was one of the three best and could name all the legal texts, highway junctions in Germany and all the rivers on a dummy map in my sleep, I was quickly told that my career ended at police sargeant. There was no scholarship or anything like that. I found out that most of my colleagues were power-hungry civilian failures who had nothing to offer in human terms except a big mouth. They waved their guns around and thought they were more fun than anyone else.

I realised how unfair our legislation could be when the ban on wearing masks at demonstrations was introduced. As policemen we sat on church steeples and photographed people protesting against nuclear power. If there were teachers among them, they had a big problem.

After a few months I started trembling all over when I had to go to the shooting range. When I saw for the first time what pistols and machine guns could do, I was terrified of walking around with them. Even greater was the fear of using the guns in action.

I witnessed how colleagues from Biberach were killed in the line of duty. From the riot police we had to go looking for suicides and corpses. I was glued to every word of our team leader, with tears in my eyes, when he reported how he had to inform a mother for the first time that her little child had been run over by a lorry and was no longer alive. He told us how he then drank himself into a coma for two days.

I did not want to experience all this. I could no longer do this job. It was not possible. Besides, I hated being told when I was freezing and when I had to sweat and what the appropriate clothing was for that. I died a thousand deaths because with my confused emotions, my whole future planning went down the drain and I had no idea what to do with my life as a result. There was no plan B.

Nevertheless I quit my dream job after one year. I even had a psychosomatic breakdown in the barracks and was brought unconscious to the hospital by the emergency doctor. Two days in intensive care without finding anything. Then I went home and back to the barracks.

On the day I announced my resignation at home, I flew out of the apartment without a second thought. I was forced to leave immediately. It was pure luck that the parents of my best buddy Harald's girlfriend in Hechingen had an empty granny flat that I could move into immediately. The next day I got my furniture and stuff from my room and left home.

From that day on I only saw my stepfather twice. He did not want to understand me. In his opinion all that crap about dreams and life was not worth a damn. I would have had a guaranteed job with the police for the rest of my life. He was not interested in what I did and achieved in the years to come. Once again I became a disgrace to the family.

When I announced that I was gay ... Let's leave that. Just this much: My mother never had a problem with that, on the contrary. She loved her first son-in-law more than me.

In love

The third happiest day of my life so far was the 7th of March, 1993.

After a never ending bus ride from Pirmasens to Berlin, I arrived with my fellow students in what was then the not-quite-yet capital city. In the meantime I had completed an apprenticeship as a hotel specialist and at the same time I had studied tourism marketing and business administration. I worked in the hotel 5 days a week and studied at the weekend. We were on our way to the international tourism exchange in Berlin, where we were supposed to learn something: Countries, people, adventure on the narrow-gauge railroad. For me it was the first time that I had come to Berlin. I had therefore bought a travel guide. On the bus I skimmed through the pages and what do I see in the middle of the book? A headline that said Berlin is the gay capital of Germany. "Aha" went through my mind, which was being forced to be heterosexual. Well, that is exciting. I was still not sure about my sexuality. I had a guy once, but it was so incredibly disastrous and disgusting that I was determined not to be gay. Over time, this intention lessened. The girls weren't a turn on and I felt that I didn't feel like wearing high heels and handbags and that sex was so ludicrously boring because it was extremely unattractive. I read through the two pages and memorised the "SchwuZ" in the Hasenheide. It sounded like a nice disco and I was sure that I could visit it at night. Just to see what kind of guys gays are. If they are any at all?

When we arrived at the hotel, we freshened up and quickly went out on the town. Unfortunately, all of our fellow students were lured into tourist traps and ended up in bars like "The Loo". They drank and I always hated that kind of party. So I did what I often do. I went off without a word, disappeared and headed for the Underground. I think it was the U7, which I got on just before midnight.
In the Underground I noticed two men dressed in leather from top to bottom. I had never seen gays in public before, but I was sure they must have been gays. As a boy from the Swabian Alb, I thought to myself that the two of them would surely be going to SchwuZ. What an idea, as if there was only one gay club in Berlin! Back then I didn't know that there were about 163 gay bars and clubs in Berlin. I still don't want to end up in some of them. Chances would have been

high that they would have gone to a club I couldn't get out of in one piece or seen things that would make me break out in a cold sweat.

I write that and still have to grin. Oh dear, oh dear. Anyway, I followed the leather clad men inconspicuously at a proper distance. I was walking about two hundred metres behind the guys when one of them suddenly turned round and shouted loudly through the Berlin night: "We're being followed". I stopped as if rooted to the spot. Didn't know what to do and finally caught up, red as a beetroot and rather sheepish. "Where are you going?" one of them blared out. Clearing my throat, coughing, whispering "erm to the SchwuZ" I said, in a high pitched voice. "You've come to the right place," they said, grabbed hold of me and dragged me across Kreuzberg to my first gay disco. "Oh God, if anyone sees me," shot through my brain in panic. The gay disco was packed. The music was not really my taste, but after four beers I thought it was OK and I dared to hit the dance floor.

It didn't take long before a really nice young man was smiling at me from the side. I did not know where to look. So we cast furtive glances at each other for half an hour until he finally approached me and introduced himself as Rasmus. At that moment Whitney Huston was being played. "I will always love you", she warbled. We jokingly called her the Heulboje, the howling buoy.

Rasmus was immediately really nice. He was not pushy, not poofy, did not make a weird impression and I liked him very much. He had just returned from New York a few weeks earlier, where he had spent a season abroad. He had fallen in love there and was suffering terribly back home in Berlin. His mates Armin and Horst couldn't stand his whining anymore and so dragged him to the club.

I had been back from Africa for five months. I had been on the road for a year to cross the African continent from Senegal to Madagascar. So we had something to talk about. We talked and we talked and suddenly it was six o'clock in the morning and it looked as if the club would close soon. He asked me if I wanted to go with him to Reinickendorf. It wasn't a sexual thing and I didn't have that in mind. He was too nice and our evening was too nice. Yes, I wanted to. When we arrived at his house, we sat in the kitchen, made coffee and had breakfast. We were still telling stories and sat at his little table in the kitchen until about noon. I think I made lunch then. There wasn't much in the house, but I could make a Swabian potato salad. In between we had actually kissed for the first time. My first kiss. I still remember. When we fell into bed, it was late in the day. The first time, other things, you know, had to wait until the next day. We spent a whole three days and nights together.

I didn't go to the international tourism exchange at all. I didn't see my colleagues either until I showed up at the bus on Sunday afternoon. It makes me wonder when I think about the fact that nobody called the police and looked for me. Anyway, Dieringer was being nicely "alienated", as I was told. We were both very muddled up. I had this permanent grin on my face and everybody knew that something extraordinary had happened. Of course, nobody had the slightest idea that in the past few days and nights, touching a penis was included. I remained silent as a grave with a broad grin on my face.

On Tuesday I received a postcard from Berlin. "No woman, No cry" was written on it. I danced and hopped, laughed, screamed and sang my way through my apartment in Pirmasens and had to call 23 times until Rasmus was finally at home. The time without mobile phones, and only with an answering machine, was pure torture for people who had just fallen in love. I was thankful that I had a phone and didn't have to drag myself to the phone box.

Rasmus said that he was in love and wanted to see me again. That hit me immediately and I cried my eyes out with joy and danced through my attic apartment. Oh, how I learned to hate the period of the answering machine as a result. But I kept all the tapes, all his messages, every single word, every single letter he wrote, carefully stored in a box until the day I was ready to do TREES of MEMORY decades later.
As a result, we lived togeher not only through the stormy times of young men newly in love, but also the most incredible and happiest decade of my entire life so far. We grew along with the technology into a new age of mobile phones and computers, our apartment doubled in size every two years and we travelled around the world. We discovered people, countries, adventure and ourselves. I suddenly had value. For almost 12 years he was the man at my side. The guy I wanted to grow old with. I can still say, now as before, with complete justification, that it was the most precious time of my life and gave me a life that I could never have dared to dream of. There was only one thing I did not have: a steady regular job that would bring me prosperity.

I chose adventure, I only did the jobs I wanted to do and I don't regret it. One day I ended up at IA TV, the forerunner of today's TV Berlin. I did a work placement and then some voluntary work. There I had the greatest colleagues of my entire professional career. To this day I have not forgotten those times and I still think of each and every one of them often: Ralf, Horst, Timo, Susanne and the many others. What has become of you? Where are you?

I ended up in television and after so many years and training I finally found my professional home. I was happy and content and I worked my way from job to job as a freelancer. I will be eternally grateful for this gift of the universe. Whether looking for the Titanic, making the first ascent of a mountain in Antarctica or hanging in a waterfall while ice climbing, my life became an adventure playground and I enjoyed it, even though I never really earned much money. It was not important to me. Nevertheless, money was something that determined our everyday life and to an ever increasing extent. My boyfriend was already earning very well at the beginning of his career and when he became a junior partner in the company, his income increased exorbitantly.

For us this meant ever larger apartments, shopping in the KaDeWe and insane holiday travel. We could certainly not afford everything, but a lot. In itself, it is more true to say that HE could afford many things. MY income was just about enough. Sometimes it was good, sometimes not, sometimes regular, sometimes not. At the beginning it was not so bad in our everyday life. But the more luxurious it became, the more difficult it secretly became for me. I was great at spending money and could accept it without any problems. But I did not really feel good about it. But in a partnership, that is how it is, just without a marriage certificate, you share everything: table, bed, fun, worries, money. This is how I was brought up.

So we lived in our paradise with our Egyptian Pharaoh dog Sabou, later the Carthusian cats Amor and Bantu and in between the snake Adolf. We discovered not only the world, but also the Berlin club scene. I always liked Techno. So we dived in and were soon a part of the scene with all the trimmings. There was no club door that remained closed to us and the bouncers usually just waved us through. At some point on Sunday afternoon we went home quite drunk for a long night's coma like sleep. Sometimes we came from the Ostgut at noon and went home for breakfast and showers. Often with many friends in tow. At 2 pm we were already back at the Open Air Club, where we continued dancing until 10 pm. From there we went directly to the GMF to the next dance floor. The fun had to end at three o'clock in the morning because we had to go to work at 9 o'clock. This went on for about 6 years. During this time we also experimented sexually and more or less voluntarily gave ourselves space to play around. Some of what the other person did was known, some remained a dark secret.

As exciting as this was, it changed us. It changed our relationship. In combination with our drug experiments it was cool, but in this way we lost each other somewhere and at some point. Our behavior created our new reality. This reality had less and less to do with the respect and dignity you should have for the person you love. Self-imposed standards were increasingly

disregarded. The man I loved so incredibly changed gradually, but drastically. The same can probably be said of me.

One day he stood in front of me, one day before we were to go on holiday to Spain, and told me that he was not going home with me right now because he was going home with someone else first. Or in Rome, when without warning he got into a cab with a guy and left me alone with his buddy, who subsequently came with meback to the hotel.

Similar scenes happened again and again. I had a golden rule for myself that I never broke in my life, no matter what other crap I did. When my boyfriend asks me to come home with him, I'm there when I know that he can't live with me staying on at the club. And I would never let it be said that I'm just going somewhere to fuck and then I'll come home. For others such a relationship model can work and can certainly make lots of things easier and is more honest in a way. But it breaks my heart. Now that I'm older, I still haven't relaxed in this respect, on the contrary. In fact, I want to relax less now than before. I want to concentrate on my boyfriend, that's enough. I'm glad that my hormones are at a low and that I don't have to live through sex-oriented days anymore.

I lived a life with him that I could never have afforded on my own. We lived in 250 incredibly amazing square meters in Kreuzberg and we were popular and well known everywhere. At the same time my worthlessness returned a bit and was regularly fed, through one thing or another. I was repeatedly hurt to the core, but I loved this man without any ifs and buts. He was my great love and we fitted together so well that I wanted nothing more than to grow old with him. Our life began as a little fairy tale and that's how it should go on.

Even today the eyes of the audience start to shine when I tell them about our meeting. In the gay scene there is a consensus: this was a great gift from the universe. This is exactly how I see it too. Our relationship was not taken for granted in everything. I am infinitely grateful for that. There are too many fucked up guys here in Berlin. All of them disillusioned to the core because they lost more and more trust because of some guys and disappointments. They pass on an inherited guilt to their new boyfriend and are naturally disappointed again. In their eyes, it is always the other at fault, without them realizing that they are the more essential part of the problem. I never wanted to become like that. Above all I wanted to feel love and give love. We both did. We were loud and strong, until love became more and more subdued. It became more and more difficult for me to love deeply, even when I was screaming inside. I wanted to shake him and did not understand what had happened to us.

I didn't understand why I started to get back at him in the same way. I had a man whom I loved to bits and he loved me as well. But my feelings of worthlessness had reached a low point. After a long period of silence, my basic beliefs spoke to me and told me that I was extremely inadequate and no longer deserved the man. "You are not worth it". We were no longer on the same energetic wavelength. My subconscious tried with all its might to balance this imbalance. People who also suffer from such a worthlessness, in such cases either look for reasons why you could separate, or develop a behaviour which causes your partner to want to separate, which then fits in well with the victim state you are looking for. My task was clear in the meantime. I was going down both roads and either one or the other would happen. Unless we realised in time that everything would get out of hand. We could change and return to ourselves in the name of love and of all we had achieved together.

This could have happened if I had known then what I am aware of today. But at that time I didn't even know myself. I had no idea about my depressions. I didn't know what destructive forces were working in me. I had never heard of "underlying self beliefs". I loved this man and would have rather died than live without him, and yet I destroyed myself more and more step by step. I was devastated, I broke up our life. I destroyed what had a promising future and had worked so well for over a decade . We were incredibly happy people whose identical energy of unconditional love had attracted each other. Only because of this could our impressive relationship have happened. That is the recipe for success, if you will. We shared the same energy and thus formed a harmonious unity. This energy synchronised and duplicated itself. This is why we felt heaven on earth. We had every reason to do so, because through this we believed in love and this belief linked our individual idea of relationship and love with a meaning, which thereby triggered even higher energies. This enabled us to develop further, made free space possible and established a life in emotional security. This insane emotional success was an effect that came from a cause. Namely belief, confidence, respect, and devotion. That is why over many years we became increasingly happier. We did not have to pretend to be happy and lie to ourselves. Our inner and honestly lived happiness inspired us more and more. We built our house on the foundation of love and our life. For a long time it was unshakable and defied every tremor.

But at some point the first hairline cracks opened up in the concrete. At first hardly noticeable and not visible. But they grew. The first crack appeared when Rasmus hung up a picture of a young Berlin artist in our apartment. After about four years, the pink cloud that had surrounded us until then burst. I had messed up anyway, but I did not nail the guys' works to the wall in our apartment. This art showed me every day how little respect I deserved and let my feeling of worthlessness grow in tiny millimetre steps. I did not know this at the time. The painting was always a thorn in my flesh, but I still thought I was cool. Bugger the picture, the main thing is that the guy knows who he really loves.

Today I realise that a happy relationship is virtually drenched in love when almost every thought is born of love. When the feelings are carried by love. I imagined this was the case with us. It was, until that day when the picture hung in our apartment. Screwing others was not nice, but it was quickly forgotten and forgiven. As I mentioned, I too had skeletons in the cupboard. I thought that my beliefs were secure. The thought "I love this guy" was closely connected to the fact that my heart burst with happiness and that's how my attitude developed. From this, a behaviour developed that has lasted to this very moment.

A look at the reality that followed could have shown me that something was wrong. And no matter how I twist it, whoever hangs the work of a guy he fucked around with and confronts his partner with it every day damages the flow of energy that carried both of them to heaven. And anyone can imagine what happens to the energy of love when the boyfriend tells you the day before your holiday that he's first going fucking and then will go on holiday with me later. But many of us gays are like that and live well with it. This holiday, which I didn't want to go on at first, was heaven and hell at the same time. In both cases a journey that has branded itself into my memory and mind, both positive and negative, forever and ever.

My subconscious worked with all its strength on the murderous destruction of our lives. One day I met a young French man with whom I felt I had fallen in love for no reason. The drama was that I loved my Rasmus and I didn't want to lose him under any circumstances. Again and again I talked to my best friend. I could not understand what I had done. I just didn't understand why. My boyfriend had his faults, but we both conquered the world.
It could not be what happened at that time and yet it happened. The disaster slowly took its course. It went on like this for almost half a year. Sometime in winter, at the box office, my boyfriend asked me a trivial, funny question and suddenly it came out. "I'm having an affair." He knew immediately who it was. And then it happened. With a loud crash our lived illusion burst and poured out in a torrent of pain and disappointment over the debris of what we thought was our relationship. I had betrayed everything we believed in. I was the murderer of our relationship. That is how I felt. That's how he felt. As a result, I had my first dramatic depressive nervous breakdown and lay on the carpet in the living room for hours, crying and screaming. No one thought to

call a doctor. Nobody felt that I was sick. I was terminally ill with rage at myself. I was dying because I had lost what was most important to me. And all because I had exaggerated my sexual escapades. I didn't know even then that I had the worst depressions, which had not broken out before simply because I was so happy all the time. And then I was desperately unhappy because I was no longer worth anything.

Gradually the cancer of the soul ate me up. Pouring heaps of grass and ecstasy in to me was not very helpful. I had to make a decision and couldn't. Why not? Why the hell couldn't I? Today, the answer lies clearly on a silver platter in front of me. Because my subconscious sensed that something was wrong with our energy and that deep inside of me I had only used the lovable Frenchman, who was such a great person, to destroy my relationship. Consciously I didn't want that and today just as then what happened deeply hurts me. I am infinitely sorry. Maybe YOU will read these lines one day and can accept my "forgiveness". The same goes for Rasmus.

What I did to my boyfriend and everything that happened still hurts as much now as it did then.

Shortly afterwards I got the offer to move to Los Angeles to work and live there. I accepted. It was a way out which the universe had sent me. So I could gain distance and sort out my feelings. I knew even before I flew out that I did not want to lose my boyfriend. With horror I remember my last night together in the Hilton Hotel in Mainz. At breakfast, we took turns breaking into tears. I cried for 11 hours on the plane and puked my guts out again and again in the toilet.
Three months later I came back for the first time for a short visit and was happy to see my Rasmus, again. He had not forgiven me. He went home early from a dinner at a friend's house. I wanted to stay. When I came home two hours later, he was not there. A phone call to my friend Francis, who worked in a notorious bar a few streets away, confirmed that he was where I suspected him to be.

A few days later I flew back to Los Angeles. A quarter of a year later Rasmus came to visit me for four weeks. We had each other again. I was happy. He was at a distance. When he went out alone, he was canoodling around with a friend of mine, as it turned out later. Rasmus flew back again and I met Ramon, with whom I still have a nice friendship today. But after one year my longing for Berlin and Rasmus was just too great. I wanted to go back again. Away from Los Angeles, which I had learned to love in the meantime. Away from Luis, with whom I was definitely a little bit in love. Back to my old, new life. I had made a decision and that decision was for Rasmus. I firmly believed that we could make it.

Unfortunately, I couldn't get a job in Berlin anymore, so I had to move to Frankfurt am Main for two years, where I accepted an exciting job with a TV provider. This was not good for Rasmus and me. But in retrospect, it was already clear that the attraction we had for each other and the energy we shared had long since been irreversibly destroyed. A miracle should have happened. That did not happen. I moved back to Berlin. Frankfurt made me so sick. I wanted to live my life with Rasmus. One Saturday in October, I couldn't go on. It was still very warm outside. I wrote Rasmus a long letter and explained myself and my action. It broke my heart while writing and I cried buckets for hours. I gave him the letter, he should read it. I cannot say things which are important. I have to put them in writing. He read it on the terrace. The neighbour from across the street opened the door and loud music boomed from his living room. There are no coincidences and the universe told us something at this point that we had ignored when it played our song. Whitney Huston warbled loudly "I will always love you." This song was playing when Rasmus spoke to me for the first time on the dance floor. It was always our song. It is still our song to this day. A few weeks later, I moved out.

For the next 2.5 years I spent every free minute getting stoned with drugs and, whenever possible, I spent my time somewhere on the dance floor. At some point I ran out of work and lived on odd jobs and friends sometimes filled my fridge. I drowned my depressions, which I didn't know existed, in a sea of ecstasy. I thought it was normal to suffer for a long time when you break up after such a long time. My friends say today that they were afraid that one day I would die. Personally, I didn't think it was so bad. Looking back, the amount I consumed was nothing compared to other people. It was enough for me. It helped and at the same time it was killing me. Whether the drugs aggravated my depressive state cannot be said. The doctors confirmed to me that there is no reliable evidence for this. But let's put it this way: it can be assumed that it did not make it any better.

September 2019
After more than three years I met my ex again. In all the difficult times, especially after Jose's death, I didn't really get any support from him. He showed his compassion by yelling at me on the phone that I should go to the fucking psychiatrist to get rid of it. I shouldn't bother him with it.
On my own suicide attempt I received two text messages in which he vilely insulted me. In a later phone call he hung up on me when I tried to explain what his insults had done on top. Rasmus has changed insidiously and radically

over the years, especially since he got married and is subject to an influence that has cost him many close friendships.

Rasmus had given me "time with him" for my birthday three or four years ago. I was very happy about that. Unfortunately he never spent the time with me as promised. In response to his last text message to me I replied that there was no point in staying in touch anymore. Our differences are too great. His world is dominated by money and values that I no longer share. Rasmus works to increase his wealth. I have given everything to dedicate myself to TREES of MEMORY.

Shortly afterwards he asked for a meeting. This made me happy again and I was excited about our evening and I hoped that our old love still held a connection that neither IT nor life would separate. He greeted me with the information that he only had 1.5 hours because he had to meet with friends who wanted to buy a house.

In this hour together he told me old stories and revelled in memories that no longer had any meaning. I heard who grew fat and who was still a couple. He overestimated "How are you" with cliches. I learned nothing from Rasmus. I don't know who he is, what moves him, what touches his heart. I haven't seen or heard anything about the man who changed and influenced my life so drastically. Not one word came from his heart or from his soul. In front of me sat this round man who defined himself by his possessions and the obligations arising from them. His life takes place between Berlin, Ibiza and Bavaria and with every third sentence he emphasizes that he doesn't need all this. In his omissions he did not feel how much he contradicted himself, lied to himself and maintained a strange façade that I could not grasp. He needs exactly this life, with all its comforts and three major holidays a year in luxury hotels around the world. He had already been working towards this when he became a junior partner. It's what he always dreamed of, and for many years the two of us lived and enjoyed this life. If that is what he wants and if he is happy, that is good and I am happy for him.

For me, the definition of happiness has changed dramatically in recent years. For me, two factors became clear during his monologue: During our relationship I idealised a man who had not existed like this for years and after that I obviously only saw the positive for a long time. Which is perfectly OK. I don't see it negatively, because I loved him with all his strengths and weaknesses and we were as we were. We had the greatest time of my life. But more important was the realisation that evening, which quickly became clear and felt like a slap in the face of life, which screamed at me to wake up and finally understand what was happening to me.

For Rasmus, his whole life was always about what would become of him and what he could call his own. For me, my whole life has been about how I become. Life is not about what we become, but life looks at how we become and then decides what challenges we have to overcome. That's why this window of time squeezed in by Rasmus was the enlightened answer to all the questions that have so occupied and weakened me over the years. If you can define yourself with your "how" only by your "what" and without the "what" there isn't anything, you can have all the money in the world and collect as many works of art as you like and gather rich people around you and the deep emptiness will not be filled by them. The handshake of a rich man who is happy to have made even more money simply cannot be compared to the tears of a person whose life has been changed simply by taking him in your arms or by alleviating suffering through listening and sympathy.
I do not want to swap my life anymore. Rasmus' perspective on life is as it is, good and right because it is consistent. He has worked hard for it, always dreamed of it and did everything right. He followed his visions and made them come true. We are still similar in this respect and this common ground once connected us very much.

My reality is also good and right and its development suits me and my circumstances. I have taken on other tasks and deep inside I am happier and more fulfilled than ever before. In fact, I am so happy that I could die tomorrow with a smile on my face when the universe calls for me. I found the love of my life in Rasmus and for that I will be grateful to him for a million years. We had the most exciting time ever and nobody can take this gift away from us. To have found the great love in someone like him will always fill me with gratitude, even if our paths have separated. It had to be this way. "My way is my way, is my way" sings Klaus Hoffmann.

Should I ever marry again, I know that it would not be for money or possessions. Not everyone can say that about themselves. Having nothing turns out to be a blessing more and more often, even if it is more difficult to get through life with little. Since I exchanged having with being, my life has changed radically for the better. No matter what else may come.

Nudged back into life

It had been six months since Jose had taken his own life.
In September 2016, I wasn't any better than I was right after his suicide, quite the opposite. I continued to cry myself through the days and nights. I dragged myself to class and regularly burst into tears in the middle of my lectures. The work helped me to get through life. At the same time, I was no longer able to cope with everyday life emotionally. As a freelancer you unfortunately have no choice and have to go to work if you want to pay your rent and bills. If I had had a permanent job, I would certainy have been on permanent sick leave. I would have gone from one specialist hospital to the next. Who knows, maybe I would have let myself fall into the safety of the German pension system and would have been sick until early retirement. At that time I would have had nothing against it.
Today I am glad that I was forced to earn a living. That gave me structure and kept me on the path to recovery. Without this "must do", the physical and psychological lethargy would have become a permanent condition, which would have made the depression worse and with it the suicidal thoughts. Being on sick leave is okay for a while, but there is a great danger of losing yourself in it. 'Wanting to' and 'being able' are also in this case two different descriptions of a state that do not always work together. Turning will into a skill is part of the task and a difficult struggle that is worth fighting for every day. But at that time I had hardly any energy and my courage to live dwindled to almost zero.

So there I was, standing in the shower at seven in the morning. I could hardly stand upright. My stomach ache from crying was bothering me. Once again I hadn't slept a wink during the night. I felt more and more that I wouldn't be able to hold on much longer. Sure, I wanted to live, but where would the energy come from?
I increasingly lost interest in my immediate surroundings. I no longer went outside the door. Friends had been buying food for me for weeks. I spent the days and nights working, brooding, crying, asking why, and visiting my psychologist. In the shower I realised again that all this was useless and that the days were not getting any better. The darkness of the future intensified and there was no glimmer to be seen or felt on the horizon. With crossed arms

and closed eyes I stood for minutes under the boiling hot water jet. Warm water is often the only thing that does me good and gives me warmth. A substitute for missing hugs. I feel really safe in the shower. The worse my condition is, the longer and hotter I shower.

Suddenly, as if someone had flipped a switch, I no longer felt the beating of the water and I didn't notice the burning heat. "Hike around the world," the thought, which silently filled the room, shouted at me. There was no space for anything else in my head, well the entire bathroom, even the apartment suddenly seemed like a sack that was about to burst at the seams at any moment. Just filled with one thought: "Hike around the world".
 "I think you're out of your mind," I suddenly screamed into the emptiness. "What is this shit? Leave me alone," poured out of me. I was sure now that I would go insane. I started to cry. I couldn't take it anymore. "Now I'm completely mad," shot through my mind. I had clearly lost my mind. "Plant trees", was the next thought. Just as powerful, just as demanding, just as intolerant of any contradiction, no less ... somehow. "You've got someone crapping in your brain," I shouted and hit the tile mirror with my fist until my knuckles bled. I gradually collapsed and cowered in my bath in a fetal position. What should I do? Was this the future? Schizophrenia? Voices in my head that were not voices? Orders from the shower head? I curled up in the bath crying and sobbing, holding my ears and whimpering for it to go away. And then the next thought came. Much louder in its silence. Much more powerful. Dramatically more decisive and so surprising that for a brief moment I forgot to breathe. A thought that drove everything I had just experienced crazy again and left me paralysed with my mouth open, speechless and paralysed. "Let me help you," resounded through every twist of my brain. What the fuck, English? Why English?

"But, what ...", I staggered back into a standing position and stared at the bathroom wall as if hypnotised. I felt the heat of the water threatening to scald me. The water splashed down on my scalp. I turned off the shower, grabbed a towel, dried myself and realised that I was already too late. As if in a trance, I got dressed, ran out of the house, grabbed my scooter and drove to work.
I have no idea anymore how exactly I drove to work. Suddenly I was there. The memory of the last minutes in the city traffic was erased. Arriving in my broadcasting room, from where I was giving lessons, I turned on the computer. Soon 10 students were staring at me via webcam and waiting for the lessons. I tried to the best of my knowledge, but my mind was like a fairground. Thoughts played 'catch me if you can' and landed on the carousel, on which they were spinning merrily in circles. My brain felt as if it was about to start boiling. What was wrong with me? I could no longer concentrate.

Something was inside me, wanted to get out. I felt so strange. I was scared. I panicked. My mind suggested something bad is about to happen. When I could no longer continue teaching, I gave the students a task that would keep them busy for at least four hours. I had an irrepressible urge to sit at the computer. I had to write. After the Word program opened, a condition set in which I can only describe as "the writing just happened". It was hard for me to believe what was flowing from my fingertips.

Tree in remembrance of suicide victims.
Each tree represents a person who has gone, a suicide victim. Each tree is meant to warn and urge society, the victims and their bereaved relatives not to stigmatise people with depression or suicidal thoughts, as well as their relatives, and not to sweep the taboo subject of suicide under the carpet.

Help and sympathy for the traumatised bereaved.
Each tree represents a wife, husband, child, sibling, parents, whole families and friends who are in shock and have lost the most important person in their life. These relatives deserve help and compassion and need people to support them and help them back to life.

Love is like a tree.
Each tree is the image of an individual relationship, love or friendship. Just as every love, small and tiny, began as a glance in a café, just as your own child grew from a teeny weeny egg and a wafer-thin sperm, so the little trees grow into stately trees and, like love, become more remarkable and beautiful with age and size.

Trees to give encouragment to people with suicidal thoughts and depression – a form (mine) of suicide prevention.
Each tree stands like a candle in the darkness, as encouragement for all those who believe they have no hope. Who, like me, are sitting in the abyss of hell and cannot believe that life will get better again and that happiness and fulfillment can ever be present again even when there seems to be nothing left to fight for. Depression can be treated. It is possible to heal depression and suicidal tendencies. We can all help when relatives fall into a depressive crisis that becomes a tangible illness, in the course of which suicidal thoughts arise and torture those affected.
These trees of life, as a remembrance of the deceased, speak to people who, surrounded by the cold and darkness, feebly resigned, no longer dare to open further doors in the dark dungeon of the mind. But they have to, because somewhere down there, behind the closed doors, is a candle for each

individual. The candle that brings light and points to the key which opens the door to a fulfilled life. A different life with a new path in life.

Trees as a symbol of the continuity of life.
The trees of memory stand like a circle around the earth. A self-contained path that represents love, friendship, courage, hope and the continuity of life. An eternally visible symbol, which should give people all over the world hope and courage to discover a new perspective that leads back to life.

TREES of MEMORY saw the light of day in these lines. I had written down a completely consistent concept. Everything was there, the logo, the colours, and even the texts for the website, as it can be found today on www.treesofmemory.com Footpath of Life, a hike round the world to plant trees of memory..
My text also said when it should start: On the second anniversary of Jose's death, Easter 2018. I had 18 months to prepare.

Does God exist?

I am often asked whether I met God when I took my life. Whether I noticed the white light. Or whether I had a near-death experience. I have to disappoint. Unfortunately I was not floating above my body, I was not pulled out of my body through the wall into a white, warm light full of love. I did not hear any voices and nobody sent me away from a place where I would have loved to stay.
Nothing, nada, niente was there. My last memory is blacking out. It felt like a free fall on the biggest roller coaster you can imagine. It was a bit like the feeling I had when I bungee jumped off the world's highest bungee jump bridge in South Africa in 1999, when I dropped 265 metres.

In fact, God does not exist in my reality. At least not in the way we are so often led to believe. For me, there is no white-haired old man who casts the good into eternal life and the bad into eternal purgatory. In my world there is no superior authority that decides about life. I am not on a desperate search for the ultimate redemption that promises me eternal happiness. No, what I perceive, hear and feel is different. In my universe there is only consciousness. It is matter without particles, it is so to say the great I, which does not demand, does not advise, does not praise and does not punish. A consciousness that one day perceived itself and realised: "I am".
Doesn't the Bible already say that in the beginning was the Word? From the "I am" this consciousness asked itself "What can I become? Why, how come, for what reason did consciousness suddenly exist, where did it come from and what does the empty space around it look like, this need not be answered, for that is what makes it divine. It has always been there, just as space was there before the beginning of time. Where did it come from, or if you ask yourself the question where God came from so suddenly, you would imply that there is something greater after all. Does not occur in my thinking, but even that would be theoretically possible. From the small to the big, as outside, so also inside. Everything we know exists super-nano tiny, such as the DNA spiral structure, and its equivalent of extremely huge, such as the spiral galaxy Messier 101, which was recorded by the Hubble Space Telescope.

Infinity and divinity could be expressed in that everything we see and know is seen in proportion, no larger than an atom and we are part of an unbelievably gigantic organism, which is part of an incomprehensibly exorbitant organism, which is part of ... etc. Before one or other of you get your feathers ruffled and think that I've completely lost it, please be aware that you don't know anything. Be aware that I know nothing. No human soul is certain about any thought. Our thoughts are nothing more than fantasies and games in our existence, which we would like to be able to understand. We will learn the truth when we die, but perhaps not. You are not right, I am not right, nobody is right, we are all right. Why do we argue? Why are the world religions banging their heads together? Everyone's right. Everybody's wrong. This is the only true state of being, and anyone who claims otherwise is simply insane or has come to visit from another dimension of the universe and therefore knows more. You can choose now. To argue whether science or religion is in possession of the only reality is stupid and arrogant, if you simply have another version of a theory at hand. There is no difference between you and me. Only our belief, which is like taste. You cannot argue about either.

Okay, so once again. No god, no being, but only consciousness that wonders what it could become and has given this task to every being in the universe. The meaning for all of us is: What can I become? From this it can be deduced that it is in our own hands whether we follow a positive or negative vision. We decide ourselves how we are remembered.
Recently I heard a beautiful explanation in a film which sounded consistent: "You are in heaven when everyone remembers you in a very positive way and you are missed. In hell if you are forgotten or are only remembered in connection with horrible experiences and thoughts".

The question "Who can I become", the realisation of the vision, followed by the renewed question, which leads to a new vision which can be attained, determines the path that our souls will take. In this way, I think that we, that is, our personal being, is evolving. Our consciousness wanders from life to life and experiences every possible reality in every possible way until we are ready for the next dimension. Everything we experience is nothing more than a projection, a kind of mind game of the divine ego. We are all part of this consciousness. Each one of us experiences different aspects of this consciousness. Although we all feel very different and you think of the other as something better, we actually belong together because we all originate from the same ego. Mankind should have understood long ago that we are all one. But unfortunately we have not the slightest idea what this means. We think that Oneness means to synchronise and that we should always hang around together. This thinking is reflected in many couples. We are together now, so we have to do everything together, eat the same food, have the same friends, etc.

This has nothing to do with being One. Oneness, for example, means that we are all human beings. We are living beings who think and feel, who feel love and pain. Every human being is the same, there are no differences whatsoever, because the colour of the skin or the shape of the eyes is nothing more than another design feature and makes no difference within the human being. In one case the body protects itself from the sun's rays and in another the body has to absorb every ray, no matter how small, if it wants to get enough vitamin D. Only we sick and blinded spirits have brought differences into being because we want to be better, because we must have power and because we think we are special. But would a mother of non-identical twins come up with the idea of making different creatures out of her children just because one is blond and the other has black hair? We all share the same mother and father. The consciousness that has always been there and will always be there. Forget our poorly developed body, which only causes us problems anyway. It is a receptacle for our soul or whatever word you might use.

We play the game of soul migration until we become part of the great consciousness again and return to the totality from which we were created. Our realities are nothing more than individual subjective thoughts. Once we are one step further, we create our own reality as individual consciousness and thus become the creator. But this is also nothing more than a thought of our self. The absolute truth does not reflect our individual revelation, because we cannot perceive it in its entirety as a human being with these limited possibilities.

The goal of our wanderings through the dimensions and life forms is to return to consciousness filled with the nothingness. There, where everything dissolves and every duality finds its centre and becomes neutral. There in the nothingness is the only place where I can see everything and where truth takes shape. We cannot see it, but we can feel it. From this feeling, pours out endless knowledge.

It is said that you have lived through everything and must have experienced everything in order to subsequently forget all this again. Only then can you feel the truth again. We humans can only become emotionally neutral if we have experienced every feeling at least once and know about its existence. Only then can we accept situations in a relaxed manner and accept what we encounter. In nothingness you feel so many things that you suddenly feel nothing. Every emotion cancels out another emotion and lets a new emotion arise.

Put yourself in your childhood. There was nothing that you have already experienced. No good, no evil. You travelled from A to B without knowing any boundaries in your mind and changed the locations of your adventures as often as mothers change their child's nappies. You have travelled through time and space from a single point. Only the negative and positive experiences have suddenly limited your space, time and horizon. Your mother said "You can't" or "That's not possible" and you accepted what she said with amazement, although you had other experiences. In the nothing we see again everything without space, without time, without limits and for every question in this world there is the right answer. I also have a less muddled example. Before you became an expert or professional, in anything at all, every experience pushed you to your limits. Everything was new. It was always different. The emotions went up and down. 20 years later nobody can fool you. You know your field like no other. No matter what comes, you take it calmly and don't even have to judge. Having experienced everything there is in your field once, leads to emotionally neutral worlds of experience in which your thoughts no longer have to hold on to any details. You may forget them because the knowledge is within you.

The reality is that there is no reality. We must learn to perceive and understand every space, every time, every perspective. We can understand that they exist and when we have all the knowledge together, then we can get back to the big "I am" because we have experienced in the meantime what can become of us. It no longer counts what has happened. Only what my "I" is capable of is of any importance, because from it the "I am" arises. It is important to be aware of the fact that your thoughts create your own reality. There is no escape from this - never!

Who can I be? Who am I? In meditation, when you are at one with yourself, you are in the middle of question time with the universe and you are piercing the great consciousness for answers. If you can manage to be still and listen to the silence, then you will find the answer. Is it the right answer? You find out by asking yourself if it feels easy or difficult.

This is the description of my new reality and reality of life, which has shown itself to me in different ways over the past three years. It is no less silly than believing in a white-bearded Lord in Heaven on a throne of clouds, worshipping a holy cow, or thinking that a god finds it good to kill people of different faiths. The exciting thing is that everyone out there is right, because in their reality there is the old man in heaven, the holy cow, the murderous creature, even the celestial spaghetti monster, which decides on personal fate.

It does not matter at all whether you are Hindu, Muslim, Jew or Christian. Everyone is right in his reality and the only thing that unites us is the unchanging fact that we are all one and have the same origin. We are less than we think we are and far more than we think we are.

Death as a puppet show

1. Deadly thoughts going round and round

In the summer of 2012, I was tormented for the first time by violent, never-ending suicidal thoughts. A few days before, I had to face by chance the end of my marriage. Hurt to the depths of my heart and soul, I fled to Italy to stay with my sister. In Bologna I wanted to regain my strength and think about what to do with this stupid chance discovery. I didn't get round to it, because my mind was occupied day and night with death. The "how" was clear, the "when" still open. These dark thoughts had nothing to do with my otherwise cheerful disposition. Why would I kill myself over a guy? I thought to myself, "All I have to do is walk out the door and in a week I'll have a new one, if I want one". But the thought of wanting to die kept me in a firm stranglehold. Two weeks later I went home. The confrontation with my husband over my discovery ended in a mess.

The physical symptoms, which had been haunting me for a year, got worse and worse. I forgot everything and anything. I couldn't remember where I had put the keys and on the way to the toilet I asked myself what I actually wanted to do. 50 metres from the front door I lost my bearings while walking our dog Golfo. When I was talking to someone, I stared helplessly because I could no longer follow a conversation. After only a few words, I couldn't remember the beginning of the sentence. What was the beginning of the sentence? What is he talking about? What do I answer now? I did not know. Days later I collapsed in the supermarket crying. I didn't know where I was and didn't know how I got there. My limbs were tingling and I could no longer feel my arms and legs. I gasped for air and panicked. It should stop, preferably immediately. The last thing I remember is calling my friend Robert. He took me to the doctor straightaway and then to the hospital. I immediately had myself admitted to the psychiatric hospital's secure unit. I was afraid of the voice in my head which vehemently demanded my death. In the hospital I developed a fear and aversion against people who wanted to look inside my mind and who had the audacity to explain to me what makes me tick. How dare they evaluate my thoughts and feelings? To claim that none of what happened to me inside my body was real, aroused sheer horror and extreme anger.

Today I am very grateful to all the doctors who treated me. I was constantly afraid of myself. The pain just wouldn't let up. I cried day and night for almost four weeks. The physical suffering was so great that I was afraid I would lose my mind. But it was already gone or at least the far side of knowing good from bad. I was in a psychiatric hospital secure unit and realised: Whoever is here expects nothing more from life. We were locked up and most of the patients were sedated. Me too. Thank God. The non-stop crying was a nightmare.

After four weeks I was admitted to Psychosomatics 1, where to my great surprise I was diagnosed with depression. Me, the sunshine and party king had depression? I found this extremely difficult to believe and accept. After another three weeks I was transferred to Psychosomatics 2.
A bed there had become free. As a patient who had voluntarily been admitted to the psychiatric secure unit, I was considered an emergency and was at the top of the list. I am often asked whether my decision to go into a psychiatric hospital was the right one. Well, it was not funny. I am not proud either. To see the psychiatric hospital secure unit from the inside was a white knuckle ride in my life and definitely not something that belongs on a bucket list. If you can avoid it, you should not be admitted. On the other hand, there are factors which make everything clear. Without admission, without emergency treatment, my family doctor would have given me a referral to a psychologist. I would have had to call 50 to 100 therapists to get on various waiting lists. Possibly months would have passed before I could get an appointment for any treatment. Months later, it might have been clear that an outpatient appointment would not be enough and the doctor would have started looking for a hospital place, which has to be approved by the health insurance company. That would have taken months to well over a year and by this time I would have taken my own life, with a probability bordering on certainty, because I would not have made it through the first week until the next doctor's appointment. Admission at my own request accelerated the process enormously and brought me to where I am today. I can't influence others who are affected what they should do. Those who put their personal freedom above everything else risk committing suicide under certain circumstances. Those for whom treatment and healing is the most important thing in the world will do everything and accept every limitation in order to lead a normal life

again as soon as possible. I would have been dead long ago if I had followed the thought "I don't want to go to the specialist hospital". I wanted to live!

During the following four months I got to understand myself. I was shocked to realise how many decades I had been depressed. I discovered the roots of my illness and understood what the supports in my mind were. I understood what made me tick. I analysed and compared the individual stages of my mental state when one of the supports broke away. Numerous circumstances, events and actions made sense. For example, if I lost my job, I compensated for it in my relationship. This gave me stability and security. The traffic light immediately went red if, in addition to the income, the man at my side went missing. The emotional protection as a comforting component was missing and the third support of my being threatened to collapse. I learned a lot about the way I met the challenges of life. I learned to look at my personal pain from a completely new angle, to understand it, to despise it and to meet it afresh. I informed myself about myself and took my self apart like a mechanic would take an engine apart to find the fault. In this case, however, you do not find a broken part, but recognise how many gears, screws and pistons there are and which part, with what force acts on which bit.

In the course of the treatment I saw the answers which I gave myself to cope with various circumstances and which of my reactions eased or increased the suffering. In a normal course of life without problems we simply function. No one thinks about why you act one way or another. I realised how I had to face life in order to slowly but surely get out of the trap of depression. Nobody else could do this for me. The entire knowledge of the various forms of therapy matured within me, supported by the psychologists. The doctor cannot change my life. He can only help me to understand it and give me tips on how I could implement the details. If I am not willing to do this and generally don't feel like it, then all the therapy is a waste.

By mid-2014 I had got a grip on myself again and was able to go back to work for quite some time. My life changed noticeably. So did my marriage, which still existed. But it got worse and finally went down the drain. I did my best to build up trust again. I did not succeed. Then came the day when a shadow was discovered on my lung and I joined my cancer-stricken family. Did I want to die in a shitty and lying relationship? No, I did not want that.

That's why I left Hubert and I was happy that after many tests it turned out that the thing on my lung was not cancer.

When the marriage ended, one of my important emotional supports fell away: "relationship". My emotional hold on life was swepped away by an avalanche of events, feelings and decisions.

2. Out of the frying pan into the fire.

About three months later I met Jose. A silver lining in the darkness. But even then, a challenge that sapped my strength. He could not decide between his ex, a priest, and me. The eternal toing and froing was nerve-racking and extremely trying on my nerves. I should have sent Jose packing a thousand times and I don't know why I never did. I tried several times, but the love for him was stronger. Being without him was worse than all his relationship crap and everything he did to me with it. I believed in love and in a life where he as my partner didn't have to hide. I was sure that together we could help each other out of the depressions.

Nothing helped, it all went downhill with me. Ever steeper, ever faster. On 28th December, I was sitting at the kitchen table at eight in the morning and could not stop crying. The physical pain increased exponentially. The presure in my eyes increased and were close to "bursting". The stomach pain was unbearable. I could no longer go through with it. Not to the psychiatric hospital again. Not to start over again. Not the same shit over and over again. It was too much. In the long run, for now, for the future and for what? I cried, "I just can't do it anymore".

I wanted it all to stop, my disappointments, the suffering, the countless repetitions and all the shit with the guys I was never good enough for and to whom every cheap fuck seemed more valuable than respect, appreciation and a common future. I wanted to live happily and no longer be the target of people who were themselves the biggest enemy.

Without feeling, I suddenly hung like a puppet on invisible strings. A puppet show that was not mine. A game that I did not write the script for. The big gambler in the dark hole above me laughed out loud and unscrewed a bottle of wine. He celebrated pill by pill, sip by sip. A drama that slowly but surely changed into the dark final act. I didn't like what was happening, but I couldn't change it, couldn't interrupt it. It was beyond my power and the decision was made by someone else. My brain took over the reins and what happened in those minutes was no longer part of my consciousness.

That was not Mario. There were no thoughts of friends, my mother, my siblings, my husband Hubert, who would find me stinking in the apartment in a few days, or Jose. It was a one-man play. A drama in three acts: Birth, life and now it was time to die. It was different to what I had ever thought, hoped for, planned, desired. At birth we are all brought into the world with good wishes and thoughts by the family. When dying, many people no longer even have the happiness and comfort of someone holding their hand when the soul sets out on its journey. We take our last breath alone. Other people, no matter how close they were, no longer play a role at the moment of passing over.

It was almost the start of a new year, 28 th December and now ten in the morning. None of my friends were in the city. My ex-husband wasn't and Jose was on his way on holiday. He was a beautiful acquaintance at that time, with whom I had fallen very much in love, nothing more. 120 km away, on the motorway, Jose had a bad feeling. A malignant feeling that spread in his stomach and rapidly grew bigger and more powerful. None of his messages to me were answered. Fear and worry increased and on the spur of the moment he turned round and drove back to Frankfurt at top speed, despite ice and snow. In the passenger seat was a priest, raging with fury, who gave free rein to his hatred of me (as always) and Jose dropped him off at home before driving to my apartment. With the help of a neighbour, Jose opened the apartment and found me. Already dark yellow and not breathing, as he told me later. In the ambulance, which they had called for, my lights went out for good. It was done and the curtain had fallen. I was dead. But somebody must have shouted "Encore" and they brought me back to life. At some point I woke up in the intensive care unit. My mouth and throat were so dry that I could only make a rattling noice. I felt pain all over my body and a thick tube was stuck in my penis. If that was death, I wanted to be away, quickly.

3. The voice after the party.
The third and last time I was overtaken by massive suicidal thoughts was in August 2017, when I asked my friends in Berlin to take me to a big music event before I started my hike with Trees of Memory. We landed at VooV, a Goa-Trance festival that we had visited three times before and where we had a lot of fun every time. My friends Hans, Mike, Anne and Uwe made every effort to make this last party-dance-festival a complete success. The day we arrived started with bad news in the media. The singer of Linkin Park had taken his own life.

Big career, fame, loads of money, loving family and a drug problem. This is how you can sum up his life. And depressions. A whole bunch of them. All of which adds up to a deadly mix, as so often happens.

Well, nevertheless we celebrated like wildmen and enjoyed every minute. There are lots of pictures of us all lopsided and wonky. It was so great. Until this particular Sunday midday, when, completely out of the blue, an evil man with an unbelievably deep and ugly voice lodged in my head and, demanding, commanding, and with unprecedented toughness, shouted at me: "Kill yourself! Kill yourself now! You have everything you need right here. There is no better time. Do it! Do it now! Do it now...!" Frightened and in panic I left everything and immediately sought the company of my friends. But the guy did not let up. Every five minutes he demanded my death. Massive, clear, not tolerating any argument. I did not know what to do anymore and confided in Hans. "Oh dear, oh dear", he said and it was clear that from now on I was not allowed to be alone for a second. I was afraid again. Not of me, but of the power of the scary guy in my head. And this guy didn't let up. Every five minutes he wanted me dead. Also on Monday, 24 hours later. Once again, for the record: Every five minutes a voice in my head screamed, "Kill yourself!"

It became so alarming that I had to take a break on the motorway to Berlin. I couldn't drive any further. The voice was accompanied by the worst dizziness and I constantly had the feeling of losing control of myself and the car. I was justifiably worried that the devil in my brain would steer the car against the pillar of the next bridge. Hans was sitting next to me, and there were a few other people on the motorway. I stopped in a lay-by and tried to breathe peace into myself.

In the late afternoon we had finally made it and were in Hans' apartment. "Come on, finally do it! What are you waiting for? You are at home in Berlin! There is no better place for you! Here you can leave. ...“ My potential murderer and executioner was still there.

Actually I wanted to go out of the house on Monday evening and chill out somewhere. I did not dare to leave Hans' apartment without an escort. I was afraid that the demon in my head would push me in front of a train from off the platform. I could not leave the house. Tuesday was still no better. I started to consume Atosil and Tavor in large quantities to turn off the voice. It got weaker and was no longer so horrible and powerful. At night I took sleeping pills so that I could at least get some sleep. On Wednesday, the man in my head only called every 15 minutes to demand my death. Nothing helped, I had to go back to Frankfurt, my job called. I felt like shit, but I had to go back. I was worried I would not arrive alive. It was to go on like this for another two days, and every single day I didn't know if I would still be alive in the evening. It was bad. Unbearably horrible. There is a technical term for it: schizophrenic episode. I can only hope that this excursion into the other world is the only one and the last one in my life. I'm not worried about it and I'm sure it won't happen again, especially since the circumstances at the festival won't be the same again.

4. No free will.
In all three cases I can say with absolute certainty that these thoughts and my suicide attempt were not controlled by my free will. I wanted to live and not die. I wanted to be Mario and not a puppet. But I had no influence whatsoever on what happened. I was lucky that I was strong enough twice not to let it go to extremes. In 2014 that had not worked out. In 2017, not much was missing. Whoever hears voices in his head wants to get rid of them one day, wants them to stop, no matter how. Nobody wants to die.

Many bereaved claim that it was free will that led their relatives to take the final step. Honestly: How do you know that? Just because there is a free will? Just because the person has done research on the Internet? Just because they bought their suicide weapon long before? Talk to those who have survived a suicide and stop trying to make suicides pretty and make heroes out of the sick. Suicide is the last symptom of a really lousy illness, its course, its feelings, its attacks can't be imagined by anyone who hasn't experienced them personally. Such a symptom can sometimes be strong and sometimes weak. If it is powerful and leaves us no peace, then we suddenly look on the Internet for ways to commit suicide or go shopping for deadly weapons or write a will. When the healthy mind returns, it panics and makes sure that we find our way back into life. We are glad to have turned the corner again. Then, suddenly, we are ambushed, the disease strikes again. We run, jump, swallow, cut or do whatever needs to be done, often at a moment when hours before the most beautiful and happiest pictures of us were taken. Driven by a cruel spirit in the black hole above and below us, we end our lives with a snap of our fingers. No thought of family, friends, loved ones. Only the end in sight and at the same time we do things we can't remember. Writing text messages, scribbling, quickly putting a last Facebook post online and much more. Then we are dead and the healthy believe that we left full of character, of our own free will, so as not to harm anyone and because we were so sad and nobody wanted to hear our cries for help.

Sorry, we are not heroes, we are not cowards, we are just victims. When the organs fail in cancer, we are all full of compassion, powerlessness and sadness and it would never occur to us to judge how the dying person fared. When our brain fails after depression has become unstoppable and has spread more horribly than any cancer, suddenly all sorts of healthy people know what happened to us and how we planned our death. No, every suicide, planned and unplanned, is a symptom that manifests itself in many ways. We have to accept that there are things and view points that we cannot imagine. Nevertheless they are there. Of course there are exceptions and of course people take their own lives of their own free will to preempt death from cancer, to give an example. And of course there are people who have mental illnesses, suffer from them for years, and see themselves as no longer treatable and so make the fatal decision.

A suicide that was based on depression or other mental illness is not a free will decision. Even the statement: "She was so sad for years, she didn't want to bear it any longer" is not dying of free will. If it had not been for the depression, it would never have come to this. If I take my own life to prevent the tragedy of a fatal illness, I personally make a decision: "I am going to die now". In depression the brain says: "You are going to die now" and our free will is not asked for its opinion. The option of treatment and successful therapy are even hidden. We are all victims of some shitty disease that you can't see and that you can't cut out, or as my ex-boyfriend Rasmus once said, making fun of me, "Then go to a psychiatrist and get it taken away."

I find it not only inappropriate, but presumptuous that people argue with me who have never been depressed for a day. Who never had suicidal thoughts themselves. Who knows best? Those who are dead, those who have this illness and have survived suicide, or those who are healthy and have no idea what happened to us? I speak about myself and I describe many conversations with people affected by the illness. I stick to facts that I have personally experienced and for which I have almost paid with my life. I do not exclude other motives in any way. Everything is possible - but extremely rare. Nobody knows what was going on in the minds of those who took their own lives. For example, we condemn people who commit extended suicide after a divorce and take their own child with them. They are murderers. Yes, they are. But they are not always vengeful monsters who want to harm the ex-wife. They are people who can no longer live without their child, who have had their most important things taken away from them and who see no way out. Sick people who want to be united with their child forever and ever. We are quick to condemn them and of course it is terrible what they have done. Such an act cannot be excused and glossed over. But there are views that those who are not affected cannot imagine at all. Stop justifying suicide in the name of your loved ones. You do not know what you are talking about.

Why do some of the bereaved argue with me? For the truth? It has many faces and shows itself in new versions every second. Those arguing come from their own life situation and perspective when they observe or act.

With TREES of MEMORY I want to encourage those who have been sitting in personal darkness for years. I was there and I too thought that there are no longer any prospects. Especially after the suicide of my partner. And suddenly the idea of TREES of MEMORY came into my mind and my life changed from day to day. I would never have thought that possible. That's the only way you can understand how I put this project into practice each day. This is the reason why I make every thought public. With all the ups and downs. There are countless perspectives for each one of us that remain hidden and do not show for a long time. This is true for the sick and for the healthy. Just because you can't imagine something, it doesn't mean that it doesn't exist. Light exists everywhere, even in the darkness. In it there is simply less hope, but it is there. It has made itself small but is only hiding. Perhaps I can help those affected to rediscover this light and the ray of hope. That is the reason for TREES of MEMORY, for my hike around the world, for this book and for everything I make public.

Do not give up. Believe in yourself. Only in you. In every coming moment, without any warning, everything can change again, just like it did for me in the shower. Give me a single legitimate reason to doubt and refute this statement, except your belief!

Silence

The door to the world closes
Peace, breathe in, island

Silence
it screams and becomes loud
Terror, hold your breath, no escape

Silence
Protects, kills

Silence
Emptiness without courage

Silence
Love that hurts
Love that protects itself

Silence
Forbidden World
Punishing world
My world

Silence

28. December 2014 09:39 added:

Silence
Up to the last note

Silence
Until everything fades away

Out
Silence

I wrote this poem two days before my suicide attempt and published it on Facebook. I was doing well. I had no plan. It just came in to my mind, like many texts and poems before.

Looking back, these words take on a new quality and the text takes on a much deeper meaning.

If only you knew beforehand what you would have on the radar afterwards.

The truth behind the stillness

Ever since my suicide attempt stillness has become very important. I look for it almost daily, run after it, beg for it to come back and find it for a few seconds every now and then and only rarely for a few minutes, when the meditation is going well for once. What is so special about the deep and silent stillness?

Back in December 2014, when my brain was trying to take my life just before I became unconscious, I first of all felt my thoughts slow down, then lose intensity and finally come to a standstill. Suddenly it was completely still inside of me. There was nothing to hear. Not the slightest vibration could be felt. Now, at this moment, when I write about it again, I smile to myself, because the total stillness felt so incredibly good. I can't find the right words for it and I long to experience and feel it again. At this point I would like to mention that I was not unconscious or dead at that moment. Both came some time later. I do not associate this stillness with the stillness of death. I know exactly, without being able to explain it with any arguments, that I will not find this stillness in death. It is nothing worth dying for. But the search for it is worth every effort. In this stillness you will find all the answers to all questions ever asked. Getting to this point is the goal of true meditation, far removed from the "we'll be in a hippy-style-mode-of-enlightenment-palaver". For this reason, meditation is a lot of work that needs daily practice and often with frustation because the 'monkey in the head' does not want to shut up. The most unimportant thoughts of everyday life run through the brain like old washerwomen chattering.

In the past two years while I have been on the road, meditating a lot and spending almost every day alone with myself and the chattering in my head, I have learned, grasped, understood and experienced quite a lot. I am no longer concerned about the meaning of my life. I am no longer looking for a meaning. I have created it with Trees of Memory and have done the best I can for my life. That is how I saved myself. I understood that an essential aspect of my existence is learning. Understanding how the big picture works, in which our life is an integral part, takes me forward in small steps. But every single insight, no matter how small, makes my heart sing, open up and allows me to notice more of what surrounds us, hidden behind all the unimportant daily grime. In this way I regularly manage to rise above myself. This is necessary if I want to complete Trees of Memory independently in the distant future.

If I manage to find stillness in meditation and as a small bonus on top of that, I feel that I can sense a strange and different form of energy, then I feel a knowledge without naming certain aspects. It is not thoughts that explain, for example, how a piston engine works. Just to make this clear. It is about a spiritual resource that is behind my personal reality and helps me to interpret and understand life differently.
I think everyone knows the feeling of knowing or suspecting something before it happens. I am not talking about clairvoyance, but about such a strange and often unpleasant, uneasy feeling in the heart. I have this often and I register again and again that the heart feels something long before the mind receives a message and I get precise information. The heart is often described as an organ that is the actual control centre between the brain and the soul. Our perceived feelings are full of information, which we usually do not interpret or misinterpret. But in fact it is our instincts that carry us through life and make our own reality something we experience, beautify or dramatically worsen. In the end, our mind is similar to a processor, which serves as a central processing unit to execute the commands given by the emotions. The intellect should help us to understand reality.
The problem is that everything we perceive is built like layers of onions. We have known this since time immemorial. Colloquially we say truth has many faces. Each truth, whether large or small, important or unimportant, part or whole, is built like a ball. It is never possible for us to see the truth in its entirety or to recognize and understand it completely. No matter from which point of view we look at it. Imagine that you are surrounded by a balloon. We only see a tiny part of it at a time. If we take a step to the right or to the left, we see a new section, while what we have just seen is already adapting to a different angle. Reality will always remain the truth, even if the viewpoint adapts and apparently realigns itself to each location and changed viewpoint.

An example of this is the fact that my stepfather used to beat the living daylight out of me on a regular basis. This cannot be argued away and is in line with the facts. His beatings scared me to death and his behaviour set triggers that still drive me crazy today. The emotional pain I had to endure is hard to describe. This is also an established truth. But today, 45 years later, I see these facts from a different viewpoint, even if my feelings are the same and will always remain the same. The knowledge about the helpless behaviour of my stepfather and his own inadequacies, which was shaped by an extremely cruel mother and the post war years, enables the truth to appear in a new light.

These, my facts, are completely different to the truths held by my mother or sister, for example, because they have not been witnesses and are not emotionally involved. My reality is embedded in their perspective and their own reality of their lives. Even the thug looks at the facts from a different point of view, which have adapted to his own reality and perspective. I am sure he is looking at his life with us, today, after his death, from another dimension. This does not change anything about the truthfulness of what was, in the here and now. Thus, our family shares all events, which are divided into infinitely different perspectives. They present themselves over and over again, although the fist in the face and the ensuing moments are always the same.

The meditation and the accompanying stillness that I perceive while hiking have shown me that it is important to centre myself and to be at one with myself. To perceive everything within me and to acknowledge it. It is existent. Whether I like it or not. What I feel and see is my perspective and reality. This is part of the great movement of life, the universe and the all encompassing truth that we can never recognise because we are always on the other side of the sphere. To find the centre means to grasp and recognise your own truth as part of a factuality that, together with an infinite number of other realities, creates an image of which we have no idea. Yes, there are not even words to describe them completely.
The goal is therefore to look inside, to penetrate into your own core, in order to be able to see every conceivable perspective of the specific reality from there.
This point or momentum is found in stillness.
I had the feeling of having reached this position just before death. That is where I want to be again.

New knowledge, unfamiliar life

In the following chapters I will show you which insights have helped me to see my life with different eyes. It reflects especially the time after Jose's death. The period in which the grief had taken on the worst possible proportions and I saw no progress. With the change in my thinking, new perspectives have arisen, which I am now putting into practice and which have long since become a tangible reality. It is already clear to me that these attempts at explanation are not good for everyone. Some people may wonder what I have been taking. In fact, it doesn't really matter what you think, because it worked for me. My reality bubble, as I like to call my life in the meantime, works, is worth living, full of fulfillment and more exciting and diverse than ever before. We all know the saying "The end justifies the means". At the end of the day, all that matters is whether there are changes for the better.

I would like to give you some thoughts with the following. It may be that you will discover a new perspective in it, which will help you to reinterpret and follow your path in a new way. In some circumstances reading between the lines you may sense a possibility to change your reality bubble. If you find yourself in a situation similar to mine, I wish you comfort and hope.
I was at the end and about to lose my life. Out of the blue, pieces appeared which I saw on TV, read in articles and books, dreamed about and much more. The puzzle became more and more extensive and at the same time more and more complete, even though it still grows and never seems to be finished. It is to be assumed that my new life picture is not the wisdom of the last conclusion. It may well be that the experiences described will result in a new picture in 10 years and that this book in its entirety is an important intermediate step without which I would not have made any progress.

Try not to evaluate my experiences. Do not put it in the good-or-bad drawer. Do not think about whether it is right or wrong. Think of it as another possibility and one of many millions of realities of our world and attitudes. Find in it whatever can support you in your process. If you do not find anything, you have found something anyway.
Then you know in which direction you do not have to search any further.

Dare to take the first step, because this is the only moment for which you need courage.

See the opportunity in loss

Every serious loss in my life has led to a huge inner emptiness. Especially after the accidental death of my biological father. Probably my youthful age and the fact that life had just begun and was picking up speed, helped me to get over the worst during this time, even if the emergency brake brought me to a standstill,

I was glad that I was already allowed to stay out half the night at the age of 15 and so I was already hanging out in the legendary Tropy in Albstadt-Ebingen. There were terrible rumours about the place. Some said there were monkeys hanging from the ceiling in cages and of course it was the worst drug hell on earth. Honestly, it was neither one nor the other. There was no more nor less smoking joints than in other clubs. At my police training it was said that it was the number one drug dealing place in Zollernalbkreis. I was never offered anything and, what's more, I didn't consume anything. I liked their music.

One day my girlfriend's brother took me to the Bhagwan disco in Stuttgart. That was amazing. I liked the atmosphere, the people, the light and especially the music. Afterwards I hung out alternately in the Tropy and in the Bhagwan disco and danced the night away. That was my dance therapy, which I still use regularly. I close my eyes and disappear onto the dance floor for six or eight hours and don't notice anything around me. During those hours I manage to switch off my brain and escape the thoughts which go round in my mind. Despite the heavy techno bass sounds I find a certain stillness and a pleasant peace within me. What dancing cannot do is to fill the emotional emptiness within me. I do succeed in finding a special kind of peace, but I cannot fill the hole inside me, which drags me into the depths.

With Jose's death, all of it became a monstrous abyss that swallowed everything inside. There were no more feelings in me, no values, thoughts, plans, no courage, no hope or joy, nothing. I was filled with a malicious, all-destroying vacuum. The longer this state lasted, the more anger, disappointment, doubt, guilt and fear poured into this space. I used to be able to counteract this by taking vast amounts of drugs. Back then, when I felt this nothingness after the separation from my first boyfriend Rasmus, I sank into techno-drug heaven, which helped me to survive the following two years.

"Drugs", some readers might moralise now. You can think what you want. It helped me and I didn't become addicted. At no time was I an addict. I don't have the gene for addiction. That has always been the case. Addiction is foreign to me, except nicotine addiction. That is history since 2017. Since not everyone is so stable, I would certainly not recommend such a procedure and only approve of it in a few exceptions. For me it was right and that was fine.

In the meantime there is a nasal spray on the market which is mixed with the party drug ketamine and has been approved as an antidepressant in the USA for quite some time. In Germany it is awaiting approval and in Berlin hospitals it is already being used, in order to help with periods of depression fast and effectively. Drugs are, therefore, not always the worst thing per se, just as deadly poison can help with healing. My doctors told me in no uncertain terms that there is no conclusive evidence of how drugs aggravate or cause depression. But you can assume that they are not particularly beneficial, especially when used improperly. I agree with that. Although it can be, but not necessarily. They have helped me get over the pain. But the drugs couldn't fill my emptiness and couldn't dispel the negative emotions that went along with it.

After Jose's death I was glad not to be in Berlin. I am not sure what would have become of me. I could well imagine that I would have become all messed up until there was nothing left of me. In Frankfurt there was no such possibility, because cocaine is too expensive and I always thought the stuff was shit. In addition, I lacked energy and adequate dance halls for a first rate intoxication. My will resembled a zero line. No matter what, I was not able to do it. I dragged myself to work, I sneaked off to therapy, I waddled from the dining table to the couch where I was comatose staring at the TV and waiting for any improvement. In between, I wrote desperate emails or Facebook postings, hoping that something would happen that would help me.

The worse my condition became, the more I searched outside for help or people to blame. To blame it on the outside felt right at first. Why couldn't the psychologists see that Jose was severely suicidal? Why didn't Jose's pseudo friend take care of him as promised? How is it possible that Jose's priest increased his fear instead of giving him courage? My accusations were nothing more than natural and understandable distractions, which in the end pushed me deeper into the abyss of inner emptiness, where the monster of fear was waiting for me in all its bloodthirstiness.

If I had had money, I would have become a shopping diva. Happily shopping as retail therapy. But in previous years I had felt that shopping and new possessions no longer made me happy. The joy of each new thing lasted only seconds. There were times when I wanted to build a wall round myself, full of possessions, money and career. The size of the apartment was the measure of happiness. The number of trips said something about my joy. The amount of friends and acquaintances gave further details about how I felt. I was doing great and I felt like a young god. A damn empty and superficial, almighty Abraxas. Filling the ego with useless stuff and illusions should help to make me complete. It should help me to feel totally happy and loved. But no matter what I did, the inner vacuum remained permanently palpable because it lacked depth.

With Jose's death, I was trapped even more in the emptiness and I could not compensate it with anything. There was a lack of energy and awareness. Neither money nor medicine could help me. The hugs of my friends did not help me to look to the future. To feel like a full human being was hopeless.

Today I understood that I should have looked at the causes of this emptiness. Jose's death, my father's death and the separation from Rasmus only increased the emptiness and had nothing to do with the causes. As long as I didn't know the reasons for the emptiness of my soul, then the perpetual return to the same and similar situations is a sure fact. No matter what great things I would do, the darkness of my wasteland would catch up with me. The older I got, the faster and more severe the big hole would come back. Everything that was new and colourful quickly became something colourless and old. Every good feeling rapidly found its emotionless or negative end.

It lasted a while and I had been running TREES of MEMORY for some time when I realised that I was maintaining the emptiness myself. It is an illusion that has become a tangible reality. Only the questions of who I really am, what my deeply hidden dreams, desires and goals are and what makes me what I am, removed the delusion bit by bit and made room for the truth. Part of this reality was that I loved Jose incredibly and forgot everything around him. I had given myself up for this love. After his death, it almost broke me. I had been working on giving myself up for the last ten years because I wanted to live my marriage with my husband Hubert in a traditional and conventional way. I completely suppressed my real self at work and didn't realise it because I enjoyed teaching. I kept myself in a strait jacket of alien expectations. I had stopped unearthing my potential and trying out new things. I was no longer me. The more my unrecognised depressions grew in the background, the more dramatically things went downhill with me.

There was not only this all threatening emptiness and the many negative emotions and moods, but also a brain attacked by the depression. Depression changes the brain chemistry. That this led to a thinking and behaviour that no longer corresponds to that of a healthy person is understandable and is confirmed by medicine. In summary, this means that the unsuccessful search in the outside world, the filling of the void with unimportant shit and the negation of my ego had made me ill. I hurt myself subconsciously wherever possible and at the peak of misery was my attempted suicide. In the months after Jose's death, all this increased again in intensity and drama. I was about to end it all for good. I was trapped in nothingness and surrounded by suffering and grief. Either I set to change this state radically, to fathom and eliminate the causes of my personal ego suffering, or I would soon be dead. I was aware of this at a certain point.

The author Fabian Wollschläger sums up the solution in his book "The Source within You": "The entrance into our suffering becomes the exit from our suffering. The exit from our suffering becomes the entrance to our infinity."

The first step I had to take, above all others, such as finding a meaning for my life or changing my life, was to define the causes of my emptiness. Only then could it continue. I found a way out with the realisation that for the past ten years I had been working against myself, leaving space and time for the illness of depression.

Honestly, it is only now in these past weeks that I succeed in making this statement. It was not possible at the beginning to get to the heart of the argument. In fact, the idea of TREES of MEMORY has only prepared the ground for me to grow in knowledge. I am writing elsewhere about the fact that feelings contain knowledge and understand what is going on long before the heart and mind. When I realised that TREES of MEMORY is a good thing and that I find a considerable number of positions in it that also benefit me personally, I followed the drive and listened unconditionally to my feelings. There was no intellectual step behind it. Only the feeling and a knowledge not based on any argument that everything would be fine.

I am often approached on the street and I am told that I am really brave to do Trees of Memory and to be on the road every day, to leave everything behind or to ruin my pension. I regularly say that this is not true, because being on the road is easy for me. It is only taking the first step that actually requires courage and following your own self and heart with determination, regardless of what speaks against or in favour of it. Being courageous means listening to your feelings, reading them and implementing them consistently.

Create your outer world from within

I needed to recognise the causes of my emptiness so that I could escape the cycle of suffering and grief. I had to fill this vacuum with things that were helpful to my ego, support my mind and serve the bigger picture in which our life is an integral part. I did not worry about the latter, because what do we know?

I was no longer allowed to see myself as a victim of tragedies. I no longer wanted to be the weird product of a recent past that brought nothing good with it. The moment had come to start a new life with Trees of Memory by creating a task which would take all my suffering and change it into a positive and thereby experience a personal healing. But not only that. I want to help with my experiences and insights. I want to become a spokesperson for people who do not have the courage to move on and to say loud and clear what the stigmatisation of suicide and the taboo does to the bereaved and their relatives.

The horror of how I was treated and the situation after Jose's death lies much too deep within me. The majority of my friends approached me with compassion and helped wherever they could. People who were complete strangers supported me. I am forever grateful for that. However, there were also people who tried to harm me and who called me a murderer and blamed me for Jose's death. There was an accusing silence from Jose's entire family and circle of acquaintances. No one asked what really happened. And to top it all, there was my "very best Berlin friend, Brutus", whom I had known for more than 20 years. The day before Jose's suicide we wanted to meet. I sent him a text message and told him what had happened before I went to Berlin. As a result he cancelled our meeting. He didn't want to hear about my day to day drama anymore. Three days later I told him that Jose was dead. I have never heard from him from that day. No comfort, no word, nothing. He disappeared into thin air. I expected nothing else from those in Jose's circle. Despite everything, it hurt like hell and it was highly inappropriate, painful and in my eyes monstrously shameful behaviour. I never expected anything like that.
In the months that followed, I thought I had had the misfortune to have nurtered extremely false friends who were just snakes in the grass. Today I

know that I am not alone in this. A completely normal occurrence after a suicide. The moral spiral downwards knows no limits, especially when pain, grief and incomprehension are involved.

TREES of MEMORY showed me that everything I needed to fill my emptiness already existed within me, to fight the causes, to feel gratitude for any help and the courage to dare to take the plunge myself. I did not have to invent anything. I believe this is the key to every success. What you tackle can come from your own strength. We should become aware that all abilities, powers and tools are available within us to reach the defined goal. Each of us has a different toolbox on board. It is like a sportsman or singer. If you don't have talent and don't have the necessary voice, you don't have an ear for pitch or can't get high performances from your body, you will never become a good singer or athlete. At best, you can tinker with yourself a bit and make a few modifications, but that will never be enough to belong to the elite. But the best shouldn't always be the goal anyway if you want to avoid disappointment.

My intention is clear: to hike around the world and plant trees in remembrance, to help, to prevent suicide, and to give hope. And to help a little bit so that we humans do not hurt ourselves in the worst hour of our lives and push ourselves into the abyss in which we are already half hanging. For this I do not need any outstanding knowledge. My will for adventure, some creativity, perseverance, my professional skills and experience, sufficient optimism, as well as the drive to create positive change are enough to reach my goal. Things like fitness, good shoes and proper equipment which I had to get, was not the problem.

If I want to create something with my inner being, I have to be aware that I have to make a distinction between being and having. These two layers determine progress, your own development, and after a death, they allow us to let go of grief and to live again. Everything that can be seen materially belongs to having. My equipment, my cash, my credit card or some knowledge. If I were to lose all that, it would be tragic, but not irreplaceable. I can always acquire missing know-how. Being optimistic, courageous or creative is attributed to the level of being. I am willing to take risks, I am a visionary and I am determined. Whatever I am cannot be taken away from me. Never. I may lose the vision, but I do not lose the fact that I am a visionary person. My optimism may be lost in the short term due to dramatic events, but I can never lose the fact that I am an optimistic person by nature.

We can never lose what we are, but only what we have. To create this awareness is of utmost importance. If you can distinguish between what you are and what you merely possess, you will never let yourself be thrown off track if something is lost. Those who focus on what they are will not go under in times of greatest sorrow and overwhelming pain. The person who is something just because of what he has, will lose everything and will never get back on his feet if the worst happens. Our being determines our path and provides us with the tools we need to move on. Those who have spent their whole lives focussing on having, will go under when what they have is painfully snatched away. Having and losing a husband is bad, dramatic and hard to bear. But what would happen if you lost the ability to be a sociable, cooperative, kind and loving partner or colleague on whom others can always rely? That would certainly be unbearable. There may be moments when you don't want to be a loving partner because you have been hurt. But this is not to be equated with the fact that you are not like that at heart.

I also had to learn to get back to who I am and not to cry about what I had lost. Once I had sorted that, I knew that Trees of Memory was made for me, because of who I am I can easily implement it and I can always get what I need, or replace it if it gets lost.

Today I can say "I am TREES of MEMORY". I have created and set in motion something that can never be taken away from me. This produces such incredible strength and confidence in myself that I am not afraid of anything and I see no reason why I should not carry out the whole project exactly as it was planned from day one. Even if I should lose both legs tomorrow, Trees of Memory will still be there. Numerous Trees of Memory will bear witness to this for many decades, perhaps even centuries.

I experienced how this one thought, "TREES of MEMORY", became a whole new world. People, situations, encounters, even my dog Tyrion were swept into my life, which I would never want to be without again.
It happened in a similar way when I decided to work as a funeral celebrant. It was just a thought that created a completely new world with completely different encounters. I can say: "I am the funeral orator." That feels good, this has been confirmed by customers in the meantime and in this way I become inwardly strengthened.

My tip: If you feel that your life should change and you are standing at a cross roads and don't know what to do, then find out what you are and what you have. This will help you to let go and to find new things. The second step, go there and let your idea become a vision from which a whole new world will arise. Maybe you don't have any images in your mind yet and you don't know where the journey will take you. Then your "being" can help you to identify

what you are capable of. Consider what you can use to bring your ideas to life. If you are missing something, look at it realistically and find out if you can acquire it or let it be.

Be honest and subjective in your observation. If you have everything you need, then believe in yourself and your future dream. Don't make the mistake of thinking that you are just a little spark hoping for a dry straw bed that you can set on fire. No, you are the fire that burns from the beginning. You are not the consequence or the product of your life and your life's story. No, you are primarily the cause and the creator of your life and the universe that surrounds you. wie Fitness, gutes Schuhwerk und eine ordentliche Ausrüstung musste ich mir anschaffen, aber das war nicht das Problem.

Triggers, Memory and Vision

Memories and visions have in common that they are only imaginary pictures in our mind. By remembering scenes or making a vision become reality in our mind and by taking a look into the imaginary future, we separate ourselves from the here and now. We use the possibility to let space and time disappear and can travel to any useful point in our universe and life. The present was reality, while the future is only fiction and does not exist in reality at any time.

What do memories and visions do with us? The memory of Jose is connected to many different emotions for me. Emotions that are not always beautiful. I still feel extreme anger because from day one of our relationship he refused to acknowledge his depression and to have it properly treated. I feel immense anger at myself because I allowed him to play his games with me. It made me sick. I was so much in love that I no longer paid attention to myself. It is still unclear to me how it could have come to this. What was it that got me there?
I look back in panic at that terrible moment when I realised that he had taken his own life. I can still feel how upset I am about the fact that there were people from our "circle of friends and acquaintances" who knew that Jose was dead and yet nobody informed me. So-called friends, my neighbour, his ex, his brothers and sister or even his parents, no dead soul has come to me and to this day no one wants to know what happened. They all make up a version out of rumours and untruths. Much of it was even put out into the world by those who heaped guilt on me. This lack of respect to Jose, and especially to his daughter, is hard to beat. I cannot understand them and would not act like this. I would want to know what happened. But I do realise that by assigning guilt, it makes grief is easier to bear. That is unfair, but unfortunately human. I wrote a comprehensive letter to the family and reviewed the entire 2.5 years. I never received a response to it.

To learn about the death of my boyfriend through a rest-in-peace post on Facebook, after all that had happened, is extremely distressing emotionally. I saw the post and wondered what it was all about. He had read my messages. Jose could not be dead. At the same time a friend of mine asked me if what she heard was true. "If it's true..." she wrote. I will carry that moment in my memory for the rest of my life. Every post, every sentence that was sent to me and every single phone call that didn't happen because people didn't answer the phone while they started spreading rumours on Facebook. Only those who have received a suicide message themselves, no matter under what circumstances, can imagine how the roof of the world collapses in on itself and buries everything that was, is and will be. It was only comparable to the death of my father. That too tore my soul into a million pieces. But at least back then I had my life. That was snatched from me with Jose's death. It is nothing more than what once was. There is the time before his suicide and the time after. In between lies the darkest and coldest period of my life's journey and the constant struggle for survival. Is there an appropriate word for this, which describes this memory? Horror, I would think of that, nothing else.

I am grateful however that the memories have left me with some great times with Jose. All in all, far more than the bad impressions of our time together. Every single laugh of his resembled a gigantic outburst of emotion. His laughing eyes had a magic twinkle like I have never seen in anyone else. Our many trips, which we had at weekends and many a hilarious, cheerful evening drink in the Frankfurt bars. The moment when he said for the first time that he would love me and the day when he truly chose me, after all the miserable back and forth. Our holiday in Israel, when he insisted in the hotel room that we sing Christmas carols, will always put a smile on my face. He had printed out the lyrics for it especially. Or when I think of the moment when we both saw the city wall of Jerusalem for the first time. A sight that blew us away. His eyes beamed because for years he had wanted to go to Israel and with me it happened. His ex, the priest, was always there and said for seven years that he would not take Jose with him because he would not go to the Holy Land with a heathen. The surprise was written all over Jose's face when I said that I wanted to fly to Israel to visit friends and see the country and asked if he wanted to come with me. There are no coincidences.

The many occasions remain and are emotional, almost impossible to put into words, when he stopped the world with his magic embrace and I, surrounded by absolute silence, could only see the two of us. When I concentrate on this, I hear the boom boom of our hearts, feel the gentle up and down of our chests, feel his breath tickling my ear and smell the scent of his skin and hair. Boom Boom Boom, Boom. It is still there, as if it were only yesterday.

Unfortunately, the problem is that all the good, beautiful and funny moments are drowned in a sea that is unbearable because the negative emotions were so forceful and intense - much more noticeable than the positive ones. I don't believe that the pictures in my mind will ever be changed and I will only think of the hopeful ones. Too much has happened to be forgotten.

In the meantime, the day to day memories of that time are increasingly making their way into my life and connect themselves to my everyday life as my underlying beliefs. I wake up at night and see Afshin sitting in bed reading because he can't sleep. That was the same with Jose. I want to buy apple pie and I can't because Afshin hates the raisins which are in it. Jose shared this disgust with him. I have discussions with Afshin about the fact that he has all the signs of depression and I feel like I am going back in time. I get the same stupid answers and the same reaction of denying it. He has a go at me because I portray a bad picture. I know that all too well. I constantly come across memories that suddenly become triggers and rob me of sleep and get on my nerves. It is moments, glances, statements, excuses and actions that create sheer and naked horror. The accompanying fear robs me of joy, steals my present and produces panic attacks again. And on top, Afshin has a go at me with a lot of aggression because he doesn't want to be compared to Jose and finds it insulting that he might have depression. He regards such a suspicion as an attack on his personality and a belittling of his character. He does not understand that my love for him makes me act this way.

Not surprisingly, I suffer from triggers that are related to my stepfather. If someone like a builder makes me look stupid in the supermarket, my mind cannot decide between an anxiety attack and cold-blooded murder. If I get yelled at, by whoever, my whole body shakes and I can only get a grip on it with pills that calm me down. If I see someone who looks like him, I almost get quite a serious screaming fit and shortness of breath. If I am confronted with similar patterns of thinking or behaviour, I do not know how to deal with them. If someone were to hit me, I would be afraid that my pent-up anger from the past 45 years would explode and I would commit an act of passion that I would bitterly regret. A few years ago I intervened on the island of Mainau in Lake Constance when a father bullied his son, constantly reprimanded him and finally hit him. I completely freaked out and yelled at half the café, that's how angry I was.

I search in vain for beautiful memories in my childhood. Before I was seven years old, nothing existed. Everything that did, is sort of erased. Only two scenes are clearly recalled. I am lying in my child's bed and in the middle of the night my mother comes in. She gets me out of bed, dresses me and we run away. I was wearing a black patterned jacket. This lay in a cardboard box in storage for many years. I sent it to Africa to my friends, who became parents in 1990, together with other children's clothes of mine. I cannot remember how and why we came back home. I have no picture of whether my sister was also part of this scene. But I feel my mother's fear, the haste in which everything had to happen and I can clearly see how we ran. She carried me in her arms. It was not warm outside. A few years later I see myself on my child's bicycle, with my mother and my little sister, riding from Rangendingen, where we lived, to the end of the village in the direction of Hechingen. After the place-name sign we turned left up into the forest. There was a small stream where someone had put little wooden water wheels. It was a warm day with a bright blue sky. I wore short blue trousers and braces. These are my only memories as a toddler. Later memories are dominated by fear and violence.

When I think of my mother, I have mixed emotions. I am disappointed to have a mother who did not take care of her child out of love for a single day and never let me feel her love. It makes me angry to feel her striking my naked arse with a carpet beater. I am appalled that she never apologised for it. She refuses to acknowledge that she messed up. I am frustrated because she prefers not to have any contact with me rather than coming to terms with our past. It makes me unspeakably sad that she didn't come to Frankfurt when I was in the hospital after my suicide attempt or after Jose killed himself. She knew him because I introduced her to Jose and she cooked at meal for us at the time. She called me, told me that I was not to blame for his suicide and that was that. Summer 2017, I broke off contact with her and the whole family. Since then I feel better. And yet I think about what will happen when she dies. I don't know if she is alive. I have no idea whether my grandma is still here. Do I want to know? Yes, no, no, yes, maybe, but not, no... Anyway... I have no idea ... no, let be.

Not having a single positive memory of your own mother is extremely painful and hard to manage. What has helped me psychologically is my separation from her and the whole family. Nobody, neither grandma, aunts, uncles or cousins have ever contacted me. Not during all the difficult times, not before and not after. Nobody supports TREES of MEMORY, nobody told me to call in. Only one cousin kept a loose contact, avoiding the difficult topic with trivialities. But this family has always been like that. Solidarity and standing up for each other seem to be foreign words. Is blood is thicker than water? Not in our family, because in this family, the closest person is yourself.

Not so in my Italian family. My sister and her closest relatives respect, appreciate and like me, just as I have the greatest affection for them. They are my family. We do not all share the same blood, but her mother and her sisters are part of my family. When I am there, there is always a big hello. They were there when I was in such a bad way. I can go to them anytime. Emotionally and psychologically they are a great support, while the German relatives are emotionally damaging to me. Breaking off contact with my mother and sister hurts anyway because their indifference makes me extremely angry. I shift between rage, hate, disinterest and disillusion. If I consciously think of them, nothing pleasant happens. If I don't do that, I feel fine. That is why the ending of all contact was the right decision for me. They did not want me and never appreciated me, at no time. Nevertheless, they are part of me, because the feelings about what was, shape, occupy, influence and cause me to think and act in patterns that are loathsome to me.

All these are perfect examples of how the past dominates the present in a negative way. It illustrates the fear when I find my boyfriend reading in bed at night. What happened holds me in its iron grip. That is bad. It's even alarmingly bad because I compare the moment in the now with the past events and make decisions for tomorrow and my future based on this memory. That ruins today and the decade ahead for me. It happens all the time. I am often not aware of it. My actions, which are based on past experiences, bring and manifest the negative memories of the past into the here and now and, beyond that, shape what is to come. The temporary nature of the past is abolished. I do that myself. My mind and all the crazy synapses keep something alive that is long gone, over and done with and should be dead. Instead, I transport the negative emotions into the eternity of the future. This way I can't get rid of all the crap. My stepfather's beatings and my mother's hurtful indifference become as immortal as Jose's suicide. I have no life with such a future outlook.

For the time being I have experienced often enough what times in grief and pain are like which stay in our memories. Those affected exist and suffer in and through the past. They consciously keep them alive because they believe this is the only way they can maintain their love for the deceased. They think that they have to demonstrate and justify their love to the outside world. Nobody should be given the idea that a mother can have fun again. This is a fallacy which turns their lives into eternal suffering. Love does not show itself in this way. In fact, there are two of my followers who have planted a tree with me and I am very worried about them. If they don't manage to integrate love and death equally into their lives and continue as before, they will one day have no more strength and will follow their child. They do not understand that their innermost being is reflected in the reality of their life and that there will be no improvement until they have begun to realign and transform their hurt ego. I honestly do not know what I can do to actively help them. I thought to plant a tree in remembrance would help. Unfortunately I was wrong. The tree planting resembled a drop of rain in the desert. Amazingly, in both cases the tree did not grow. As sorry as I am, I see a clear connection. I wish so much I could help. But I can't transform her inner being. I can only give food for thought. Both of them have to put it into practice and let it work or at least start to try.

Back to the memories that so dramatically influence our lives. One thing is certain: I am not forced to spend my life in negative thoughts and to shape the coming years by them. Whether they are good or bad is completely irrelevant. I must find a way to free myself permanently from their effects. There is no way round setting me free of the accompanying emotions. Looking back is allowed if it is impartial or if it spurs me on. I will only find peace by being impartial and only then can I lead a life again, which makes joy and fulfillment possible and contains them permanently.

One way to achieve this is not to blame people for any hereditary guilt. For every person who enters my life, the clock is set to zero, it is a fresh start. If I were to accuse my current boyfriend of, for example, infidelity and betrayal, just because my ex-partners viewed it that way, our relationship could never stand a chance. I have to keep telling myself that even if Afshin also has depression, it can take a completely different course and he has to deal with it responsibly. It is essential to realise that not every builder I meet drinks and beats his child. If I do not want to transport the past into the future, I am forced to dissolve my underlying beliefs and make new experiences possible. These new insights will shape the people, situations and actions and provide for future positive experiences. This is the only way that there can be a future which is fulfilling and full of joy.

Forgiveness is a further tool to stop negative power being given to our memories. Forgiveness dissolves and helps images become weaker. To forgive frees us from the burdens from negative people and enables us to create a future which is guided and shaped by positive outlooks. Forgiving and turning away from anger takes away from the perpetrators of old their power over me. It takes away their ability to continue to display their hatred and accusations of guilt. The forgiveness will one day boomerang on them.

I have a further little trick. When I think of Jose and the pictures are sad, I immediately look at an extremely funny incident. This wipes away the sadness straightaway and puts a smile on my face. Anyone can consciously control that. I have experienced how recalling a funny memory can have a strong effect. All that is needed is attentiveness and a shift in the mind. Act immediately and do not allow the painful emotion of yesteryear to settle and refocus itself. Away with it and on with something funny.

To free yourself from the burdens of the past is a rewarding process that takes a long time. I'm not through it, but from month to month I can look back on the past in a more relaxed way and leave many things where they belong: behind me. In this way I release it into impernanence and into its own death.

When silence kills

My parents' beatings produced fear. A fear that continues to this day and every now and then leads to panic attacks.

Despite the violent attacks, I never gave up trying to please as a child. I thought to myself, "At some point I will do something good enough to get a loving hug instead of a beating. One day the old geezer must love me...". So my childish mind did everything in its power to interpret signs from my parents that would tell me whether or not everything would turn out all right. At least for today, or tomorrow or next week. You have to communicate and talk to each other to get such signs or statements.

I asked questions, expressed wishes or had trivial conversations. I could sort out the answers somehow, because I analysed what my parents said and how they said it. But there was often no answer and I learnt over time that the longer the silence lasted, the greater the coming anger and the more blows I would get. More often than not, the perceived silence led into an unannounced explosion of shouting and violence.

The feeling that took hold of me after a period of silence was not nice. I got a stomach ache that kept spreading like a black pulsating cloud, getting denser by the minute. From the stomach it rose to the lungs and made me breathe deeply to get air and to be able to get through this sinking feeling. Often I was on the verge of hyperventilating.

I never knew when the threatening silence would end, but I knew the day would come. This cloud of fear and panic spread through my head and became increasingly dense. My brain kept asking itself, "Why is this happening again? I did everything they wanted? I did well in school? I didn't do anything wrong. Why is this going to happen again? Why am I going to get beaten again? Why won't they talk to me? All I did was ask a little question? Dear God, please don't let it happen again ... "

That's how it went day in and day out. Every hour, every minute. I was no longer able to think about anything else. This loud "but why" took my breath away, my mind and, as I know today, also my health.

I have never been able to get rid of these dark panicking thoughts. They were mixed with the daily self-doubt. No matter what I do, I usually feel that it is not good enough. If I question it or ask for an answer to my letter that I sent to someone, sometimes there is a reply along the lines of: "You're putting me under pressure and I'm not doing so well right now, that's why I could never answer. And that's not nice of you now ..." Sometimes you write to someone and you see that the message has been read and you don't get a reply. Not even when you ask. Not even when asking a second time. Not even when the anger slowly takes over.

Honestly, and to use the words of my ex-brother-in-law, it pisses me off. When I send a message asking to be contacted because it is important for my job, for TREES of MEMORY or even for private reasons, there is no reason and no time limit in the world that does not allow a short answer to be sent.

"I haven't forgotten your message, but I'm not feeling well right now. Give me time". Or "Get back to me in four weeks..... " These few words can be typed very quickly or sent as a voice message in 10 seconds. That would be feedback which effects mental well-being. A sentence that has only one consequence: Understanding and information. It is a professional and appreciative interaction that can even be vital among people with mental health issues. Reporting back, no matter what the circumstances, expresses respect and appreciation. Anyone who knows this and yet deliberately hides behind a wall of silence is not only repugnant in human terms, but similar in result to the beatings I had to take for years.

If the silence comes from the person you actually love or who is important in your life for other reasons, the vicious silence leads not only to self-doubt but to absolute despair because I feel like I'm driving into a brick wall. Can you imagine what it's like to keep having another go to find out what's actually happening and coming up against a wall of silence?

In my case this has actually already led to massive suicidal thoughts, because silence is deliberately used as a weapon and as a result my thoughts go round in circles and turn into a hell from which there is no escape for months.

Is silence justified because you cannot find the right words? I think not. Because if that's the case, then you can always say, "I have no words, I can't explain it and that's why I can't say anything at the moment". That is as important and as valuable as saying, "I'm not feeling well right now or I don't have time until the weekend ...".

It is always worth taking a step aside and asking yourself, "What would such behaviour do to me?" Both parties should always be aware that we have limited control over our mind and brain. I can understand thought processes, I can explain them, but I cannot ensure that the dark black cloud announcing disaster does not strike again.

In the meantime, this thunderstorm in my head has turned into a latent fear that not only triggers panic attacks in my mind, but has become what is known as phobic vertigo or anxiety vertigo. Under certain conditions I get so dizzy that I have the feeling of being pulled into the depths and lose the ground under my feet. The room sways, objects distort. At the same time, I feel so sick that I am about to throw up or faint. Unfortunately, this dizziness comes suddenly and in situations that can be life-threatening. It has happened to me many times when driving a car. The last time I went paragliding it happened to me. I had such a panic in the air that I fainted. I had to make an emergency landing immediately. That's the reason why I've never been flying since then. In the car, at least I can stop immediately. In the air, it's no fun.

In the meantime, the dizziness and panic attacks have become less frequent. But the more mental stress I have, the more severe they both become again. What can be done about it? Let me say straight away: there is no medication that can help. In the actual panic and anxiety situation, what helps me personally is, please don't laugh now, singing loudly and lots of fresh air. My therapist explained to me that singing leads to a different way of breathing and can therefore help. If I can't sing, for example because I'm in the middle of a lecture or giving a speech, it helps to breathe deeply through the nose, down to the last accessible air sac, swallow once and let the air escape through the mouth.

It can also help to focus your eyes on a certain point. In the hospital where they deal with dizziness, this is called fixation suppression. I also use this option when I am in a room.

Unfortunately, that's not possible when driving a car. I couldn't do it when flying either, because the depth doesn't make the dizziness any better, although we paragliders know that height always means safety.

If the anxiety vertigo develops into panic attacks, it is important to think about breathing again. At the same time, I walk up and down and count the steps. Breathing and movement seem to be an effective means of overcoming the moment of fear. But I continually have fear about the situation which causes fear and that can really drive you crazy. Therefore, I had to think about it and create a new awareness.

For one thing, it was important to understand that fear is not my enemy. Fear is always the body's deep psychological protective mechanism. In the past, it helped us to flee from lions, bears and tigers. When I was little, it was supposed to protect me from beatings, and today it wants to protect me from stress or people who have no decency or morals. But the silence is not a danger and the person behind it is just an arsehole. So all I have to do is show the fear that I am not in danger, neither in life, in the car nor in the air.

I have also realised that fear itself cannot harm me. If it does, then I harm myself in a panic reaction. But fear itself, wants to protect me and is not a health hazard.

When the fear of fear strikes again, I have to stop the panic attack immediately and shut down. If I succeed in doing this, the brain learns and a new belief system is created. Heart palpitations won't kill me right away and neither will shortness of breath. I have both when I run to the bus. I don't have to be afraid. I don't have to be afraid of fear. If I manage to understand this, then there is a self-reinforcing effect, which incidentally also occurs in the reverse. That is, when I simply allow the fear, suffer through it and do nothing.

I am really glad that the anxiety and dizziness have been reduced to a minimum. My daily meditation, mindfulness exercises and, of course, lots of exercise in the fresh air have definitely helped. Unfortunately, I have not yet managed to stop my thoughts going round in circles, which can last for days and weeks. But in the meantime I can notice what they are doing to me, I can let them rage and then, with a lot of concentration, let them go again until the next attack. But if I see something of the silent aggressor, the mental calm is immediately lost again. I am aware that behind the silent attack of a fellow human being is just any lack of compassion, respect and communication skills and that the vicious nature of the other person will one day take severe revenge, but that does not make it better at that moment. So there is nothing I can do but let the other person know what he is doing and how shameful I find such behaviour. If nothing comes back, then that also speaks for itself and I will draw appropriate consequences, no matter who it is.

In any case, everyone should give serious thought to whether silence is really appropriate and why he or she feels that communication is not a means of clarifying an issue or emotional slights. Additionally, it always helps to be aware that we are all a product of our upbringing and circumstances and we can never know what hell the other person has been through. No matter what situation we find ourselves in, the solution lies solely in communication and not in emotionally hurtful behaviour. Our emotional memory determines what we do. Emotions are the hard drive on which everything is stored. Most of the time they cannot be erased and replaced. The destruction that silence causes can never be repaired. Jose also took his own life because he received no reply to over 120 messages he sent to me and many others. How well will you be able to cope when your behaviour is the last straw which broke the camel's back?

Guilt or responsibility?

With Jose's suicide, I was confronted with blame that knew no bounds. His friend sent emails calling me a murderer, and his ex maligned pretty much everything I did in public. Obviously every movement of mine is being noted and anonymous messages arrive continously. In his last message, my work as a funeral celebrant was commented on in such a way that my fee for this work was called blood money.

This man, a priest, wrote a letter to Jose's elderly parents during the process of his separation from Jose, in which he warned them against me. Jose had told him that I was taking antidepressants. Subsequently, he wrote to Jose's parents that Jose had fallen into the hands of a "drug-addicted psychopath" and that he would be very worried because Jose would obviously no longer know what he was doing. Jose was beside himself with rage at the time. So was I.

Anyone can understand the frustration of being dumped for someone else. In desperation, you fight with all unfair means to win back your partner or to save your ego's pride. During the first six months of our time together Jose met his ex-boyfriend several times. Sometimes also secretly. The priest was his great love and Jose was always looking for a way to talk to him and to find a way to get them back together. I was in love with Jose and his behaviour hurt. He left me several times to return to the "bosom of his churchman". After a few days, Jose regularly returned. He said it made no sense because his ex would not change and would not be reconciled. I was happy, in love and blind. When Jose met his ex yet again, I ended our relationship. It was going to be final.

The two of them went on holiday to Holland and from there I received alarming text messages. Jose came back and begged me to meet him. I softened and met a completely changed man who knew what he wanted. Finally we officially became a couple and his seven years of secret rendezvous at the vicarage were history. Having said that, the priest was and always remained Jose's great love. I could only hope that our feelings would grow together accordingly. If I had been the priest I would have fought as well.

Perhaps I would have done foolish things as well. Some things can be excused. For a man of God, the behaviour of the past years clearly overshot the mark. Officially, in this job, being celibate, you should not have a heterosexual or gay relationship. He is just a man full of mistakes, weaknesses and longings. I can only hope that one day, with the necessary forgiveness, he will find the peace within himself that my heart reached some time ago.

Jose's parents were only reassured about his ex's letter when they were invited for a meal for the first time and I cooked for them. Since Jose's mother had been taking medication for decades, due to her own depression and suicidal tendencies, she knew everything about my pills. From that time on, I attended all family celebrations. We never had a really good relationship with each other because of our great differences, but, with the exception of one of his brothers, all of them treated me respectfully as the successor to his ex.
Now Jose is dead and who is to blame for that? That's right, me. The ex was right. I am the devil and I drove Jose to his death. His cousin wrote the following post on Facebook after the founding of TREES of MEMORY: "It's unbelievable that you now want to make money out of Jose's death."

If Jose's parents blame me, if his brothers and sister think I drove him to his death and if his daughter only wants to know one culprit, then I can actually understand that. Those who succumb to the pain of grief can usually only cope with it if the guilt can be moved to the outside world. It is much less problematic to deal with grief if you can transfer guilt to someone. Love, which shows itself in the form of grief, changes into hatred and contempt for the alleged guilty person. Thus this emotion meets someone again. The love for the deceased flows into emptiness, it never comes back.

The grief and the pain of his ex-boyfriend are understandable. I am the reason why Jose separated from him. Jose is dead because we argued. I went to Berlin and threatened to leave him if he didn't seek treatment. It all sounds logical and it is easy to point the finger at someone. Anger and hatred illustrate the hopelessness of feelings and almost act like healing medicine. On closer inspection, these emotions cause lasting damage and prevent a new beginning.

Rationally speaking, it is worth taking a closer look at the subject of guilt. First of all, it is necessary to replace the term guilt with responsibility. Guilt is a morally influenced concept that has been brought in particularly by the church. A word that has nothing to do with the facts. No one is guilty, and you can't burden someone with guilt. But you can and may and should ask about responsibility. Also in my case.

Yes, I was the final straw. Yes, our quarrel triggered a reaction in which Jose took his own life.

But am I responsible for the fact that Jose's mother is suicidal and that he had a disposition to it? Am I responsible for the fact that Jose's grandparents were already severely depressed and passed this on to his mother and her son? Can I be held responsible that Jose stopped taking his medication against better judgment? How can I be held responsible for Jose's refusal to receive medical treatment and to go into hospital? Would his family also blame his father if one of his mother's two suicide attempts had succeeded? Do I have to be held responsible for the fact that Jose suffered from depression and, by his own admission, had been suffering from suicidal thoughts since he was 16 years old? Do I bear the responsibility for the fact that Jose was no longer happy in his relationship and therefore wanted to separate? Do I have to take responsibility for the fact that Jose claimed to have attempted suicide twice in their relationship and still did not receive treatment? Can I be held responsible for falling in love? Am I responsible for the fact that my fear of his committing suicide became so great that I could no longer live with it? Is it my responsibility that Jose skillfully hid his true feelings from the outside world like an actor? Am I responsible for the fact that Jose was in contact with my friends all the time and that the last message to a close friend, who wrote to him day and night, read, "I should go to the hospital, but not immediately. I'm going to bed now and I'll get back to you in the morning." Is it my responsibility that Jose knew very well that he was ill and made this point to his daughter in his farewell lines, which I have in front of me and still did not go for treatment, even for her sake? Am I responsible for the fact that on Maundy Thursday the police did not look for him, although I called them several times. They didn't get back to me because every time I called the police, Jose presented himself as the little innocent, saying that I had psychological problems and I wanted to harm him. Am I in fact responsible for all of this and could I have changed any of it and could I undo it?

I have asked myself all these questions a million times and could not magic out of a hat, "Yes, you are responsible for this", even with the most malicious way of looking at things,

The bereaved do not deserve any blame from others, because their own is enough to make them no longer happy for the rest of their lives. We must be aware that depression and suicidal tendencies are illnesses. None of us would think of blaming a mother, a father or wives for cancer or a stroke. How can it be that with the death of a loved one so many people do not shy away from punishing with guilt, responsibility and recompense? The answer is because of their pain, grief and helplessness. For this reason, I forgive his parents, his siblings and his daughter for what they did to me with their accusations of guilt and their silence. I forgive them that I was denied attendance at his funeral and that they do not allow me to see his grave in order to say goodbye. I wish his entire family, his ex-boyfriend and his friends that they may find peace in their hearts. Forgiveness is a powerful weapon and a valuable remedy in the grieving process. We all received a life sentence with Jose's suicide. We should support and hold each other and we should mourn his death, which is not negotiable and cannot be reversed.

I have found peace and I carry Jose in my heart. I always meet him there with both tears of laughter and of sadness. We will grow old together, because I loved him. Through TREES of MEMORY Jose has already become immortal and will always be remembered. This will not be changed by anything or anyone. I am sorry and I regret with all my heart what this illness has done to family and friends. I hope that you can feel Jose and with it the certainty that he is doing well and that he has taken a different path in the meantime. We must not worry and we can trust in love. It is eternal.

The meaning of my reality

My life should get a new direction and TREES of MEMORY was just the beginning. I went on a new path, both physically and mentally. With every step I took, I changed. I felt that the world around me was also changing and my life was taking on a new shape. The many thousands of kilometres I spent alone in the forest, meditatively putting one step in front of the other, were accompanied by questions and answers, by which my life could be filled with meaning.

It is important to take that first step which makes the vision a reality. Only then can the images in my mind take on a tangible form. However, this is only a part of the reality that would vanish into thin air if I did not give it any meaning. If I don't give meaning to the idea of my life, my visions and what came out of them, then other people will give meaning to my life. Whether I would like that, I doubt it. Everybody who is on the Internet knows about the trolls and the envious people who make everything and anything bad. You can take the wind out of the sails of any critic if you define, live and make the meaning available. Whoever then stands up and judges you, sets himself apart.

Another good reason to define the meaning of my vision myself is the fact that every truth has multiple forms and countless points of view. Those who want to judge choose the dark sides from these possibilities and tell a story that has nothing to do with my intention. Therefore I have to fill my truth with my meaning. With this I set the basis for the awareness of others. The distortion of facts can have a fatal repurcussion on the perceived reality as I show in the previous chapter "Guilt or responsibility".

Which reality of Jose and me is the right one? What do his parents, daughter, siblings and friends see? What reality do you see, as a reader? Every outsider gives our relationship a unique meaning that has nothing to do with my actual reality.
I cannot change that. None of them sat at the table with us, lay in bed with us, or were there when I or Jose cried. When we got to know each other I didn't giveit any particular importance. Why would I?

Meaning and Emotion

At the beginning there was only the vision. A thought that was planted in my mind and which relatively quickly became a plan: Hiking round the world and planting trees in remembrance of suicide victims.
What looked like a fixed idea to outsiders quickly took on life saving significance for me. I never doubted for a moment that this was the right decision. My anger at everything that I had to go through after Jose's suicide was so great that no matter what came, I wanted to work to spare others from this fate. I no longer wanted to see the bereaved stigmatised, harassed and driven with the most repulsive gestures into madness, grief and some of them to death.

I felt that it was important to put everything on the table and to speak for everyone who suffered. I was not afraid for my existence, reputation, future and whatever else might be in danger. I lost all my possessions. Nothing could be taken away from me anymore. I learned that the only gain could be to give value to my being. My suffering should be good for something. Only in this way can I contribute something to alleviating the suffering of others, at least I hope so.

It was, and is already clear to me, that I am no messiah and no miracle healer. I don't want to be that at all. But under certain circumstances some word, some gesture, some of my future actions may have a positive effect in changing a direction.

The personal meaning, together with all this, was gradually enriched with emotions that were divided into light and dark. Either I lived and implemented TREES of MEMORY or I would be dead in a few months. I didn't want to be dead and therefore I had to give my vision not only a meaning, but it was necessary to determine the emotions that went along with it.
As I continued to explore the subject and make plans, I sent out more and more messages that contained emotions. Not necessarily to the outside world, but deep into my own subconscious. The feelings that flooded into me became visible in my writing and in public communication. They became a means for other affected people. We were on the same wavelength and the

bereaved could feel what I had experienced. They noticed that I had to go through the same hell and was not willing to let third parties make me a punch bag any longer.

Those who created their own version of my story, and thus gave it its meaning, could no longer cause me any personal harm. They no longer hurt my feelings and could no longer fuel my own doubts or further develop my initial feelings of guilt. The meaning that some of them gave to the events was lost in the emotion of their hatred. Their grief grew stronger and with it their self-destructive emotions, which were nothing more than the polarity of love, which no longer found answers in death.

The past must not become forever

We are constantly hanging on to our past. We remember with pleasure funny and great experiences. We relive painful memories again and again and the greater the suffering of the past, the greater the the heartache when we look at the situation again.

Unfortunately you cannot plan or specify that the mind will never again journey into the past. Unfortunately, our brain leads a life of its own, which we cannot always escape. Therefore our existence is subjected to a constant comparison. The brain works out what similarities the present has in common with the past. It subjects both time periods to a profound analysis. The goal is to give some meaning to the present experience. In doing so, the conscious mind refers to the experience of the past.

I experience this clearly in relationships with friends and acquaintances. If a behaviour or a statement appears that Jose has made before, the comparison is immediately made. Subconsciously, I evaluate the situation, which thereby acquires a meaning that it does not deserve.

I will try to explain it with an example. When I first met Jose, he suffered from massive sleep disorders. Whenever I woke up in the night, Jose was lying in bed playing on his mobile phone. At first I didn't think anything of it. Later, I knew that the situation was serious. When I wake up now, my boy friend Afshin is lying next to me and usually long before the alarm clock rings, he is awake and reading his Kindl. He has insomnia because there are many things that trouble him. He finds no rest. Immediately my brain compares and comes to the conclusion that it is the same situation. "This is bad", it tells me. As a result I observe Afshin more intensly and discover more and more signs that indicate depression. I approach him about it and I reap almost the same statements as I did from Jose back then. I would see ghosts. It was not all that bad. Everyone is in a bad mood at times, etc. When I refer to my experience with Jose in such a conversation, Afshin freaks out completely. He can't understand how this sets me off and how big my concern is. For this reason, my past with Jose becomes the future with Afshin. My conscious mind has made a decision because it has analysed the situation. The meaning which my mind imposes on me is, "You must be vigilant, because it could happen again".

Of course this is not good. Not for me, not for my mind and not for my relationship with Afshin. With these fears and interpretations I create a future based on the past, which thereby makes the past become forever. De facto I have no chance to live a normal life. The past should remain behind. That would be the natural course in everyday life. But the way I tick at the moment, I have decoupled time. The events that have caused me pain and that have caused me suffering cannot be eliminated. Added to this are the negative emotions that guide, influence and then make every decision. Suffering lives on through me because I constantly bring it into the present and by doing this I save it and stop it from being temporary. It is difficult for me to tell my mind that the story of my life cannot be changed anymore. It seems almost impossible to experience a present that builds a future neutrally and without judgement.

.

But what happens if I concentrate on everything that made up yesterday? I give my thoughts space and freedom to materialise. In this way my fear becomes an event again, from which I actually wanted to protect myself. I must learn to use the power of my imagination in such a way that I can be the creator of my world again. In addition, I should find that at any time I can give a new meaning to an event, an action, or even the word I said. If my boy friend keeps telling me that I don't have to worry and can prove this by the way he lives, the negative analyses of my brain will change more and more into a positive message. This just takes time and is not something that can be done overnight.
Focusing on this new information allows life to take a turn for the better. Each of us carries within us a universe of all possibilities and perspectives. It is up to me to decide which perspective I allow to become real. I can always use the power of imagination to create new worlds for myself.

There is a clear statement: If I want to expand and change my life, I have to expand and adapt the imagination in my life and direct everything I do towards it.

Principle of cause and effect

We all know this principle and there are many proverbs, whose origin lies in this truism. "What goes around comes around" is one such proverb. Or the popular saying "The farmer reaps what he sows". Actually, this basic rule is simple and plausible. You can extend this rule to all areas of life. Everyone can test that it works at home or at work. Be grumpy all day long and you will find that your partner or colleagues at work will also start to feel bad. It works the same way the other way round. Be cheerful and lovable, bring something tasty for your colleagues and the mood will quickly and visibly change towards a harmonious cooperation. Ok, if your work colleagues are selfish fools and they don't want to notice you and your efforts, you have to be charming and lovable all the time if it is to bear fruit one day. Constant dripping wears the stone, you can only hope.

Back to cause and effect. On a small scale and in daily life we already know what it is all about. But what does it look like when we extend it to the level of our life as a whole? Does what we do in our life, or what we have left behind, have an effect?
On closer reflection, each of us can think of a person whose work has been the cause of decisive changes for the future. Think of Martin Luther King and Black Rights. Or the other Luther who divided the church. Marie Curie, who is responsible for the discovery of radioactivity and who invented the mobile X-ray unit. Mother Teresa and many ordinary people who dedicated themselves with their foundations to health, medicine, welfare, art and much more. All activities that do good, have a positive influence on people and are passed on and in use often for hundreds of years. They become reasons for new actions.

People like the ones just mentioned have probably accumulated good karma. But what exactly does that mean? Karma comes from the Indian Sanskrit and translated means "deed" or "action". It is often translated as "action". Karma speaks of nothing other than doing good or bad deeds. To equate karma with a valuation or judgement, as is common in our language, is not correct. Right or wrong? Good or bad? Please remember that this purely human evaluation does not exist in the universal laws. In the Asian religions, karma connects cause with effect and so follows the universal principle. It follows the law of polarity, because good and bad are inseparable and lie on the same axis.

Furthermore, the law of resonance comes into play: Like attracts like. Therefore, the principle of cause and effect is a just principle, because all deeds fall back on to the originator in their effect. According to the Bible, what did Jesus say in the Gospel of Matthew? "He who takes up the sword shall perish by the sword." This is nothing more than a metaphor for the age old law of cause and effect. Incidentally, the Bible is full of pictorial comparisons that are not newly invented, but merely quote the existing universal laws.

He who sows love will reap love. The one who attracts attention only with envy and resentment will reap envy and resentment. The one who sends out hatred will encounter nothing but hatred. So far, so good.

Beware of thinking: "I only have to love the woman or man intensely and sincerely enough, then he or she will love me one day too. Can work, but is unlikely to work. Love stalking, to challenge the principle of cause and effect, tends to backfire. It does not work at all. Remember that the effect of your actions might only show and unfold in another life. Karma has the task to show you how it feels. Everyone should experience for himself what he has done to others. From this you can recognise yourself and the truth. You learn from this. When I look at these theories more closely and apply them to my life so far, I can already see many incidents that prove that everyone gets what he deserves. Pride comes before the fall.

Unfortunately, I personally had to learn that. When I was with my first partner Rasmus, the world knew no limits for us. We were on a steady path to the top. There were moments when I forgot for a while the reality around me. There were many times when I took the as-is state for granted. I made mistakes and there were situations where I was not good. I did things that I would not do today. I have learned lessons from that time. I am sure that I constantly feel the effects of my actions in order to learn from them.

What puts me at ease today is not so much the prospect of everyone getting their come uppance, but rather the causality, from the principle of cause and effect. For a while I was very angry and I started to look for those responsible for my misfortune. That just did not help. There is no one I could pin the blame on. Not even my parents. It may well be that in a prevous life I laid the foundations for my violent experiences. What if I was a thug and crushed my own child? Now might be the time to feel this experience in my own body, to learn from it.

Every action, every thought and every emotion comes back one day, one to one. Therefore I take responsibility for myself and my actions. That is why I should learn that I have to take on responsibilities in a focussed way. I should always focus on it and never forget that the distance between action and effect can be quite long, sometimes over one or many life times.

I see the workings of the principle again and again. Take my stepfather, for example. In my opinion, he is a malicious, resentful, lying, drunk and violent person who got what he deserved. His bricklayer job, his lifestyle and his diabetes weakened him early on and that is why he took early retirement. I don't think he was even 60 and a few months later he had a diabetic toe amputated. In addition, from then on he went blind and several operations did not help. The former loud, bellowing soccer fan now sat in front of the TV at a distance of 30 cm and could only see light and dark. Then came the first stroke, quickly followed by a second one. After that he lay in bed for five more years and had to be cared for until he suffocated. From the day he retired, life made short work of him. He could have dropped dead right away. Instead, he had several awful years and not one more single day that was good in any way. I am sure that karma had a hand in that.

But who knows what I'm going to have to face? As a child I often wished him dead, begged for him to be killed by an excavator shovel. It's not good for my karma either. At over 53 years of age, I no longer wish death on anyone, but I wonder why unscrupulous African or North Korean dictators always get off lightly. I hope, however, that karma will not forget these monsters.

In Buddhism, bad thoughts go against the principle of right thoughts and right action. I cannot imagine that I can undo or neutralise events or thoughts by apologising in spirit. What is done is done, thought is thought, and everything that happens has its justice, and it does so immediately. Immediately, because in the universal understanding every action and thought causes an immediate reaction. However, it may take years for the effect to occur, even though the effect was created long ago.

The stupid thing is that in this present life we just can't remember what we did wrong. In the next life definitely not. The consequence for our whole life is that we go through life happily and self-determinedly on the one hand and at the same time encounter predetermined "reactions" that we have triggered in the past. Therefore, we determine the course of our life ourselves all the time and decide for this or that action. It is our individual decision whether we want to lead permanently one or more positive lives. If we know and sense this, we can accept the bad times and learn from them.

It is important to understand that bad karma is not a punishment. It is solely the consequence of our actions and has nothing to do with punishment. It also

does not follow any thought of redemption. We certainly have the chance to transfer negative actions from the present life into a positive by closure.
How is that possible? That is not complicated. If at some point you stole money from your classmates' jackets in the locker room while they were playing sports and later you can remember who it was, then send them an anonymous envelope with money. If you weren't such a good child to your mother when she was young, show her how important she is to you today and regularly bake her a cake or take her out. If you accidentally killed a child in a car accident, adopt a child and raise it. An eye for an eye, a tooth for a tooth also works for the better. What about modern Robin Hoods? You took it from the rich, then give it to the poor.
Stop, it isn't like in a good film. A thief remains a thief and I'm not sure that redistributing what is stolen will do your soul a service, even though it is honourable to take from those who have enough, and who don't want to hand it over, in order to give it to the needy. But always remember that the one with enough money, by being successful or inheriting, has not only earned it but has also done something for it. Some pay a high price for it. For these reasons I have stopped seeing myself as a victim of the situation. If I was a father who beat his child in another life, I got what I deserved. The only question is whether this law goes on. Will the old geezer in a future life as a child be beaten accordingly? Maybe so. But it cannot be ruled out that he was a victim before and now became a perpetrator in the game of life. There are thoughts which say that with the corresponding counter-reaction, or the other side of polarity, a balancing out has taken place and the issue is closed. You could say: The soul has achieved its learning objective.
.

I for my part can understand even terrible atrocities with this concept. If I kill a child as an adult, I will be killed when I am young or my own child will be killed at an early age in a terrible way. How often do we say: "This child did not harm to anyone and had to die innocently, so young and so brutally, that is not fair". Death in this world is definitely bad and unjust. If then different fates and souls are interwoven, it becomes more complicated and feels much more unjust.
A thought game: There is a mother and father who lose a child, and perhaps this is a reaction to a past equivalent deed in which the two took someone else's child. We also have the child with its own soul's history. In fact, the question arises whether, according to the universal laws, these persons were reunited and only the configuation has changed.

Before you evaluate my thoughts now, find them despicable or otherwise triggered by emotion, please realise that your view of life and fate is also only a theory. None of us knows with certainty how this great movement of life actually works. Not even the pope, who is also only a representative of an ideology. If Catholicism were the only real truth, there would simply be no other models of religion.

I do not judge anyone here. I am not saying that it is so. In my life bubble I support the theory that helps me to bear all the injustice of this world. And if your daily "Our Father" and the belief in heaven and hell helps you to understand, endure and forgive the events around you, then that is as good as my theory. We are all right and at the same time we are all wrong. Furthermore, every possibility is a view point that has to be experienced according to my understanding. If I am the doubter today, I can be one of the convinced tomorrow. We don't know and it's not worthwhile beating ourselves up for religious ideas, whose foundation consists of the visions and interpretations of people like you and me.
Let it be and exist as a possibility, just as I also recognise your faith as a possibility, even if I don't want to share or defend it.

At this point I would like to state that I have no explanation for suicide. I can imagine that the soul was not prepared to solve upcoming tasks and that this life was simply just too much. From a scientific point of view, it has nothing to do with it but that the altered brain chemistry triggers an action that does not correspond to our nature.
Who can give the right answer? God? Can it be by chance that all the universal laws were caused? The more I think about it, the more I come to the conclusion that our saying "There are no coincidences" is not to be objected to. If there is always an opposite pole and there is a reaction to every action and everything in the universe is influenced or made possible by polarity, what would be the opposite pole to chance? I know, "planned causation" someone might say. But then the question would be who planned it? It is damn hard for me to believe in a God who spends half the day creating coincidences or making situations look like coincidences.
The idea that there is a system that, if the worst comes to the worst, searches for some person who has nothing to do is a bit strange and for me it is absurd. No, coincidences cannot exist and if they do, we have not understood the law behind it, if there should be one. Honestly, after all that has happened and how it happened, I don't think I fell into a bad situation by chance. The fact that I consistently decided against what would have been good for me and I put up with everything, no matter how badly it hurt me, suggests that it was no coincidence.

I have a big task to solve and I don't know which one. I also have no plan.
One week before Jose's death I met Tasos at an exhibition and we got along well. Although we only met each other once, for two or three hours at this

exhibition, this complete stranger came to rescue me after hearing what had happened. He stayed for several months and took care of me and helped me to get through the daily routine and life. He guided me through the horror.
When TREES of MEMORY appeared, four months later, he left and has been gone ever since. We often sat on the couch and wondered if our meeting was destined to happen. He showed up the second the drama took its course and then left when I could live on my own again and didn't need anyone to take care of me anymore. I am sure that there are no coincidences. But no matter how: I will forever be grateful to Tasos and the non-coincidence and he has filled an important part of my heart. No matter what.

Addendum
The subject of cause and effect still captivates me, especially since I constantly come across it. I am sure that my actions are the cause. My actions, as the stimulus, will one day show an effect. These effects will in turn become triggers again. My life is created from this cycle and everything that is connected with it. I try to be the cause and the effect in a good way and in the Buddhist sense to lay the foundation for good action and right thinking. In the books it says that you should show compassion and kindness, then you will get both back a hundredfold.
Is this so? Sometimes I doubt it. Unfortunately, I often do not succeed in showing compassion.

If I have any advice, this is it: Examine your life and see if there are things you could make up for. If there are, do it. Even if the karma thing does not exist, it will open up a whole new level of experience because you will feel much better. Check what reaction your actions might trigger and ask yourself if you want to feel good in this life or at least later in life. "What you do not want done to you, do not do to anyone else".
What is this saying based on and why are there so many trolls in the world who are steeped in malice and incompetence?

Karma
The fault lies with the sufferer

As you know by now, I am firmly convinced that we are subject to a constant rebirth. Why? Because I believe that only rebirth brings the form of justice into our world that we all feel the need for. Why was I lucky enough to be born into a country as rich as Germany and why do other souls find themselves in the worst regions of this earth? Why are there people like Hitler, Stalin and any number of other murderers who can carry out their barbaric deeds without being punished? Why are some always rich and others always poor? Our world, that is, what we can see of it, is everything but a just place. If we all had only one life, if nothing came afterwards, and if each of us had only bad luck or good fortune, I would kill myself on the spot, because I wouldn't want that.

Of course, I can't say what the purpose of rebirth is. There are many theories. We could work our way back into the consciousness from which we emerged. We could slip into a new dimension at some point and become a creator ourselves. These are only two theories, out of many on this subject. I do not have an answer.

What I have learned in the past few months, however, is that rebirth is subject to a strict law that is closely related to karma. In addition, I sense with a strange and benevolent certainty that karma could be even more radical than I ever imagined.

I have been interested in Buddhist philosophies for a number of years and also occasionally go to a small Chinese monastery just down the road. There I sit and meditate and learn the basics of Buddhism. Unfortunately, with my birdbrain, I can't remember so many things, and churning out dates, facts, names and concepts, as well as endless lists of this and that, is a bit like learning vocabulary: so not for me. But of course that doesn't mean I don't understand what it's all about and what I have to follow. But I have to confess that although it all appeals to me very much and definitely helps me in my daily activities as a recommendation for action, it does not touch me deeply in my heart. I can't feel it and reading it is as inspiring as studying the Bible, the Koran or the secret teachings of the Upanishads, all of which I have read.

Some time ago I stumbled upon Dada Bhagwan and his science of happiness Akram Vignan. I watched a video about him and although the video only told me about his life, I started crying and something touched me very deeply in my soul. At that moment I began to want to know more and since then I have been reading. From that moment I have experienced a sense of ease here and there that I did not know before and I am still at the beginning.

He talks about how in this world, or in karma, there is only one justice and that is: "The fault lies with the sufferer". This law, or justice, governs the whole universe and all our lives. Those who have earned something through their actions are rewarded and those who have incurred punishment are punished. This is a radical feature in all our lives, in both great and small matters. Everything we do will have its consequence in the next life. Those who accept and understand this 100% will sooner or later have an easier life. Whoever chases after his ego and does not accept that everything that happens to you is the effect of your own actions, which you carried out at some point, will not understand or see justice.

The suffering that runs through our lives is the result of the mistakes we have made. We receive the punishment for a mistake. If we accept it and do not seek revenge, the mistake will be removed and we will be liberated. Thus, every bad deed and every malicious thought or wish we hurl at another soul will bring a punishment in the life to come that must be lived through and atoned for. We all experience the bondage of being, only through the mistakes we have made, because karma is tied to them.

If we live with good intentions and treat all living beings in such a way that we do not harm them through thoughts, words and deeds, we are free. The person who brings punishment to us is called an instrument. Thus, a pickpocket who steals your wallet and is very happy to get the money is an instrument. While the person who suffers from the loss is the punished one. We would cry out that the thief is to blame for our misfortune, because the world always blames the instrument. But Akram Vignan says, "The fault lies with the sufferer". That is why our world looks the way it does. We blame the instruments and seek revenge, setting in motion a never-ending cycle that grows more severe and more painful each time. As a result, people's mistakes double and problems increase enormously.

You may shake your head now and think it silly. But what if Dada Bhagwan is right? Just imagine it for one day with all the consequences. He has another nice example. If we step on a thorn on a road, it is a punishment. It only affects me, for example, because many hundreds of people had crossed the road before. Nobody was hurt, only me. Would I attack the thorn or seek revenge? Of course not. I would just accept it. Why would we want to beat someone to death who intentionally hurts us?

This law, Dada Bhagwan says, is exact and no one will ever be able to change it. It is the only justice that exists. When suffering occurs, the cause is always your own past mistakes.

Sounds terrible if you have to suffer a lot in this life, as I did as a child. What happened to me was deeply unfair and not justified. I couldn't have done such bad things as a 9-year-old to justify being beaten half to death. If the explanation, apart from all sorts of psychological reports attributing whatever to the perpetrator, lies in the fact that I was punished for my own wrongdoing in the past, it makes a lot of sense. It's very painful and it really scares me about the future, but it also holds a certain peace.

Acceptance of everything that happens to us is always the first step towards improving the situation. Those who do not accept their depression, their suicidal tendencies, the loss in death, cannot be freed from it and will continue to suffer. If I always know that I will always get exactly what I am entitled to because of karma, life is much easier, isn't it?

I feel in my case that the sentence: "Whenever you experience some kind of suffering, it is a consequence of your own mistakes", is a statement that must and will drastically change the way I live. This feeling that spreads in this process feels good and light. When I acknowledge the suffering that is brought upon me, my karmic account is balanced, bit by bit.

I wanted to bring this idea closer to you and if you are touched by it, if it does something to you as it has done to me, then my thoughts about it have served their purpose and found you, even if you are only the one in a million. This is also one fragment of many that has helped me to deal better with everything that has happened and to recover a little.

My resistance

I am sure I am not the only one who now and then gets ruffled by something or someone. I build up a resistance as soon as I dislike what this person says or the behaviour they display. I have already built a thick concrete wall between us. The same applies to situations, for example at work. It has often happened to me that I suddenly found myself in a working group that I didn't want to be in. The job was stupid, the employees were not my favourite and then, to top it all, I had to work on things I hated.

Even resistance to objects is possible. Your boyfriend or girlfriend buys something that you absolutely can't stand. For the sake of peace of mind, you don't discuss it for long and accept it being there but its appearance offends you. I still remember a stupid Rosenthal teapot that Rasmus once bought. How many times I was about to drop it from the shelf. During the move I tried to incite my mates to drop the box in question. Unfortunately nobody dared. Ha, even now, at this very moment I start hating this old thing again with its strangely rippled handle.

Twenty years later, this ugly black, white and gold pot manages to constantly fill me with resentment and I can't even remember why I detested it.
Any resistance to a situation, a person or an object that I have built up in the present can prevent me from having a future which is independent of it.
If I concentrate intensely on a resistance, especially when it concerns people, and direct all my actions and thoughts towards it, this leads to an extremely emotional burden. After Jose's death, I focused on the people who had done me wrong. This automatically resulted in negative actions and feelings that became a cause, which have, or will have, their effects in the future.
The resistances that I now build up, keep alive or expand, are cause and effect at the same time. They give rise to my life's story and give it a new direction, depending on which cause I encourage to work. When I look at it more closely, I constantly have my future insight.
I am grateful that I have found myself in time and the people to whom I mean something. I dedicate my thoughts exclusively to them, which contain nothing negative. This has resulted in four valuable years, which have led me into a fulfilled future. All others have fallen prey to transience and that is good.

A successful start in life

When a new life is born, I always feel it is a small impartial miracle of nature. No matter whether human or animal, with every new breath and in the blink of an eye the living being goes on a voyage of discovery and perceives its environment, its reality and the basic conditions of life. Most mammals walk within the first hour as they are genetically preprogrammed and driven by instinct. It is part of survival.

On the other hand, we humans lie in our beds for months on end and are dependent on the help of our parents. We are cared for, fed, changed and colourful toys help us to explore the magic of the world full of curiosity. Everything is beautiful, is colourful and we fall in love with everyone who meets us with love, cuddles and kisses. Unless it is grandma or an aunt who spits on the handkerchief then cleans our face with it.

The second we show a little independence, our world of adventure abruptly changes. It becomes wider and at the same time more limited. Suddenly, parents show a new side. "Youre not allowed to do this and that" and "You can't do that" are statements that not only limit our space, but our ability, our drive, our thirst for knowledge and the innocent souls whose task it is to become a light in this world. Parents teach fear instead of opening our eyes to the infinite possibilities of life and nurturing our courage. Some of the educationalists do this gently and determinedly, others are uncompromising to those who don't wish to or cannot listen. My parents belonged to the latter group. Themselves disadvantaged in life and beaten by father and mother, their pain was probably not great enough to spare their own children such a fate. Completely incomprehensible to me, they went the same way using violence. I heard so often "a good hiding never hurt anyone," and "others have survived the carpet beater on the bare arse", I shouldn't make such a fuss.

Under such conditions I was often forced to change direction, although my heart and little soul wanted to take new paths. The pain inside me increased. Over the years, the suffering became an illness. And it took many decades before I realised that my soul's pain is the wisest teacher of all advisors.

Nevertheless, I have suppressed this knowledge. Only when the ground was ripped away from under my feet did I realise that I had been going along the wrong path for too long. It would not have taken much for me to have perished in the labyrinth of all the fake stories

Today I know that a single cause is enough to produce an infinite number of effects and repercussions. 30 merciless smacks on my bare arse, week after week, the fist of a bricklayer, punched month after month right in the middle of my face as a child, create emotions that I still cannot escape. I learned early on that I have to interpret everything that is happening around me in time if I want to avoid a beating.

Today, when a bulky guy with a spluttering voice yells at me, my body shakes all over. All the memories immediately come flooding back and with them a list of meanings that have been stored in my mind. I cannot control the feelings that arise from this. To detach them from the experiences is almost impossible. Its disastrous because these perceptions dictate my behaviour and actions. I set new causes, which have an effect far into my future. Therefore, my past quickly becomes part of my future outlook again, which is obviously no better than what happened 45 years ago.

Of course, I have learned over the course of the last 53 years that I can only recognise whether something went well when I compare it with the past, in which the same situation did not end well. So today I know that the boy friend at my side is not the right partner for me just because I think I have already had the almost perfect man.

At the same time I wish I could stop interpreting men or different situations, compare them, evaluate them and put them in a box with a judgement. I hoped with all my heart to get back the unaware, childlike impartiality in every aspect of my life. Then I would feel much better. It would be so good if I could flip a switch that would turn off these processes. I try to do that regularly.

When I meet a new man, he actually doesn't get my inherited guilt put on him and I throw myself into a funny adventure with my naive curiosity and hope that it will be good for the long term. This works until the first situation comes along in which I think "this has happened before". Already I am again in the middle of the interpretation trap, in which I give it a significance and the subconscious programming seeks to match it with feelings from the past.
The other day my boyfriend didn't get in touch with me for three endless hours, although he had wanted to come home right away. This is a bad situation when you are the survivor of a suicide. My memory recalled a whole

bombardment of fear. The outcome was that I yelled at the poor guy for a quarter of an hour when he came home and told me about the fun and beer with his colleagues. It would have been better for me if he had let me know. So our massive argument, which he still cannot or does not want to understand, has effects far into the future and is part of numerous reasons in our agreement to separate. He thought he had done nothing wrong, the poor guy. He could not attach any importance to the fact that he had not sent a text message saying "I'm still drinking a beer, so it may take a while...". This does not matter in his reality. In my reality bubble, a short message takes on a relevant meaning to which a fearful implication is attached. Therefore my mind dares to assign a meaning to his indifferent reality. The overall situation, about which I have allowed myself to make a judgement, has turned into a condemnation within seconds.

At this moment, during the argument, my evaluation of the situation has ensured that I have given the present a new meaning based on the past, the effects of which will shape my future. You already suspect it. Nothing good will come of it.

The principles and processes behind it made me ill and don't do me any good. But it is up to me to reconstruct them in such a way that the same processes will lead me to health, take away my fear and lead me out of grief. The underlying beliefs can remove the pain caused by Jose's suicide.

This is a task at least as powerful as hiking round the world. But it is possible. It is up to me not to be triggered any further. My opposite number can't help that his reality bubble is full of light-heartedness and he had nothing bad in mind.

Wishful thinking, realities and your decisions

In spite of everything that happened to me, and because the limits that were set so drastically for me had taken away any room to breath early on, I have become a great dreamer whose visions usually knew no limits. My fantasies were the salvation of my narrow minded existence and like Pippi Longstocking I regularly swam to a small island where I created the world as I liked it. There were no limits and I could be everything. "You must not" and "you cannot" did not exist. Amidst my palm grove and the gentle waves of the azure sea, there was nothing but dreams of the future. Big, colourful, powerful visions that felt so real that I saw no other way forward but to want to live them, come hell or high water.

And so it came about that the little adventurer made a name for himself in discovering the world. In my dreams I explored the planet and set out to uncover its secrets. Africa especially appealed to me. The longing was so great that when I was 23, I put on my over sized hiking boots and let my dream come true. My first big trip abroad led me to Africa. It took me one year to cross the continent, starting in Senegal and flying home from Madagascar. This trip taught me a lot about life, people, hardship and wealth, travelling, as well as myself. I have been able to take experiences with me which bring me back down to earth when the desire for prosperity strikes me again.

In the course of my life I have learned again and again to believe in myself and to follow myself. When I did so, my dreams came true, no matter how absurd they sometimes were. I could fill a book with them. I am not doing that now. But you should hear about a dream that started when I was ten years old.

My grandpa had everything you could move with a remote control: helicopters, aeroplanes, cars, ships. He owned a metre high replica of the Titanic. The engine packed in and so he was no longer interested in it and wanted to throw it away. I loved this ship and I was able to persuade him to give it to me. I didn't want to stand at a lake and let it sail. That was too stupid for me even then. But it was fine in my room.

So the Titanic stood beside my bed for many years. How many times I imagined myself sailing across the seas with her. I had seen all kinds of films and I always had the thought:
I want to see this ship live!
We know what happened to her. In 1912 she sank to a depth of 5000 metres and killed 1,700 people. She was found in the Atlantic Ocean by Robert Ballard on 1st September, 1985. Again there were films of the wreck in the darkness, prepared for Hollywood. Again I was dreaming. 15 years later Ballard gave up the maritime rights to the Titanic. Extremely wealthy people from all over the world were then ready to secure these rights - because you can make a fortune with them. One of them was Graham Yasopp. Treasure hunter. Worth millions. His father had found the Bismarck and pulled sunken gold from a warship for the Russians, for which he received around 300 million dollars. Graham wanted the Titanic. Maritime law requires that salvage work on a wreck be documented.

And what happened? I got a call from Alex from the film production. Without much explanation, he asked me if I would like to go out and look for the Titanic and make a film about it. I was so excited. I jumped up and down with joy and surprise. About three months later, I was on an $85 million salvage trip. A few weeks later, with the help of our diving robot, I saw the Titanic lying at the bottom of the sea . I saw her with my own eyes, only not as beautifully lit as in the Hollywood films. Naturally, the universe could no longer fulfill my dream of going on board, but it did its best and gave me the greatest possible gift. The universe always does its best. This is as sure as eggs is eggs.

My dream became a reality and I have to admit that I never believed that this would be possible. All I can say is: There is no reason to stop dreaming and even less reason not to believe that dreams build the reality of the present and the future and that shitty times will get better again.

After searching for and finding the Titanic, good fortune led me to a 22-metre sailing boat, the Pelagic Australis. I was allowed to be an accompanying journalist and to document "Breaking the Ice", the peace expedition of Israelis and Palestinians. We sailed together on a cockleshell boat from Chile to the Antarctic on 1st January, 2004, where we made the first ascent of a mountain. A mountain that today bears our name: Mountain of Israeli-Palestinian Friendship. The pictures and magnificent experiences which I was allowed to make on this trip will still make me happy on my death bed and I thank every atom in this universe for letting me experience this. By the way, it can be found on the Internet at www.breakingtheice.org/antarctic

Years earlier, in 2000, completely out of the blue, they rolled out the red carpet for me and I got a job in Los Angeles that I didn't even want. But do you miss this experience? Not me. I lived and worked there until I got fed up with my boss's selective perception and the insincerity of Hollywood and the whole country annoyed me more every day. Two weeks before 9/11 I turned my back on the American dream. I still miss Los Angeles today because, despite everything, there were many circumstances that I loved, that suited me well and did my mind more good than any medicine. 300 days of sunshine a year and the sea on my doorstep were among them. If I have that, hardly anything can happen to me mentally.

Years later I finally turned my back on my daily life with TV and became freelance with my own small business. Shortly after that I was offered the opportunity to teach. That was 2008 and a new vocation was born. I still teach today and now, as I write this sentence, I am in my last week for the time being as a lecturer. Corona stole the contracts from me. But also my subconscious says it is time for this to be over. Deep inside me, a long time ago, I unconsciously made decisions that led to events which heralded the end. Corona now only puts the lid on it..
What next?, you ask yourself. Mmm, I ask myself the same thing. I would like to earn my living in winter as a funeral celebrant and I will work to make it happen. But it won't be the end of the road, because one day I won't have to take a winter break anymore from TREES of MEMORY and my hike round the world. How will I earn the money to continue my project?

Yes, TREES of MEMORY is also one of those things, an impulse, a motivation, a part of me, the consequence of what has happened, a great help and the meaning of my life, which I simply put into practice. The most glaring life project ever. Jose's death had completely snatched my life away and torn it into a million pieces. It became a life's work that reassembled these jigsaw pieces and gave me a new life. It was the icing on the cake of my big, colourful, entertaining, not always carefree life story. So far it feels like it will be better than all of it ever was before.

If you are interested, then you are welcome to visit http://www.treesofmemory.com to see what fruits my "letting go" and my "new beginning" have brought about.

All the things I was allowed to do, I have long called a gift of the universe. In fact, I owe them less to a great master in the vastness of the universe than to my insistence on living my dreams and my ability to grab it and try it, even if my reasoning initially argued against it. Every decision to live a dream, to implement a small vision and to get stuck into a big fantasy has always radically changed my life, especially in the past four years.

I have never regretted a decision nor has it done me any harm. No matter what, it fit into my life, it suited me and my intuition on which I relied. These alternatives appealed to the me that my parents beat up and the non-conformist me who crucially did not conform with the "what" generally considered good or bad, right or wrong, true or untrue. I set my priorities at every age, in every decision. The results of my adventures and the episodes were always more important to me than money or career. I ignored the objections of those who meant me well and the attempts to block it by those who always wanted to harm me. I have bravely faced the concerns, worries and fears, even my own. In my mind there was no scenario that showed me images where something would end disastrously. What could happen to me? I could not lose anything. Especially not what I did not want: wealth and career. I always wanted to live happily, feel myself and be myself, and now more than ever. Whether this is good or bad is judged at this moment only by the fact that you are evaluating me and you want to put your evaluation and the meanings of your outcomes and experiences on me, forgetting that my reality has nothing to do with yours. My character and the meanings I give to things are not part of your life. Seen from your point of view, all this may feel terrible and uncomfortable. But it would only be bad if you had to do the same as me. For you, the pursuit of career, money, family and luxury travel may be just what you are looking for, and it fits your character traits. This is good for you. It would be a disaster for me. Therefore it is neither good nor bad, right or wrong.

Every one of us makes decisions every day that will influence our life and that of our surroundings. At every moment each one of us acts in accordance with his experiences, beliefs and emotions and this gives rise to effects which are often only seen years later. That it to say, when the lowly bank trainee one day becomes head of a finance house, the young girl becomes a mother, the old man builds a school in a third world country or a reader follows his true calling in two years.

I would like to invite you to go on a journey. Take a trip into the possibilities of your self. If one day you decide for something new, you must be aware of what is more important in life. Is it the freedom to be yourself or is it the fears and worries that keep you from any change?

Now, for a moment you can decide for yourself which of my experiences you would give yourself. Allow yourself the possibility that you a.......... ... and observe. Take the liberty to forgive any judgement of "nonsense". But you could nevertheless look at what we both have in common. It is within the realm of possibility that somewhere there is a sentence that makes you sit up and take notice, brings change and can give you something new on your journey.

Decide now, or postpone it and decide later. No matter how or what, it is good as it is and shall be what it becomes.

My helpers

I got to know my helpers when I watched the "Dead Poets' Society" in the cinema in January 1990. I was 23 years old at the time and at last had in mind to pack in the dream job as a policeman. This film and Robin Williams changed my life. "My Captain, my Captain". I cried my eyes out when I left the cinema. I felt that I was on the wrong road like never before. It tore up my thoughts and feelings into a thousand pieces.

On that day for the first time I surrendered to my innermost nature on a grand scale and listened to the strong feelings. The world of bogus arguments was to fall silent and I abandoned myself to the consequences that were to come. A few days later I quit the riot police and put the kibbosh on my childhood dream, which had made me so unhappy. The same day I was kicked out of my home with a great commotion and lots of yelling. One day later I moved into my own flat in Hechingen, which my best friend Michael had shown me in his neighbourhood. I wonder what he is doing today? I tried to find him from time to time, but nothing. He has disappeared from the face of the earth, like so many good friends from back then.

I can't find words for the tragedy surrounding the suicide of the great actor Robin Williams. What would have gone through my mind if a clairvoyant had told me that the subject of suicide would one day connect us?
I have made up my mind that one day, when I arrive in the USA with TREES of MEMORY, I will try everything to plant a tree in memory of this hero. It must succeed, my Captain, my Captain.

There are several quotations and poems that have always accompanied me from those days. They fill my heart, they express thoughts, they always give me courage and they make me smile. They make me carry on: Earlier, today, tomorrow, the day after tomorrow and in the distant days of the future. At that time in the cinema, I sat rigid in my seat and every line was a slap in the face that pulled me out of my powerlessness.

I thank these ancient souls for coming into my life and for always accompanying me with the following words, building me up and sometimes wiping away tears of hopelessness. They gave me the strength for the first time to oppose the illusion.

The power of their message still works. It is not impossible that they now have an effect on you as well, dear reader.

Walt Whitman
(1819 – 1892)

"The worst and most widespread disease that plagues us all, our literature, our education, our behaviour towards each other, is the unhealthy worry about appearances.

"Until the mind is changed, all outward change is null and void."

"The pendulum indicates the moment, but what indicates eternity?"

The following poem is taken from his poetry anthology "Blades of Grass":

O me! O life! of the question of these recurring,
Of the endless trains of the faithless,
Of cities fill'd with the foolish,
[...]
The question, O me! so sad, recurring –
What good amid these, O me O life?
Answer
That you are here – that life exists
and identity,
That the powerful play goes on,
and you may contribute a verse.

He delivered the decisive sentence that would dramatically change my life from that moment on:

Robert Frost
(1874–1963)

from the poem "The Road Not Taken"

Two roads diverged in a wood, and I –
I took the one less traveled by,
And that has made all the difference.

Henry David Thoreau
(1817–1862)

 wrote in his book Woods:

I went to the woods because I wished to live deliberately, to front only the essential facts of life, and see if I could not learn what it had to teach, and not, when I came to die, discover that I had not lived. I did not wish to live what was not life, living is so dear; nor did I wish to practice resignation, unless it was quite necessary. I wanted to live deep and suck out all the marrow of life, to live so sturdily and Spartan-like as to put to rout all that was not life, to cut a broad swath and shave close, to drive life into a corner, and reduce it to its lowest terms, and, if it proved to be mean, why then to get the whole and genuine meanness of it, and publish its meanness to the world; or if it were sublime, to know it by experience, and be able to give a true account of it in my next excursion.

E. E. Cummings
(1894–1962)

from his poem "Dive"

Dive for dreams
or a slogan may topple you
trees are their roots
and wind is wind.

Trust your heart
if the seas catch fire
and live by love.
though the stars walk backwards

Honour the past
but welcome the future
and dance your death away
at this wedding.

Never mind a world with its villains and heroes
for God likes girls,
and tomorrow and the earth.

What am I for?

As a teenager, I spent endless nights around the campfire and with friends tried to find the meaning of life. We didn't find any answers. The useless number "42" left us as helpless as any other viewer of the film "Hitchhiking through the Galaxy". I had to turn 50 and live a big, fun, colourful, senseless but perfectly normal life until I found out the hard way where and how I would find the meaning and the answers to my questions.

The other day I heard in a report that our universe is home to good and bad angels. Both have their tasks and are by no means to be classified as well-meaning and mean creatures. The white messengers of heaven try to move us in a meaningful direction with positive suggestions, so that our soul can learn and develop itself further, so that it can make use of its potentials. We all know that some of us, I am one of them, are sometimes a little resistant to advice. In such a case, the black angels come into play, who teach us the hard way what's what and whose the boss. They push us brutally and without mercy onto a path and drive us along until we have understood of our own accord what is good for us. This is why they are called demons or just the evil or black angels.

In reality they mean well to each one of us and use as a last resort the language we understand, according to the motto: "And if you are not willing, I will use violence".

I think this is a beautiful idea that has helped me not to rail as much against my fate and to accept life as it is. It was not easy and I was far from acceptance for a long time. But in the meantime I have accepted my path and realised that it is spot-on and that it gives me a life for which I am grateful and which gives me fulfilment again. I have understood that I am the only one who can give meaning to my life. I could have developed, invented and determined the meaning of my life years ago. Life would have been different if I had known, and not repeatedly forgotten, that I am the creator of my happiness.

In the meantime, I believe that we need a school subject that helps us to develop the meaning of life.

At school we learn a lot of meaningless rubbish that hardly anyone needs in life. We don't learn how we can manage to integrate happiness in life through our actions. We are not taught how to practice mindfulness and how a meaning of life can protect us from depression, life-weariness and suicide.

Viktor Frankl, who is well versed in having meaning at the centre of life and hope, reports in his existential analysis that a meaning in life has value for mental health. I am convinced that if we could fill our lives with meaning at a young age, depression and suicide would play only a small or no role at all. Especially if this meaning is a little bit bigger and more important than our own modest life. But it doesn't matter whether you hike around the world planting trees for suicide victims, rearing old breeds of domestic animals or growing pink fir trees. It does not determine what society values, but what it does to ourselves. I give life a meaning and with that I myself become the meaning of life. I am always the beginning and never the end.

With this meaning, born from my visions and dreams, I am part of this great movement in which our life is an integral part. In this way I go further and join in the game of the powers that be and here and there set a new rule. What remains of me in the end is the poem that is recited, the song that I have sung, my care that I have passed on to the children, my smile that is carried through the world from person to person. Perhaps my thoughts will touch generations and my picture will be painted anew every day. The trees I have planted, if all goes well, will still be standing in 1000 years. The animals you reared will walk the earth until it goes under. Our associations and foundations could outlast time and help many generations. No matter how big or small our legacy will be, no matter how important or insignificant our heritage may be, what remains is the memory of us which makes us immortal.

I know of course what you are thinking now: "What's the point of these same old lines", "You are the architect of your own happiness" and "Give your life meaning"? Yes, I have not reinvented the wheel and I can hardly sell you truths that have not been known for a long time or that you have never heard. I have taken note of all these thoughts for decades. Have I ever consciously used them with all my senses? No. They slipped between the fingers in the life of fun and in stressful times, they were worn out and fell into oblivion. Until at some point, long after Jose's death, all that information gradually came back into my consciousness. Even then I thought: "What's with these antiquated traditions?"

One day I started to analyse what had happened and I observed my life so far in retrospect. I saw how I reacted and what it caused. In a flash the penny dropped. I began to test it. I responded to the association's board of directors, "How can this be done?" when a problem appeared on the horizon, I kept saying that, "I didn't know. You can trust me. It will happen if needs be".

Since I started with TREES of MEMORY, life has been going exactly as it should. No more, no less. It is not raining millions from the sky, but the association is growing. I earn money in the winter and if it doesn't happen, then a door opens. I experience a great sequence of effects, the causes of which I have consciously designed. Sometimes this happened unconsciously, because my intuition knew before I even suspected that ...

That is why what I have heard a thousand times before is suddenly new and real. I try to back up everything I have experienced with examples and events. In this way I hope that the new meaning of words will have an effect and that something will be created that will surprise you as much as it surprised me and will continue to leave me speechless.

Give life a new meaning

Anyone who loses a partner, a child, a sibling or a parent unexpectedly and without warning often experiences how life changes dramatically from one moment to the next. Nothing is the way it used to be, and in the event of suicide, the relatives feel that the world will never be the same again.

I also experienced this after Jose's suicide. I had the feeling that everything around me and inside me imploded. I knew immediately that this was the most enormous turning point of all time.

Plagued by a renewed suicidal tendency due to my self-reproaches, extreme panic attacks and depressions that could hardly be surpassed in their darkness and power, I was rarely able to leave the flat for almost six months. It was so bad that friends went shopping for me.

I cried day and night for more or less six months. The pain and grief were immense. But the worst of all feelings was that I no longer saw any point carrying on. There was nothing worth living for anymore. The friends, my job, my family, nothing mattered anymore. Even my little project for the homeless "The Winter Knitters" got lost in a void of meaninglessness.

It wasn't as if I had previously lived a life enriched with great meaning. I was pursuing the things I loved. A little writing, reading, travelling, friends, work, partys, no children and no family which I must provide for, no family which worries much about me... that is it. Meaningless and nothing exciting ..... that was the purpose in life and suddenly it was gone.

Life lost all meaning the second I received news of the death. A glance into the future revealed nothing but endless darkness. To simply carry on at some point as before was and still is unthinkable.

Then came the day when I was in the shower early one morning and Trees of Memory was delivered as a full package, as I call it. Unexpectedly, this strange idea was in my head. At first I thought I was really going crazy, but hours later it was clear to me: Mario, either you do this or you're dead in four weeks at the latest. I had no alternative and I still feel that way.

A few weeks later, when I went public with TREES of MEMORY, and as many people were fascinated as well as horrified, I was allowed to present the project at the annual meeting of the Frankfurt Network for Suicide Prevention. There I met the patron, Dr. Walter Kohl. Nobody laughed at me, on the contrary. I received immediate support. Later at a dinner together, Walter casually said: "Surely you are familiar with Viktor Frankl's book, Yes to life, in spite of everything: a psychologist experiences the concentration camp".
Erm.. I didn't know it.
Viktor Emil Frankl was an Austrian neurologist and psychiatrist. He founded logotherapy and existential analysis, which is known as the "Third Viennese School of Psychotherapy". As a Jew, he survived the Holocaust in the concentration camps of Dachau and Auschwitz. In this book he describes how the human soul and mind changes when years are spent under such conditions. The only thing that kept these people from killing themselves or provoking the immediate murder of themselves was nothing but hope. The expectation to get through all this, to be liberated, to have their family again, to be able to go back to life.

Then the prisoners were freed. And they found that all their family members had been murdered. They came to the cities which had been flattened and no longer had any home or property. They were surrounded by people who, despite everything, preferred to see them dead rather than alive, surrounded by Nazis and traitors and hardly any country would take them in. What had kept them alive was gone: hope.

Many of these people did not survive the years that followed. But others succeeded in doing what was almost impossible to imagine. They found a new lease of life, they had families, they could laugh again and grew old. These people were able to give their lives a new meaning.
Viktor Frankl calls it meaning centred living.

Without knowing this book, I or my soul, who knows, has done exactly that. My life was given a new meaning. One that goes far beyond what I had before. I never doubted for a second that it would do me good to implement Trees of Memory. My heart and my feelings said with surprising ease: Do it.

My brain went into overdrive and screamed the whole day that I have completely gone mad. I kept having panic attacks and then something inside me switched and said: trust it. Follow your heart. Do it and you will see. That's what I did and that's how everything in my life changed. It even got to the point where I was able to gradually reduce the medication for the treatment of the depression, which I had been taking for four years.

Since March 2018 I have been hiking around Germany as the first stage on my way around the world and have so far planted about two dozen trees of memory.

Before that, there were people who were so fascinated that they founded an association that has doubled its membership after only one year and in the meantime offers active support for the bereaved families. I hike through the world day after day and I have tears in my eyes so often because I am grateful that I am allowed to do this and meet all these people and I am alive again.

I have given up everything for this project. I gave away or sold everything I had and I gave up my rented flat. All my possessions fit into 5 moving boxes. I was prepared for the feeling that the letting go of my worldly goods would be an advanced payment for which I would get something great. I still have that feeling, though the specialness has long been part of my current path. I have received a great gift when I look at the events of the last two years. It cannot be put into words.
Giving life a new meaning has saved my life. It was difficult and in my case it was as radical and final as Jose's suicide. But what I am doing now fulfils me more than all the money in the world. And it suits me, also because of its extreme focus.

You don't have to give up everything, but you can. You don't have to want to save the world, maybe the dog breeding you have been dreaming of for years is enough. Knitting for the homeless is as helpful as collecting rubbish on the beach. Starting your own family, club or foundation is meaningful. Working in an organisation can change your life. This is reported by some of the members of the association who, with a lot of enthusiasm and commitment, promote and expand the association TREES of MEMORY e.V. By the way, we are still looking for people who would like to volunteer as contact persons for our "First Contact Points" or who would like to support the association in other ways.

Everything is possible. It is important to find a meaning that makes you forget the dramas, that fills you with ease and that refocuses and centres your life. You just have to feel your project, your plan, the new task and the sense of purpose, with such power that it leaves you in no doubt. The power which would give you all the energy to do what is necessary in order to commit yourself completely to your new task will come knocking loud and clear on your door. It doesn't matter if it is something big or small, extreme or normal. The important thing is that it is yours.

I have learned that it depends on what answer you find to the sinister tasks that life presents you with so mercilessly. When the dark angel comes around the corner and hits you in the face hard, he wants to hear and see answers. This insight saved my life and lets me laugh, live and love again today.

I believe that it is not so difficult to find meaning when you ask yourself what your heart is desiring and how you can combine it with other things. I don't believe that you can sit at your desk and invent a meaning that you can't feel, as you would with a marketing strategy. I think that you can open your heart and feel it. Get in touch with the self, the soul or whatever you want to call it. Now that sounds terribly abstract or aloof. But it is not. You just need a little bit of courage to allow it to happen. If you succeed, you will find that it no longer matters how much you earn or whether the flat is small or large, because everything revolves around being able to do what you feel and what fulfils you.

Saying yes to life by giving it a new meaning. Sometimes even your loss and pain can help you do this. It is possible to transform these feelings and then they no longer paralyse you but give you the energy to get up and move on.

Do not worry about what others think. I also annoy many, even friends. But none of them has ever walked in my shoes. Do not worry about the others. It's all about you alone, because you lie in your bed in the evening and you will feel how you are. You will see how much positive feedback you will get from others. The annoyed ones live their carefree life, which is theirs but not yours. Letting go means, among other things, separating from people who want to control or change your life or who are annoyed for selfish reasons. People who, with their egocentric negativity, do not enrich your life, do not support it, but harm it. None of us has to make this a problem for ourselves. It is about you, your life, your health, your future and your happiness.

The hope and the key to salvation lie buried exclusively in yourself. It is important to find them. To give your life a new meaning will help you to do so.

If you have lost someone, life will never be the same again, it will realign itself, get other qualities and make you miss many things painfully. But it will be all right again. Painful memories may be a part of it.

Say yes to life. Nobody can take that from you.

Sunny Boys in relationships

When I think back and look at every fling and affair, as well as my long and important relationships, it becomes clear how significant similar goals and energies are which have connected me to the men. A happy and loving relationship can only develop when both are attracted with the identical dynamics of love. Not the one who is madly and undyingly in love, as I felt with Jose, or the other who just thinks it's so-so.
Unfortunately, I was not always blown away in love and there were two or three stories in which I was rather moody. Nevertheless, I gave it a try, because I hoped that more would develop or that there would be similarities that made it worth living together. I think it's worth giving it a chance for several weeks.

But I am half Italian and a loud cry of "a heart in love" is somehow part of it. It was not good at all, because it overruled existing shortcomings. In the meantime I tend not to listen anymore to a heart that's shouting out. I want someone who understands me. Someone who has the intellect to put mental factors in order and who has defined goals in life for himself, which he follows. Intentions that can be combined with mine. They do not necessarily have to be identical. I find that it can be agreed upon if my opposite is a security conscious person and I leave it to fate how secure my life becomes. The important thing is that we don't impose our ideas on each other and have the ability to push the boundaries and dare to try something new.

This consideration makes it clear that there are many factors that contribute to the fact that surfing together on different waves is possible. It is a bit like having two surfers. One is on a wave as high as a house and the other on the slightly lower one in front of him. When both of them master the sea simultaneously and encourage each other, they reach common goals and build up positive energy together. Then it doesn't matter whether you swim five metres higher or not. Unless you absolutely want to go where the other one is and you can't for a thousand reasons. Then it becomes a competitive struggle. In addition you are constantly accompanied by a frustration that intensifies. At the beginning of an attempt at a relationship, everything is usually nice and smooth, perfect and nobody thinks of anything bad. Then there is this one moment that changes everything. I had such a typical moment with an affair. At that time I should have reacted immediately and left.

We only knew each other for a few weeks and I spent a few days with him. One evening he came home late because he was having a drink with his colleagues. He then told me that the next day his colleague's dog would come to us because she was going on holiday for a week. He thought that would be fine because I was at home all day with my dog, which I then had. I was outraged that he hadn't asked me if it was OK with me. I was angry because it's stupid to promise to take a dog without first checking to see if the two animals will get along. I was pissed off because I was the one who was supposed to walk both mutts, which caused me a lot of stress with a strange bitch and my own animal, which is not used to the city, which is afraid, which has not learned to walk on a leash next to another dog. In addition, I was unwell at the time and was supposed to recover in bed. When I expressed my clear displeasure, the guy gave me such a ticking off, he would never ask anyone for permission whether or not to do a kind deed for a colleague. I was lying awake half the night, struggling with myself whether I should just leave the next day. Whatever the reason, unfortunately I did not.

The very next evening the man learned his lesson and saw how stupid his behaviour was. As a result he tried half the night to dump the dog on other friends, which unfortunately did not succeed. Russell, a beagle, was a clever guy, but the animalistic I-want-attention-hell, after he thought he'd been abandoned by his mistress and master, resulted in him howling the whole place down when I just took the rubbish down. He also messed up my dog because he showed him that it was much better to lie on a human couch than on the floor.

Anyway, looking back, that was the first crack in our relationship. Many more were to follow and each was more significant than the one before. Any disharmony became a cause for the future when it became an effect in the present. I endured it almost exactly one year to the day, then fortunately our paths parted. It was a lesson for me which I hope will not be repeated.

My relationship with Rasmus is still such a highlight because we lived it from an inner and unconditional happiness. We floated on cloud nine for many years because this happiness was stable and strong. We committed ourselves to Fortuna, to good luck, which continued to grow. The more joy we experienced, the more intense each moment became. Sometimes it was almost unbearable, it was so beautiful. Everything we did and invested was mutually dependent. Until that moment when each of us made mistakes and the sexual urges were stronger than love and reason. Until that point when we hurt each other for the first time and trust was no longer there. You can compare it to a yeast dough that rises further and further in the heat and is beautifully round. The moment you poke it with a knife, the air escapes and it no longer looks great. Then you have to knead it again, reshape it and let it rise again. It can still make an excellent bread, no question about it. If the dough remains sunken and unprocessed, it won't be round any more.

All my subsequent relationships, to be honest, did not even manage to rise nicely and fill up because important ingredients were missing. I no longer fool myself or try to do so. Everything that doesn't fit or that which was, to talk nice about it, only becomes a paralysing lie. A past that I do not want to repeat. The mere claim that you are happy is like quicksand. Nothing can stand up to that. How many times have I said "we are fine" even though I felt deep inside that this was not true.

Today I still have no patent remedy and I know very well that love can be a huge arsehole that deceives us wherever it can. I believe and I hope that I will once again meet a person who has had basic experiences and whose sexual urges are, as far as possible, behind him. Someone who knows that the secret ingredient of a happy relationship is the creation of moments of happiness and bliss, coupled with the same or similar values and goals. (Hey, read it again. This sentence was important.) Someone who has experienced first-hand that the production of suffering, unhappiness and injury in the long run always becomes the cause and effect for destroying the relationship.

Almost three years after Jose's death I suddenly fell in love. I was grateful and wanted to be blind because it felt so good. It soon became clear that we were not only on different wave lengths, but that our very own frequency could not be understood by the other person. It felt as if I was using a CB radio to play a radio programme. My mind was suffering from it faster than I could feel or think. But any relationship, no matter how easily ailing, is a huge burden on mental health. I realised that it is more beneficial healthwise to remain alone than to absorb the poison that unfulfilled longings, wishes and hopes secrete every day.

Alter the way we live?

Depression, burnout or their symptoms - suicidal thoughts do not come from anywhere. There is a cause for every illness. Whether it is medical or spiritual, because an unsolved problem from the past made us ill, should not be discussed here. The fact is that depression is the most pathological unhappiness, which is accompanied by zero future prospects.

From my own medical history I know when my depression started and who might be partly responsible. I deliberately say "partly", because nobody knows when the melancholy breaks out, who gets it and what is necessary for it. As much as I would like to pillory my parents for this, I have to admit that there are many shitty parents and children who have been brought up with violence and have not developed depression or anxiety. There are no studies that prove that this or that is "guilty". Of course, it is easier for the likes of us to blame others and share responsibilities. For example, that cruel parents should deserve this is not fair, no matter what. The number of unknown factors of this illness is too high to present a simplified explanation.

People who suffer from depression usually have a whole bundle of negative burdens that they have to carry around with them. There is the past as the cause with its effect in the present, which becomes the future. I was able to compensate for this for a long time with a great job. A job that was not there to make money. A job that I loved more than anything and felt like a great hobby for which I got money. As a TV editor, every day becomes a small and sometimes big adventure and only in the editorial meeting do you find out what's in store for you. No two days are the same. The perfect job for someone like me.

When I felt that I had to change, surprisingly I went in to teaching and quickly found pleasure in it. It was a worthy replacement. This job also involved a lot of travelling. Sometimes I spent four weeks in Hamburg, then a few weeks in Düsseldorf, from there I went to Munich and at the weekends I had a stopover in Frankfurt. In these cities I usually lived in a room that I had rented through Airbnb. During these years I always stayed in the same flats. I got on well with the landlords and we had fun. But it was just not my home. I missed my dog, at the beginning my husband and the flat with my things. That didn't do me any good. Slowly my mind started to decline, which I did not register.

My marriage situation was bloody awful from day one and today I wonder what made me marry this guy with whom I have so little in common. We lived a life that was characterised by everybody doing their own thing. There was zero common ground and we did nothing together. I went out alone because that was not his thing. I mostly met my own friends and I went on holiday without him. Even when I got out of hospital, he let me travel all by myself, instead of appraising the time with me and making a new start. These were years without any emotional support and love had long since ceased to matter. After my breakdown I tried for two years to set the clock back and make a new start. I thought we both deserved a chance. We learned to paraglide together. A hobby that should give us a common ground. Halfway, my husband packed it all in because my pace of learning was too fast for him. He would have had the chance to go slower but he preferred to give it up. With that he threw away the last attempt to save us. That is how I see it and feel today.
In short, this marriage was messed up a long time ago and if I am honest with myself, the relationship was nothing before we got married. I don't know what got into us.

I had the baggage from my past and the weight of my job, which became a burden because of constantly having to be somewhere else. As a TV editor, you're always on the road, but you have an adventure every day, work until you drop and fall into a comfortable hotel bed. With a bit of luck you might even get a decent wage for it. As a lecturer at further education institutions and universities you earn between 22 and 38 Euros per lesson. Preparations, follow-up work and marking of exams are usually not paid. I had to pay the Airbnb costs, the travel costs and the flat at home and all other expenses. As a freelancer, health insurance and taxes are payable in addition. You can calculate what is left at the end of the month from 22 Euros per hour.

The past, the travel stress, the unadventurous teaching, was accompanied by relationship problems and now and then money worries. This is not a good combination. Especially not when I learned in the hospital that my mind is capable of compensating for deficits at any time. If the relationship is right, the job or the lack of money is not so bad. If the job is fun, I can put up with a bad marriage with little money. If I have enough money, I can easily put up with the lack of marital bliss or the not so great job and compensate. Gradually, without me noticing, I found myself in a situation where nothing was right anymore and the psychologically important pillars collapsed. Marriage messed up, too little money, too much travel stress and a job that I enjoyed less and less.

I had nothing more with which to compensate. If the weather was good, I wanted to go flying. Sometimes it worked. Often I sat on the mountain and couldn't take off as it was too windy. Besides, flying is not a cheap sport. The whole situation literally cried out for a trigger that would lay my life in ruins.

The first trigger came when my beloved dog Meon died. I was in Hamburg and got a phone call from my husband at 7pm in the evening, saying that he was afraid Meon would die during the night. Meon was suffering from cancer. I tried to get a train immediately and I still can't believe that I had no chance to travel to Frankfurt after 7 pm that day. So I took the first train at four in the morning and arrived just after nine. I spent the whole day with Meon, who could no longer walk and at some point looked at me with big, infinitely sad eyes. I knew that it would end now. We called the vet, who put Meon to sleep in our flat at 18:45 in the evening. I hope I never have to experience anything like this again in my life and pray that all the other dogs will die in their sleep.

The second trigger came with a pop-up message on the I-Pad addressed to my husband. My marriage was a farce and what had happened in the background without my knowledge was such lousy malice that morbid fantasies of violence come over me when I think of the people involved. My brain imploded and that was the moment when out of nowhere suicidal thoughts first appeared. I immediately flew to Italy to calm down with my sister. That was not possible. My brain went completely crazy and I could think of nothing else but taking my own life. My panic was enormous. I didn't know this and I was terrified of myself. So I flew home again, where I collapsed three days later in a supermarket. As a result, I voluntarily let myself be admitted to the psychiatric secure unit at the Frankfurt university hospital. There I was my own prisoner in relatively bad conditions.

I knew that apart from the medication that was supposed to correct my bio-chemical imbalance and all the therapeutic measures, my life would only be permanently healthy if I underwent radical changes.

After I was discharged from the hosptial, it took quite a while before I was able to work again. It was only in tiny centimetre steps that I approached a life that was not marked by fears, panic attacks and severe attacks of depression. But at least the thoughts of suicide had disappeared. My husband struggled to express his regret and help me back into life. Unfortunately, this did not change the fact that nothing connected us and the fundamentally destroyed trust was irreparable. But I worked on it. The paraglider training should help. It did me good, at least I had a goal again. At first I couldn't change my job. But I was grateful that I was allowed to return to my job in all the educational institutions. So one day I went back to work, still in a relationship with no future and had considerably less money than before, because I had accumulated many expenses due to the long period of illness, which I had to pay off.

The day that changed everything was connected to a visit to the doctor. I was not feeling well and I had strange breathing problems. Everyone in my maternal family died of cancer. Mostly between the ages of 40 and 55 something was found by chance and by then it was already too late. After twelve months at the latest, the patients were dead. I always had a latent panic about an illness that is growing undetected and is recognised too late. So I begged my doctor to check my lungs with an X-ray and all the paraphernalia. My grandfather died of lung cancer, his sister died and so did my Aunt Anita. I had every reason to be fearful. The lung X-ray showed a mysterious shadow that the doctors could not interpret. I had to undergo further examinations. The distances between them were enormous. Who knows if I would even experience the last check-up. "Was that it?", I asked myself again and again. I'm out of the loony bin, I'm in a crappy relationship, I'm not having fun at work and now I'm going to die on the underground on my way to the doctor? That could not and should not be. I didnt sleep for two precious days of my life and thought about it day and night. Then on Sunday morning I separated from my husband, who immediately moved in with a friend, until I found a one-room flat months later, where I moved in temporarily.

About three months later I met Jose. I had no idea that the real drama would come with that. In the meantime, all the medical results were available. Smoking had irreparably damaged 37% of my lungs, but apart from that everything was fine. I was head over heels in love with Jose and this one pillar supported the fragile roof of my entire mind. The job, little money, the flat which was clearly too small at 37 square metre, didn't matter. I was in love. From here to the moon and back and twice more than Jose and all the people put together. My life had achieved the turnaround and now it was time to live, celebrate and create a future.

The years before that, my mind was severely weakened by the latent dissatisfaction, the unhappiness, the lack of everything and everyone. A huge hole opened up, into which I first slowly slid. Later I fell into the darkness until I hit a rocky outcrop hard. I did not know that I would fall much deeper. The rock on which I landed actually seemed very stable. Moving out, getting my own flat and finding a new guy by chance were the changes that saved my life. My mental supports could be rebuilt. If nothing else had happened afterwards, I would not be sitting here today, with this new life, which was also only made possible by radical changes.

Anyone who wants to free themselves from their depression should be aware of the need for profound and radical transformation. Anyone who suffers from their relationship must end it, no matter how many children and common property are present. Those who are not up to the responsibility for staff at work must lower their sights and do something that eases the strain. Anyone who is out of their depth at work has to give something up in order to have some hope again.

Although it seems like a painful loss, giving something up can bring inner freedom and riches and become a liberating reward. Anyone who pursues a profession that is no longer enjoyable will only be happy if a new direction in professional life opens up new opportunities.

Nothing will change if the causes are not tackled. You think it feels more differentiated in the short term if you shift one thing or another a little. In fact, new houses cannot be built with old, broken bricks. The reduction from 5000 Euros gross to 3000 Euros can lead to a new life full of quality, fulfilment and joy. This is even possible in a 50 square metre flat. Anyone who has experienced how reduction and giving something up can lead to a positive new beginning, will automatically give a life-affirming meaning to what was supposedly a negative climb down. This leads to new beliefs, thought patterns and actions that will bring happiness into the future and change life from the bottom up. If this is not given a chance, if the step back is enriched with negative meanings, every action will be directed towards it. Thus the present and the future will not become better than the past. Whoever defines and experiences change as compelled, will fall flat on his face instead of starting a new life's adventure with joy.

Just dreaming of doing everything differently one day does not bring about amendment and improvement. In the end you have not implemented anything at all and on your death bed you will say: "If only I had lived my dreams and longings, now it is too late".

We have two options: We make a decision and we tackle it and create changes that will make a big difference.

Or we dream on.

Fear

Why does it always take a long time for me to embrace change? The answer is simple. I am a creature of habit and sometimes I find it difficult to let go of the old and the comfortable. The uncertainty of the new attracts me on the one hand, the fear of losing something, of possibly paying for it or of jumping out of the frying pan into the fire, keeps me firmly anchored in the situation. Even a stupid relationship can keep me in its grip, because I don't know what's coming and because as you get older, as a gay man, you quickly disappear to the bottom of the leftovers, where no one will want to dig you out. On top of that, in my case, I struggle with myself until I am 100 per cent convinced that nothing can be saved, no matter how I twist it or turn it around.

When I look around, the same story appears in many situations. Partners are left only when life has become unbearable and too much damage has already been done. If I want to lose weight, I wait until the look in the mirror gives me the creeps and there is no longer a one night stand who thinks he can have fun with me.

I have always known that smoking is unhealthy and as a member of a family burdened with cancer, I waited 35 years until the ominous shadow on my lung X-ray finally made me give up smoking.

There were times when I threw up every day and I didn't know why or suspected that it had something to do with the current circumstances of my life. Namely, whenever I was unconsciously afraid that one of my mental supports might break away.

In most of us, fear slumbers as an omnipresent monster, which we awaken in the blink of an eye so that it can show its ugly face. Only when the horror, the pain, the vomiting, the panic, the darkness and whatever else becomes so great that we can no longer bear it, are we ready to allow changes or to tackle them. Some of us don't even manage to do that anymore because the nightmare has already become part of our lives and it is no longer apparent that we can break away from it. The dark thoughts become more powerful and heavier every day. They are becoming more and more solid and no scientist in the world knows how this feeling can turn into depression that throws our brain chemistry out of balance and makes us do things that have nothing to do with a natural instinct for self-preservation. The uncertainty of death becomes a saving light in the darkness and for God knows why the fear of death is not as bad as the prospect of making radical changes to improve and heal our lives.

What may appear to be an unjustified accusation is not meant that way. From my experience I know that there are huge gaps between "can do" and "want to do". What looks like the flight thought of a coward is a powerful and malicious symptom that forces people to do things that were not planned. They struggle and up to a certain point try to change the course of events. But without any immediate success, the fatal realisation that all effort is in vain quickly takes hold.

Others, who are not ill, just very unhappy, simply lack the necessary pain and the daily vomiting has not yet become a tormenting ritual. I have often thought, " it will go away again". My life wasn't doing brilliantly, I was in a trough at that moment and I knew that after rain there would be sunshine again, but I didn't feel crappy enough to overcome my worries about change and the hardships that come with it. I wrongly assumed that until I am scared shitless there would be plenty of time.

At the same time, fears of change sabotaged my ways of thinking and acting. I went through the day on autopilot, always with the faint hope that things would change. All I had to do was firmly believe in it. The only stupid thing was that I had no images in my mind of possible change and no visions that I could implement. I began to sabotage myself, so that everyone and everything would make decisions for me, only I didn't. At such times I was no longer the nice work colleague I used to be and did not do my job as well as I was expected to. Deep inside me the sabotage squad was working, destroying my framework without me having a better plan up my sleeve.

Some people, and I am rarely one of them, do not trust themselves. They lack self-confidence. The negative beliefs have been implemented so deeply over decades that they have become unshakable beliefs. I am not good enough. I cannot do this. I will never learn to do it, just to name a few excuses. Bad habits also contribute to the fact that change cannot happen. If your girlfriend always does the dishes anyway, why should you do the dishes yourself, even if it would improve the relationship? Some people do not help their colleagues on principle, which does not contribute to a better working atmosphere. You don't contradict your boss, no matter if your potential is smashed against the walls of despondency.

In addition, family members and friends let us know that they do not trust us with anything. They want to keep us down and we believe every piece of information, especially at a young age. "You can't do that" and "You don't have the talent for it" as well as "That's not on" were the most common statements I heard all the time.

There was a piano teacher in our street and I wanted to learn to play the piano. Every attempt failed because I was told exactly that: "You can't do that" and "You don't have the talent for that". My parents had no basis whatsoever for this claim. They did not know.

All my life at that time I was constantly put down and they tried to make me believe that I was too stupid. I couldn't even carry the rubbish down the stairs properly. But I was beaten into the football club because the old geezer played football. It didn't matter whether I had talent or not. I hate football. I'm too slow, not agile enough and I hate running. That's why I had myself set up as a goalkeeper. The day after I got my player's pass, I went and pushed it through the coach's letterbox and resigned. I got a good hiding for it. Still, I felt more powerful than the old geezer.

Fear is a weapon and a monster. Both destroy the soul of the child. They prevent us from using our talents and turning our visions into reality. It is necessary to face the fear, to endure it and to learn that there are no consequences to panic about if you allow your ego to live out what does you good. Acknowledging that you have no talent for this or that saves frustration, failure, broken dreams and gloating from others. Having no particular abilities is not bad per se, because it is an indicator that shows us what we can do. But we should always first check to see if we really have no talent at all.

Eliminate your own dogma

Beliefs can kill and dogmas can be killed. The former is quite justified and the latter is literally not quite correct. Actually, it should say: dogmas can be redefined. The problem is that it takes a while for a new doctrine to gain a foothold in our subconscious and to stabilise itself so that we not only believe it, but feel its truthfulness.

But what do we understand by a belief? Beliefs arise from our individual experiences, our memories of them and the feelings that trigger such a memory. And to top it all, we give this whole package a meaning. Both the feelings and the meaning can be positive or negative. But unfortunately, many memories contain quite bad emotions, to which we have added crazy or sometimes even almost delusional meanings. Such a horrible package screams at us from our subconscious all day long and warns us not to have any positive experiences.

Let me try an example that is familiar to us dog owners and those who are afraid of dogs. Suppose a person had the unpleasant experience as a child of being bitten by a dog. This situation was then accompanied by fear and pain. We can all understand that. The memory consists of the image of a dog running towards the child or the child stroking him and the dog suddenly and without warning biting him. Usually it was not even a real bite, but rather a strong pinch.
This memory is automatically accompanied by feelings of fear and you clearly remember the pain that the bite caused. In addition, this incident is given a meaning. "Dogs are evil. Dogs bite." Now the belief system is complete and can work its way deep into the subconscious and lodge itself there. Out of fear this child will never touch a dog again. If even a small dachshund runs towards a person, who is no longer a child, the internalised fear screams out. The result is usually a terribly unpleasant person who is not prepared to try to have a positive experience. I often meet this exact situation with my dog Tyrion.

Anyone who knows Tyrion knows that a lamb like therapy dog was lost on him. Tyrion is able to work with any other dog, with any human being and is the most sensitive four-legged creature I have ever been allowed to spend my life with. I always offer such highly frightened men and women the chance to stroke the dog. This has not been accepted by a single person concerned. No matter how much I'm yelled at, I don't put Tyrion on a leash because it's my way of proving to them that he will pass them by without interest and won't even sniff after them. It is a positive experience, even if they refuse to acknowledge it and I force this experience on them. They force their hatred on me, I force them to realise that nothing happens. Despite the fact that nothing happened, that the dog walked past them at a distance of two metres by my side, they swear like a trooper and treat me like the last terrorist who wanted nothing more than to ruin their day, yes some think I wanted to kill them.

We always see the world the way we want to see it. One person thinks "I want to harm him", another "it doesn't matter" and a very small number of people judge: "Look here, the dog hasn't done anything to me".

Almost all of us have negative beliefs. I remember that in the early 70s my mother brought home a homemade Margarita pizza from an Italian work colleague. It had a lot of cheese on it and lots of oregano. My God, it tasted crappy. It was so bad that for many years I refused to eat pizza and avoided oregano like the plague. Remember: pizza, cheese, oregano and the smell of it. Feeling: I feel sick. Meaning: Pizza tastes crappy and oregano makes me puke. Action: I do not eat pizza.
It took at least five or ten really good pizzas for my brain to learn that pizza can taste very good and that oregano does not harm me.

Another belief that I'm still working on is parental indoctrination, that I can't do anything, that it won't work, and that I don't have the talent for it anyway or that I'm too stupid. The feeling that goes along with this is inadequately described as extreme worthlessness and self-hatred. The meaning I have given to this is that I don't have to try many things, I would fail anyway. If I have to do something completely new today, when I am over 50, the feeling that comes up is the fear of failing and showing how stupid and untalented I am. I have always been a real stubborn man, even to myself, who refused to believe that I could fail. Can't and can't you, are red rags to a bull and inside I scream in fear: "And whether that works and whether I can do that, we'll see!". This became my driving force. In everything I do, I try to prove to my parents and the rest of the world that I can do it. I am accompanied only by the fear of failing and being scared of proving myself a complete idiot.

This is indeed as exhausting as it sounds and it is an essential part of my depression. At the same time, this behaviour has ensured that I have this great colourful life. I seize every opportunity, explore every new space and constantly test to see if I can manage it. This has led to the fact that I have completed four vocational training courses, that I have studied, that I have made documentary films, written cookbooks, founded the homeless project the Winter Knitters, taught at renowned universities, obtained my pilot's licence and implemented TREES of MEMORY, to name but a few things.

This book, which I am writing at this very moment, is also such a fear project. Deep inside of me my stepfather's fist is pounding on me and he's screaming that I'd better do something decent instead of doing shit I wouldn't have a talent for anyway. The importance of writing a book is hard to bear, because I have to write it up facing my own fear. And it's all stupid. I have proved over the past 50 years that I can do a hell of a lot and that I am capable of acquiring knowledge when I really want to and that I have a reason for doing so that drives me on with joy.

Of course it would be nice if my documentaries were to make it to the cinema, but that must not be the yardstick. Yes, writing a bestseller and selling a million books is terrific and indescribable. But that is not my goal. I do not have to be perfect either.

If you think this book is crappy, then do it better. I can also live with the fact that there will always be people who don't like something. If you reduce the quality of what I have done to numbers, you judge by your own standards, which can by no means be universally valid.

My films were not screened in the cinema, but my film about Hessen downloaded 300 000 times in Japan and the DVD has been sold over 20 000 times. My cookbooks have been bestsellers for 5 years and have sold in the mid five digit range. Some say that TREES of MEMORY has no meaning because I have only 30 000 ridiculous followers, if any. But can you reach millions of people with a suicide theme? My success is messages like this one I received a few days ago via Instagram from a young girl: "Hi Mario, I found you on TikTok and I really liked you. I've been following you on Insta for a while now and find your approaches and thoughts really good & above all comprehensible. It hasn't been easy for me lately and your videos help me to look ahead and keep my head up, even if it's not easy".

If I can only reach one person with my thoughts and help them, then I have reached my goal and am successful. I don't have to give lectures in front of a sold out hall, even if I think that would be great. No, it's the three or the 50 who come that are important and each individual person is 100 percent success for me. Thank God I was able to internalise that a long time ago. I don't have to write a multimillion Euro bestseller, even if it would do the soul good. But if just one person tells me one day that they have been able to draw something positive from my experiences that has influenced their life, then this book will be successful. Nobody can speak badly of that, because millions of books, which end up in the rubbish, fill the bank account, but have no further meaning. Has a novel by Konsalik ever changed a life or even saved one? In my life bubble, success is not equated with wealth. That may not be the case in others' lives.

The beliefs that my parents beat into me no longer hold. I was able to transform them by proving the opposite to myself. But fear still always resonates. That is dangerous, because emotions are much more alive than rational thinking and reasoning. The worst thing is that our actions are not determined by reason but by feelings.

How often have you suffered because of your beliefs? Do you sometimes fall to pieces through your own fear? Do you feel your memories? It is the beliefs that affect and influence our present and whose effects lead us to sabotage and destroy our infinite possibilities in the future, even before they could take the form of a vision.

I still have to be constantly aware that my brain compares today's situations with the memories of the past and makes a stock analysis. What is the same? What is the difference? Does it cause discomfort or pleasure? Once that is done, my brain makes its judgement and yells at me that I should follow my emotions from back then because they are still valid in the current situation. "This will end badly for you", it shouts. Or when my boyfriend doesn't answer after work because he went for a beer, my brain tortures me on the basis of Jose's suicide, thinking that something terrible might have happened. This rubbish mind set does nothing else but bring the experience of the past into my present, and the erroneous analysis and judgement based only on an assumption creates my future because I act according to the instructions. I have to keep reminding myself that the negative experiences of the past, no matter how long ago they are, will build my present and future if I do not stop them. If I don't fight it with all my strength, I give immortality to the negative parts of my life's story, because they rule over me until death.

To be honest, I don't feel like it. The past has only one purpose and that is its transience and invalidity in the now. Just because someone over salted the soup once, not all cooks are fools and all soups inedible. It is up to me to disempower the emotions of the past. Only I have the chance to enrich the same experiences with new feelings to which I can give a different meaning. The only one who can do this is me. To come back to the example of the pizza: Either I bake myself a pizza that tastes better or I keep trying out pizzas in restaurants until every single pizza proves to me that it is delicious or not.

People can run away cursing from dogs for 80 years or they can ask every dog owner for decades if they can stroke the dog.

It is not the responsibility of my surroundings to treat my beliefs, or triggers, with respect and to spare me. Most of the time people don't even know me and my past has been definitely unknown. It is up to me to free myself from this painful straitjacket. I should analyse which beliefs make my life difficult and which triggers I have to get rid of. That still doesn't work 100 percent, but increasingly more often. At the same time, I do not have to allow people, who know my beliefs and triggers, to vent their deceitful lust for power on me just because they enjoy seeing me suffer. Such people, who exist from time to time, are temperamentally and psychologically bad. They carry baggage around with them, which consistently harms them. They want to distract from themselves. Others cry out that they don't know what triggers are and therefore could not use any. Well, I don't know every law either, and I am still punished if I break it. There is a reason for it if you are good-looking, have some money, are not stupid, have two or three great kids, but no partner can stand you for long. Or that you can lose any job in a very short time. Or that I send every new acquaintance packing too quickly. It's not always because of the others. Mostly it is because of your own beliefs, which sabotage us and destroy our lives. But also in this mental world it is crude and inappropriate to allocate guilt and feign innocence.

What happened to me was not self-explanatory until I realised that I could change my beliefs permanently. Again and again I had to tell myself that they were making my decisions. Sometimes this happens in secret. Out of a dark hole the voice crawls, which either makes me a euphorically bubbling spring or makes my thought evaporate uselessly like a drop on a hot stone. Whenever I thought that I have made it now, I had to experience that the beliefs deep in my subconscious still work and act. "I believe and I know" are reasonings for insecurity, which strengthen negative views rather than solving them. If I know nothing, my diffuse and stupid answer will be decisive and close open doors for me. If I accept that I know nothing and know only one of an infinite number of perspectives, then I can offer all the possibilities of this world a suitable framework to teach me something better. The good thing about it is that I can accept and use it.

It is not possible for two beliefs to work against each other for one and the same thing. Either I panic in front of the dog and behave accordingly or I don't. Either one or the other. It takes only a while for the new experiences to create a new set of beliefs and to cast off the old one. At the beginning they stand side by side and the old one shouts a loud "but" to the new one. But the voice quickly becomes much quieter and goes silent. It does not come back because it has dissolved.

OK, if the person who is afraid of dogs was suddenly bitten again, after 50 positive experiences, then all hell would break loose. "I told you so", the person would scream. Then you have to refer again and again to the 50 positive experiences of stroking and explain why the dog bit. By the way, it is the same with dogs as with people. There are psychopaths.

The emptiness within me

When I go inside myself and look for myself, I find some airless cavities that join together to form a great emptiness and which are always pestering me. Sometimes they feel terrible and sometimes less so. For example, there is a room that is filled to the brim and at the same time emptied to the last drop. The theme of loneliness is such a space. Even in a partnership I usually felt lonely. Sitting together on the sofa and being miles apart at the same time is not a nice state. That didn't get any better after Jose's death. I desperately tried to get this emptiness under control, but neither a one-night-stand, my friends nor my family could fill this space. I think that loneliness is one of the most difficult emotions to describe.
I am lonely. What does that mean? What does it feel like? I don't want to discuss either of these things at this point because everyone feels it differently and yet we all know what it means. I want to tell you about how I was able to get rid of loneliness.

No matter what I did and no matter what people I brought on board, when I tried to fill the emptiness from the outside to meet the loneliness, it remained what it is: an empty, black, stinking hole that could have pulled me into the abyss if I hadn't realised that without having created my own depth, I could not fill any emptiness. This is true of everything that can be defined as a space devoid of emotion. This emotion will not disappear if I let myself be entertained. This was clear to me one day.

I had to turn to my inner self if I wanted to find the truth, my ego, my special features and my personal possibilities, in other words material to fill the vacuum. This began with questions: What makes me special? What sets my heart racing? Why do people like me? What can I do that others cannot do? What makes me different from them or my friends? What do I enjoy? What can I use to express myself? What do I dream about? What longings do I have? Why do I sometimes find it difficult to be alone? Who can take away my loneliness?

The answers to all these questions slowly began to fill my emptiness. Like the rain that enters a cave and floods it, my voids filled up. The more I occupied myself with my emptiness, which was at the same time my suffering, the less it became. The encounter and the penetration into my suffering and the emptiness associated with it simultaneously became the exit from it. This exit opened a new space, a new infinity of possibilities. In this universe I only had to find the right thing for me.

With TREES of MEMORY I had found the right thing. I just did not realise that this was the case. I did not suspect that this would only be the beginning and that I would experience further developments and possibilities. Due to the fact that I had to deal with my own suffering to the point of vomiting, I was and am able to support people in similar situations. This is the only reason why I sense which words could be the right ones and which need has to be met. I would not have learned this from books. Books cannot offer me a way out as long as I do not let what I read have an effect or put it into practice.
I read many great books that told me what to do. Did I do it? No. Why? Shoulder shrug ...The emptiness and my suffering opened me up to more than I ever dared to hope for. This is one of the reasons why I work as a funeral celebrant during the winter months. I would never have thought of this idea in my life, especially not right after Jose's death.

When I first thought about it, I thought it was absurd. Another death theme, I thought to myself. No thanks, nobody needs it. Now I am happy to give comfort to the bereaved and to be able to pass on a little of my source of energy. Only death and suffering, inside and outside, have shown me hidden talents. I realised that I can be more than just a TV editor or just a mourner wandering around the world planting trees. If I wouldn't be something that I or someone else once defined, and if I hadn't constantly committed myself, then I could be anything. If I were not someone, because I constantly defined myself as this or that, I could be anyone. So why define yourself? I will be different tomorrow than I am today anyway. If something dramatic happens in the evening, then even more so.

With the answers to my questions came abundance and I felt a new depth. It was not the answers that filled my empty spaces, but my being that suddenly increased in size. It felt like a little treasure. The inner richness increased and the outer poverty became increasingly irrelevant to me. This was what brought me more and more freedom. I was no longer dependent on having. I was somebody without being something specific. With that I could grow. I became and will become more of who I want to be.

Please do not ask me now who I want to be. I have no answer to that. I am rather the one who looks at what the universe tries to make of me.

I stand there and let it happen and feel how it does me good and makes me emerge anew. This process is not complete. It never will be, because what I am today can look different in a month's time, because I have had fundamental experiences that subject me to a new change, which I gladly accept. Meanwhile I understand this as wealth. What was before, the many having and wanting to have, left me in a swamp of inner poverty. I could no longer get out of it and thus provided additional breeding ground for depression.

In retrospect, it was like a wasting away, although it didn't feel like that for long stretches of time. I believe that this was one of the building blocks of my suicide. At some point, the fun just stopped.

To be or to have?

In the current Corona crisis we all see what it does to us when something we do not have control over, endangers or severely limits all our having. How many people see their existence endangered and suddenly realise that the basis of their existence is all that constitutes them. There is nothing else that defines it, at least many people behave that way. What if a single event rendered all your having meaningless and void or if you lost it completely?

I lost everything after Jose's suicide. My love, some of my so-called friends, my hope and my future prospects. I had my possessions, but they were no longer worth anything to me. Even when I completely refurbished my home, the new sofa or the great kitchen meant nothing to me anymore. It was beautiful and it made my vegetating a bit more bearable. That was it, nothing more. What I didn't understand then and couldn't feel was the fact that I was still ME. This loss couldn't take away my feelings, my character, my charisma and everything else that belongs to Mario. I was lucky in that I never defined myself exclusively through my possessions. There was simply nothing to brag about and I couldn't hide the inadequacies of my self. Nevertheless, the little I had was somehow important to me, it switched me off a little. Let us not delude ourselves. There are enough people who, with all their showing off, hide the fact that they are selfish arseholes. But there are also enough people who, whether they are poor blighters or rich people, would always be equally empathic, and be humane where others flash their Rolex.

Now please imagine that you no longer have anything that matters to you. You have focused your life only on your being. What would happen if they took away what you didn't care about anyway? What are you then? Who are you?

I asked myself this question one day. Perhaps it is more accurate if I say that I was forced to ask it. Who was I? What am I? The latter I could answer after a long time. What I am can rather be said by the people around me. For one person I am a fool who has no idea about anything. For the girl on Instagram I am the hero today, because one of my videos, according to her, gave her a new perspective that could motivate her again. For the guy on Facebook, I'm the messed up guy who has a room to rent.

I gave away everything I owned for Trees of Memory. Having no more possessions makes me an incredibly free person. At first it hurt like hell and I cried constantly when I let something go. Then I became light as a feather. And when I had nothing left, I could suddenly be everything I wanted to be again. I could even be where I wanted to be, because I no longer had to carry rubbish around with me. The reduction to my being gave me the freedom and the possibility to realise my vision of Trees of Memory.

"Having" put me in chains, kept me in mourning, took away any perspective. "Being" gave me back my life. Being taught me to live again deliberately and with full awareness. Being gave me fulfilment on a level I had not known before. Suddenly I had a different identity that went along with recognition. This is something I could only dream of. At that time I was somebody because I had a little something. At least that was in my imagination. Together with Rasmus I was great, because we had a lot and could show off. If I had to let go of something in 2018, it hurt me deeply and took a piece of me with it.
We mistakenly think that wealth means freedom. But what value is there in an autonomy that I have to buy? An independence that allows me luxury and lots of travel? Just because someone can travel, he is not free. What will become of freedom when all the money goes down the drain?

If you build your identity on having, you are nothing when you lose everything. I had a boyfriend once. He was all I had and in the morning at work I looked forward to the evening when I could look into his sparkling eyes again. I gave up a bit of myself to be able and to be allowed to have him. I forgot everything around me, denied myself many things and put my health aside, because love was more important to me than anything else. Suddenly he was dead. I had nothing left. Not even myself any more.

Who can I be?

In the course of time I have gained a new understanding of my consciousness and developed insights that I would never have gained without the drama of recent years. I always thought that I was the product of my parents. Of course I had picked up a few other genes here and there, but actually we are made into the more or less successful vision of our parents. Add to this our personal destiny, the circumstances of our lives and all the things that others have messed up and that rub off on us. In other words, I was a victim of circumstances. I was the result and effect of everything that surrounded me and there were few elements I could shape myself, such as my choice of career. But even that was given to me because the companies saw my grades and not what was inside me.

I felt no more self worth than the drop which, if lucky, would end up in a pond full of like-minded drops, without ever getting anywhere myself. I thought that I would never become someone. Not particularly because I did not fit into this society which classified me according to my origins and what I had. Until I was 18 years old, the first question in the Swabian Alb when you met someone you didn't know in the village was: "Who do you belong to? ". No, the claims of ownership, the value and the pigeonhole they put me in were all immediately made clear with a short question. To free yourself from this was only possible by moving away.

I had to turn 50 to find out that I had lived a life full of illusions. I am neither a drop in the ocean, nor am I a victim (at least not in the long run) and I am not the effect of other causes. I and each of us is much more: we are the source that bubbles and can fill an entire sea. We can become a wave at any time. When I understood and internalised this, I realised that each of us can become a limitless creator. What I had heard a thousand times as dull bla bla bla became an image that I could grasp.

It helped me, almost like a tool, to transform the journey in and out of my self into something I could look at with a little pride.

It opened up a whole new perspective and a question that turned upside down my whole, already confused life. It was no longer a question about who I am or who I wanted to be, but rather about the big question that I was facing, and which is the start of putting a meaning at the centre of life: Who can I be?

The answers to this question were as varied as there are possibilities in the universe. Theoretically I could be everything for the time being. Nevertheless, I had to make concessions. Astronaut didn't fit because I am too old. The Emperor of Japan has just put a successor on the throne. Nothing more came of it. To be a snowboard master was also no longer suitable. But I could become an XLsize model, maybe I could get a role in bear porn, a successful writer would be feasible and if I had thought hard, many other things would have occurred to me. The most important thing was that I realised that I can be, and am allowed to be, me.

The suicide had created a break that I could not ignore. To lose my "having" was terrible. Not being able to perceive myself anymore, almost not being able to bear it. If I wanted to know who I could be, I had to change the way I looked at my life.

"Change the way you look at your life - then you change your life too", became clearer and clearer to me. That didn't always work. But once I started it, it got better. It became something like my mantra:

 "Change your outlook. You are not a victim, not a result of circumstances, not a little drop, but the source. Who can you be when you finally burst forth?

How do I experience myself?

I accepted the fact that I felt better day by day, without consciously thinking about it. This feeling has lasted for three years and is still a process that is not finished. I continously ask myself questions like: What do you want to do? Why do you want to do it? What is the meaning of what I do? What feeling belongs to this meaning? What is the core message that comes from the meaning and my associated emotion?
I have found a goal and the meaning that goes with it and I have been moving heaven and hell, the universe and the earth ever since to make my vision come true.

The present inevitably forces me to dive into the past again and again. This is followed by the never ending struggle not to let past emotions take hold of me and to get caught up in the past. As long as my present life is reshaping itself and I feel a personal growth, I can resist the drifting away at any time. When I think of Jose, the sadness still comes and I push it aside. I immediately replace this feeling with an image and a memory in which we both laughed out loud. The beating of the heart that accompanies this immediately makes me smile. Even now, at this moment. I had to practise this repeatedly and I am glad that I have succeeded for the time being. I also found the freedom to give a new meaning to my old memories. I was able to do this mainly because the time gap creates an emotional distance, which is good. Time does not heal all wounds, but it helps to heal them and leave them only as scars.

Now I can see more objectively what events have done to me and recognise that many decisions I made in the past were a disaster. I understand Jose and his actions, which were incomprehensible at the time.
The new meanings ease my suffering in the present. I can decide at any time whether I want to hold on to my burden, wallow in self-pity, rob myself of the possibility of a future, or allow myself to live a fulfilled life, which again is accompanied by happiness. An everyday life, in which Jose will be missing. A reality, in which Jose will be there, as an immortal and lovable person who has always fought for his love.

Is history repeating itself?

I had a great time with my current boyfriend, because Afshin is a lovable child at heart, who has crazy ideas. I really love his little jokes and often get the giggles so much I can hardly get my breath. I am accompanied by a little boy who at heart wants to get on, is looking for love and above all does not want to be afraid anymore. He wants to be held all day long and you can't tell him often enough what a great lad he is, even if he is sometimes a little fool, who dawdles and wastes time instead of living, which he longs for so much. Unfortunately, his longing for love is accompanied by unbelievable fear and a trauma that would leave none of us untouched. His mother died of cancer when he was three years old. A year later his father remarried because his two children needed a mother. Two years later, when Afshin was just six years old, his father died in a fire in his flat. For weeks he was not told that his father was dead. He was not taken to the funeral. Only when he kept screaming and crying that he wanted to go back to his father, was he told the truth. After the death of his father, his stepmother abandoned the children who were then raised by their grandmother. Afshin lived with all kinds of relatives in the following years.

His sister suffers from depression and takes anti-depressants. She has attempted suicide, but she seems to be doing well with the treatment so far. I don't know much because Afshin lives his gay life in secret and nobody knows about it. At least he thinks so. I am sure that everyone knows, but nobody talks about it. In Italy, this still happens very often. As long as you don't talk about it, you are allowed to be gay and are regarded as the eternal bachelor. I believe that it is no different in Persia.

Anyway, Afshin never sleeps through the night. This was not quite so obvious at the beginning, but for months it has been a burden on him and me too. He lies awake, next to me, from 5 or 6 o'clock in the morning and reads his Kindle, because sleep is out of the question, even at the weekend. He gets terrible headaches as soon as something stresses him just a bit. Especially when he runs the risk of having messed something up that could cause financial damage due to his lack of concentration and planning. Then he spends his time in bed, taking one 600mg Ibuprofen after another without any effect. For months these headaches have been tormenting him in this way, without any apparent reason.

The subject of death, and everything to do with it, is a trigger to him and he becomes downright aggressive when I ask him to let me show him where my documents are, in case I drop dead in the forest. Not only does he become aggressive, but he downright refuses and wants nothing to do with it even as my boy friend. This means that he doesn't even know who to call and it doesn't matter to him, or else his mind won't allow it, whatever. A condition that is unbearable for me. It is not about where I am finally buried, but I have meanwhile Trees of Memory, which I would like to get sorted out. In addition I have a right that he knows what a living will is, so that I am not just kept alive regardless. It doesn't interest him one bit. How we have argued about it in the meantime. There is nothing further to be done.

OK, I can understand his trauma and maybe I would have had my problems talking about my boyfriend's will in my late 30's when I would have preferred to live with him. But for me, death is part of life and a relationship also involves taking responsibility.

The trauma of his childhood has flooded his soul with fear. Fear eats up the soul and it's the best way to do it. His fear of losing someone he loves is so great that it eats up any form of love and he would rather build a 10 metre high wall around himself than ever again allow anyone to really like him. He behaves like a little dog that has experienced nothing but beatings and violence. If you try to stroke him, he screams, bites and lashes out just to protect himself. No matter what you try, this traumatised dog does not believe that a hand can also mean love and does not need to be associated with pain. Such a dog will never gain trust in his life because he is trying to protect himself and when he is big enough, out of fear, he will kill the person who has been trying for years to gain a little trust with love. Afshin behaves in the same way.

Today at dinner, he said for the 100th time he felt he didn't know what was wrong because he felt so bad. My answer, which I had held back 80 times, expressed 5 times and this time I also said: "For three quarters of a year I have seen that you show all the symptoms of depression. And I am also of the opinion that you have depression, which is not surprising, given everything you have been through".

Afshin exploded like a steam cooker and all hell broke out. He felt insulted, attacked and his honour deeply hurt by this statement. The fact that his sister is depressed, and has attempted suicide, is irrelevant.

For years I have been dealing with depression and suicide and now I have to be accused of being an idiot, having zero IQ and he doesn't allow me to say such rubbish to him. He sees my fear, my past, my trauma with Jose's suicide like using a nuclear weapon and turns my helplessness, my fear, my worries and my love into a weapon that I use against him to do I don't know what.

I can no longer do this. I don't want this anymore and I have sworn to myself that if I ever meet a man again who ignores his condition, I will be gone. Jose "only" ignored me. But Afshin attacks me. I have tried everything I could and I will not give myself up a second time. I understand what is happening inside him and I can understand his fear. But I will not be the one to be ruined because of his fear just because he does not want to be helped.

I have tried. I was happy to be in love again. But I would rather die alone and lonely than pay a high price for love again. It hurts me deeply that I cannot rescue this child who is crying out for love, caught in his fear. I simply cannot. I hope that one day he finds the man who has the strength to stand up to his fear until it turns into love and he just becomes happy. I cannot be that man and may heaven, the universe and Afshin forgive me for this.

Love

If I'm not careful now, my brain will make another decision against me. 2020 is not even three months old and my thinking apparatus is in permanent stress mode. There's my post on the table which I haven't dared open for four days because I'm afraid of a huge bill. There are a thousand things on my to-do list. Preparing the tax return, shortening a presentation, preparing the workshop, writing the press release, finding sponsors and tidying up various speeches. The nights are getting shorter again, more restless, more tense and full of unpleasant dreams. And, as if that wasn't enough, a week ago on Sunday I broke up with my boyfriend Afshin, the first man I met three years after Jose's death. Completely by surprise, I fell in love in May 2019 and because he was also looking for a place to live, we didn't do things by halves but moved in together in September when I went on my winter break.

It's been seven days since I "melodramatically, Italian style" asked Afshin to move out. The reasons are many, simple, logical, consistent and accompanied by emotional pain. "Why? You make such a great couple," was the first thing I heard from the two friends I have since told. But what good is it looking great together if you have no common goals? If you don't share life? If you're not willing to at least try the unfamiliar? If you feel close in parts because of your own life story, but are basically separated from each other by whole universes? But the most difficult are our underlying beliefs which life has placed on us.

As a child, Afshin lost his parents at an early age (memory). This brought with it incomprehensible suffering, trauma and guilt (emotion). As a result, he decided to protect himself from loss by no longer allowing love. His emotional daily life is permanently wrapped in a heavy protective cloak. Any criticism, no matter how small, is seen as an attack on his personality. There is only a "You love me and are for me" or "You are against me". It is just one of many consequences of a childhood trauma that you would not wish on anyone and that moves me to tears when I think about it. A terrible stroke of fate that irreparably injured this wonderful and picture perfect heart that resides in this dream man and took away both his parents.

In theory we had the chance to use the bad and traumatising childhood memories that shape us as an opportunity to strengthen each other. Each of us could have looked out for the other. We would have been able to prove to ourselves that love can do anything and is able to change negative beliefs into positive ones. But it's just one of those things about wanting to and being able to do something.

Neither of us can do it, because we are not able to live love without having any expectations. For me, "unconditional love" is still a theoretical construct with many mysteries. Sometimes I think it is silly talk, because every human being wants to be loved back. For this reason alone, "without expectation" is not possible and not human. At the same time, that is exactly what I would like to see as a firm goal. I just don't know how that is supposed to work. What was it like with Rasmus back then? That was a new, fresh love, without attaching anything from our past, like guilt and fear. It was not unconditional. I assumed that I would be loved. That hasn't changed in the last 30 years.

Here the devil is in the detail. Afshin doesn't understand what I'm talking about. I feel as if I am explaining the colour green to a blind man. No matter what explanation I use, it doesn't come across. Instead of removing the cause for a toothache, he prefers to remove the whole tooth, although it is not necessary and a root canal would be perfectly sufficient. He cannot see that it makes sense to look inward. If he did, he would realise that his view of reality is an illusion controlled by his memories and emotions. This is also true for me. That is why we trigger and hurt each other. We look at each other and stare at a reflection.

I believe that by removing the illusion that harms us, we make room for the truth. Only then do we see who we really are. Only then do we have a real chance of being able to live our relationship lovingly and respectfully. However, he cannot show me who he really is. He is afraid.

This realisation makes me incredibly sad on the one hand and on the other hand I feel anger and frustration. Why? His persistent "No, I don't want to" to protect himself becomes a bulwark against the depth, against the respect and against the compassion that makes up a relationship. And there's something else I sense. "You're not good enough. You're not worth it," is what I pick up and what I feel. "Again," I think to myself. How many times have I had this awful feeling which regularly shows itself as a certainty? At least that's how it comes across, even though I know it's an illusion born of my fears.

The fact that in these past weeks love has died yet again bothers me. It felt so good. I was happy because I got to experience it again. I didn't expect that after all the suicide troubles of the last few years. Although I wished to fall in love again, I was wise enough not to seek love as some desperate people like to do. No, either Cupid's arrow hits you unexpectedly or it doesn't. There is no place to look for love or to find it. There is no moment in which it can be grasped. Time does not provide a page on the calendar that you can tear off, put in your wallet and keep until day X. Love "is". There is nothing more to say about it.

Like so many people, full of instability I too tend to want more love. I don't want to lose it. Looking back, I find myself associating the past with heartbreak and pain. Yet my unhappiness through love in the past was not so bad. The heartbreak and the mental 'ouch' only hurt for that related moment. The years of a happy relationship, on the other hand, allowed me to live deeply relaxed for well over a decade.

My relationships were a success story, but not at face value as most people define them. Relationships don't necessarily have to last a lifetime to be successful. They suit a stage in life and they change with our personalities and experience. What suits today can turn into the opposite tomorrow.

After the spiral of violence in my childhood, experiencing and giving love was in itself almost a fairy tale. But the universe meant well with me. I trusted it. That trust is always there. I can still grow old with someone. The present is not so troubled despite the current loss because I have learned a lot about myself and life in the last six months. I feel my personal development and a certain transformation more clearly than ever before. Despite all the worry, I still feel that it is good and will get much better. Why should I no longer believe in the future? Love will always be there. It is not running away from me, even if I sometimes think that unfortunately it is not running towards me to the extent that I would wish. Everyone wants love in abundance, don't they? You do too, don't you? Nevertheless, right now, at this moment, it's not as easy as it sounds.

 I feel that love is once again becoming a source from which I can draw without limit, with which I can give without knowing limits. A source that I long for and from which I have been able to draw in abundance from time to time over the past 30 years. The joy I felt every time I fell in love was great, I saw the world through rose tinted glasses, everything appeaered amazing and perfect but it was a delusion. Unfortunately, last Autumn the first magic with Afshin disappeared like a bolt out of the blue and I once again became dependent on meanings. What did he mean by that? Why is he doing this? Why doesn't he behave this way or that way now? This is a gross behavioural error on my part. It is a nonsensical need to want to see a loving meaning in what the other person does.

A "maybe Afshin will ..." is complete rubbish. That's how clearly I have to put it, unfortunately. He has, for the umpteenth time, rudely trampled on my belief in what can be brought out of him with the feet of his reality. He will always conjure up factors whose explanations are beyond my understanding and vice versa. He will not be able to put himself in another person's shoes so quickly. The meaning of my life's work will not be emotionally apparent to him.

I have gone far beyond my limit and therefore I have to return to myself if I don't want to break because of both our egos. He doesn't want to. He can't. OK. Jose was my teacher. If someone doesn't want to, you can't help them. I can't and won't love anyone who doesn't want to. That's what I swore to myself to stay alive.

Love without expectations? How can that work if you don't share anything, if you don't compromise and if you don't at least try out the unknown? What if time together, which for me is the most important thing, is not the highest good in life or at least of this stage of life? With every disappointment, with every quarrel, my dependence on meanings grew. Every word, every gesture, every action landed on the scales. Weighed against a "he loves me" or "he loves me not". Fear increasingly filled my love with conditions and expectations. Now, looking back in empathy, I realise that it was no longer love. Love "is". Nothing more. Conditions, expectations, hopes, desires, fears and whatever have no place in its space and do not make up what cannot be made up. Except the condition of being loved back.

There is another point that I had to painfully experience. He who does not love himself cannot love. He who does not respect himself cannot respect. Those who have to protect themselves emotionally, for whatever reason, cannot open the door to their heart to let love in or out. Those who have never experienced love in their own heart do not know what it is. It is like depression. A perfectly healthy person will never be able to feel what this illness means and what it is. You can get as much theoretical knowledge about it as you like. It is the same with love. Love and self-love are two feelings that are as dependent on each other as day and night, hot or cold. Either you love yourself or you don't. If the latter is true, there is no true and pure love that can be given to another person. If you did not have a family that lived in love, you will not know the feeling of unconditional love. You feel such love towards mother, father or siblings. It is always there, even when each one is different. You feel it because love "is".

Perhaps this is my problem, as well as Afshin's: same as him, I don't know any family in which love and security ever played a role. His has died away.   The circumstances of my childhood were accompanied by excesses of violence, exclusion, fear and threats . There really was no love. Except for the love for myself. Psychologists call this narcissism. But it's not that bad with me. I am not the most awesome thing on this planet. Certainly not. But no matter how many times my stepfather hit me with his fist and called me a talentless good-for-nothing, I always thought I was OK and have been able to live with myself just fine. Thank God for that. If that wasn't the case, I wouldn't be able to love. I probably wouldn't even know what love is or what it feels like. Afshin, on the other hand, does not love himself. He is full of doubts, he is not satisfied with himself, he does not trust his own decisions and does not admit mistakes. He assesses what he's made of by possession and uses it against himself. At the same time, he is constantly looking for confirmation, which I cannot always give him. In a way he is helpless and loses himself in everything he does.
Our last big fight was about him not feeling that I love and ended with him saying, "Love proves itself through actions." In this disappointment, our fundamentally different levels of being and ways of thinking are revealed. Love is not what we do, but exclusively what we are. Thus it can become unconditional and reveals itself as eternal which knows neither beginning nor end. Whether I can ever live it fully, I will see. A huge gift is worthless, whether it is a million, a ring or a voucher. Love is the attitude behind it and the heart that gives. Love is the heartbeat I feel in the embrace and the desire to touch the other.

Each of us projects parts of ourselves into the reality of the present. We constantly reap what we sow. But for some reason we are rarely aware of this, even though we have heard this truth a million times. If we realised in time that this makes us a part of our partner, who as a logical consequence becomes a part of ourselves, we could experience every relationship in absolute unison. Instead, there is only a You and a Me from which should come a We. Water and oil do not mix and even vinegar and oil, which seem to belong together, separate from each other as soon as you stop shaking the liquids into each other with brute force. But there is no need for violence when it comes to feelings, because the "I love you" is stronger than any weapon. Together with "I love myself", it becomes a powerful jackhammer that sooner or later smashes every negative belief into a million little pieces and makes room for a new loving realisation and affirmation of oneself, which is subsequently projected anew into our lives and our relationship.

"I love you" and "I love myself" stand opposite each other like hot and cold, even though this form of duality does not work that way. If you bring hot and cold together, the result is a pleasantly warm bath or even a harmonious relationship. Duality means complementary opposites. One does not exist without the other. The day would not exist without the night, just as self-love makes love possible in the first place. If we deny these two assumed opposites any connection to each other then there is an illusory separation.

As a result, there can be neither a mixing nor a connection. When we are lovingly connected, cause and effect weaken. Time together becomes a distant feeling because we experience the strength of love in its actual state. Love "is" - without beginning and without end. We look into the eyes of the person we love and cannot imagine that it has not always been so. If it ends, it is only because it becomes eternal. Ideally, we experience in this situation an enlightenment and are immersed into another dimension. Anyone who has ever lost himself in the gaze of his great love knows what I am talking about.

I could go on dreaming, raving and remembering the moments when I truly experienced just that. But what do I do? What do we do? At some point, for no reason, we return to the separation, to the you and me. Already the whirlpool of impermanence is pulling us along until at some point we are vomited out of this relationship like old rancid fish that has touched the soft palate. I believe that love is the best proof that we are connected to everything and everyone in our universe and that if there is a God or something divine drifting through our being, it, he or she shows up in eternity and in love. I believe that every baby comes into the world with this gift within them. But we behave like wild animals and if there is one thing we are good at, it is teaching the very youngest human child at an early age that love is nothing more than an illusion that must first be earned. But why do I have to earn something that exists in its essence at all times and without ifs and buts? Why are parents so cruel that they take away from an innocent being the only true thing that could make it grow into a wonderful human being? I want to scream at my parents "You are monsters" and at the same time accuse those who have taken offence at me and who poisoned me with dark malicious emptiness because they themselves have never experienced love.

Love is the only thing which is not dependent on an opposite, infact there isn'tone, because hatred is nothing but love coupled with suffering. If we dissolve suffering by understanding that the separation of "I love you" and

"I love myself" is an illusion, we create connectedness. We create reality and a great unity out of it. In this condition we will feel something that cannot be put into words. A something that everyone knows who has ever experienced a mutual love that took every breath away and left every explanation wanting.

At this very momen while I am writing this, I am thinking of how I lost the love from that time and was never able to find it again and am suffering from it today. Yet this thought is nothing more than a nasty and truly terrible huge lie with which I hope to get through life better. In truth, I haven't lost love at all. I just can't seem to reconnect with it. It was never gone, it was never lost. It never left. It never hid. It is there all the time and I'm failing to find the right frequency to reconnect with. I turn the wheel as on an old radio and all I get is static, crackles and once in a blue moon a snippet of a word that I stick to like dog poo in the tread of my shoes. So Afshin and I listen to the static in the ether, turning, searching, making and doing, drifting apart in search of the same goal.

With love, this book begins. With love, my life began. Love ended my life. Love brought me back to life. With faith in love, I continue. With love I will reconnect. Someday. Love is the common thread through life. Love leads us to paradise. Love can kill. Love makes everything possible.

Love yourself. Love yourself from now on, then love will also work out.

Arguments makes you ill

No matter whether we argue in a relationship, in a conflict with a work colleague, a friend or a complete stranger, we either feel troubled, annoyed or misunderstood. It is our own ego that acts like a dictator and believes that every other life must adapt to ours. In relationships, this kind of thing readily comes into play. I also tend to be quick to impose my view of things on my partner. That would make living together much easier. At least I think so. Too bad I'm wrong about that. On the one hand, it's a mean attempt to sway the guy and on the other hand I simply lack understanding of his reality. Worse than that, I sometimes refuse to believe that he has his own reality. I bicker too quickly, "It's not possible that you can't see, feel or comprehend this or that". If things are going badly, then we argue more. If we realise that we cannot combine our individual life bubbles, we are frustrated, hurt and quickly dig in the dirt just to be able to argue. This subconsciously creates more incentives to end the relationship. Some people bicker until they have gathered enough reasons to leave. Others quarrel with each other until their partner is exasperated and leaves. The whole thing runs according to the motto: He who seeks guilt will find guilt. Unfortunately, it almost never happens that you find innocence when you look for it. Besides, finding innocence is boring.

Over a period of time I too have developed the talent of being both perpetrator and victim, depending on where I wanted to see myself. But the goal was always the same, whether in front of or behind the dock. In the end I wanted to make the judgement. But at some point I had to realise that it didn't matter what the charges were or how I judged. I have always done the greatest possible damage to myself. My dark looks seem very powerful on the outside - just as my inner sunny nature can have an excellent external effect. The judgement I made has become a cause that has had its effect. An effect that came back like a boomerang and usually hit me twice as hard.

In the meantime I have come to realise that every argument and every act of violence, even verbal, is caused by extremely negative storms raging inside me. I often have the feeling that I can let off steam and react to the argument and then everything is over and done. But I am wrong about that. A lightning in a thunderstorm often goes out of the cloud down to the earth and at the same time shoots up, left and right out of the cloud. Every harsh word, every insult, every attack and God forbid, every physical confrontation hits me the hardest. There was once a physical confrontation. Before that I was insulted, suspected and challenged for over an hour wi the worst verbal attacks imaginable. No matter what I said, it went on. No matter what explanation I gave, I kept getting yelled at and shit on. Even though I disclosed everything, he kept going on. I had no chance. I should have left at that moment and never come back. But I was not able to let this injustice stand. I took two swings and punched so hard that he flew across the room. Okay, it helped and there was silence.

The other side of the coin was that I spent three sessions with the therapist, crying my eyes out because I couldn't believe that the man I loved could have brought me that far. It hurt so incredibly and it destroyed something in me. The matter was not settled for a long time. For my friend it was, but not for me. The argument was still smouldering inside me and I could not end it by questioning my guilt, because guilt is also loaded with negative energy and carries and intensifies the conflict.
In the end, we could only resolve our dispute by forgiving and acquitting both sides. It was a hard job, because it took a lot of persuasion to bring down the raging Italian in me, who felt unjustly treated and therefore became a perpetrator and knew that there was no excuse for it.

How can I avoid conflicts in the future? The truths we see, and the illusions they become, are joined together and inseparable as a polarity. On one side is my truth and on the other side an illusion, because I only look at the problem one-sidedly and exclude all other possibilities. The conflict cries out, rages, accelerates, goes round in circles and escalates into an arugment which I start as result.

I can pull the release cord and bring the storm to a brief halt by looking at both sides. Those of reality and those of illusion. By looking at both sides I gradually understand what is happening. I still cannot solve the conflict. It is only when I approve of other ways of looking at things that I gradually sort it out. Multi-sided thinking, interpretation, allowing and acting makes the solution appear on the horizon. I must constantly remind myself to not to see things as just black and white imaginary generalities and to emphasise and exploit the differences. If I take this to heart, despite all the emotionality and all the hurt pride and apparent offence to my ego, then there should be hardly any conflict. I am working on it to the best of my ability and conscience and I still have a long way to go.

Will I come to the point in life of allowing countless views without judgement when I approach a problem or conflict? If so, then I will never create a conflict again. So much for my wishful thinking and another remedy for a full and stress-free life that frees the mind. It is not impossible.

Basic trust and faith

When I look at everyday life and reflect on my life, from recent days, months and years, I can list countless situations in which I have been unhappy and dissatisfied. The worst of all feelings is the fact that with my depressions and with Jose's suicide my light-heartedness has gone. It has simply disappeared into thin air and I cry after it day and night. I wish for nothing more than to open my eyes one day early in the morning and leap into the day with a carefree spirit and embrace life. But deep inside of me, like above the door of the emergency exit, is a big red light which my intuition stares at all the time. Together we wait for the alarm light, the emergency siren and the order to leave the building as quickly as possible.

In fact, the light-heartedness that was thought to be lost has not gone away at all. It is buried. It is not even hiding because I am the only one who cannot see it. What stands between it and me is fear. I am afraid that it will be taken away from me again. That's why I won't let it back into my life. I call for it and slam the door in it's face before it can enter. As a result I sit behind closed doors and cry my eyes out. What is really stupid is the fact that ever since I started with TREES of MEMORY, the universe has been teaching me every day that I can have an unconditional basic trust. It constantly proves that I have nothing to worry about. No matter what happens, life will turn out exactly as I need it to in order to achieve my goals. I have a good example of this:

The idea of TREES of MEMORY was only a few weeks old and I was given the opportunity to participate in a panel discussion on social media marketing in Frankfurt. It was not planned that I would talk about my project. Suddenly the presenter led me to this project and fighting away the tears I told him about my plan. Subsequently, I was contacted by a charity and association consultant who wanted to help me. We sat together for two days until I realised for myself that I am not the person for a charity or an association. My goodness, the things that are attached to it. No, I am not. Nevertheless I stayed in contact with Martin, the consultant.
About a year later, and six months before I wanted to start hiking, a Bavarian psychologist, whose son had taken his own life, contacted me. He found my project so touching that he wanted to help me. "You need an association", he

said. I threw that out for now. He said, "I know that you are not the type for this. I have already set up an association and I will help you". That was the birth of the association.

At about the same time I met a gentleman with whom I had been corresponding for a long time. It was always very funny and so we arranged to meet for a drink. Sitting in a restaurant boat in Frankfurt I talked with Gunter about everything, including TREES of MEMORY. Gunter was very moved and felt that I was really serious. In the course of the evening I learned that he is a lawyer and that he is completely dedicated, heart, body and soul. Nevertheless I like the consistently silent Gunter very much and he is a great guy with his own mind and a few rough edges. When some time later the idea of the association became more concrete, I asked him if he could imagine becoming a board member. He said yes. Rarely has a man's "yes" made me happier. Well, now I had a psychologist and a lawyer on board. Martin, my adviser, made it clear to me that it would make sense to have at least three association board members. I did not want to be on the board under any circumstances. This is mainly due to the fact that the accusation was made publicly from Jose's family that I wanted to make money out of Jose's death. I can only counter this repulsive and absurd accusation, which comes out of pain, by saying that I am not and never will be on the board of the association.

As was so beautifully said when the association was founded: "You are the sun around which we circle". That also fits in with "sunshine", which I was often called. The fact that I am on the outside guarantees that the association can take on the values and tasks of TREES of MEMORY, which connect us all, and be self-supporting and independent. It makes it clear that I do not have access to the association's funds. Should I ever no longer be able to live up to our common values, we can go our separate ways without the association suffering any damage.
A third board member was still missing. "You need a woman", said Martin. Oh, where would I suddenly find a woman who could do the job? I have always had few, to no women in my circle of friends. The few that did exist wouldn't want to do that, so I didn't even ask. While I was still thinking about it, the phone rang. On the line was Iris, whose son had taken his own life. She told me that she had stumbled across my project and thought it was so crazy she thought it was great. At the same time she was emotionally touched and it appealed to her. "Is there any way I can support you?" Iris asked. "What can you do?" was my answer. During the conversation she told me that she had been on the board of the local football club. So there was the woman I needed so much and who has become the soul of the association. Two months later

we sat with 10 other founding members in my Offenbach living room and the association TREES of MEMORY e.V. was founded.
So much for the topic of basic trust.

I am not telling fairy tales when I say that everything will turn out as is right and fitting, if we allow it and believe in it. Even if we don't find every stage set beautiful or good at first, it is perfect and the day will come when we realise that. That is how I feel. That is how it has been proving itself to me for many years.

The only thing that separates me from the light-heartedness, the joy, the happiness, my passion, my gratitude, my recognition, my affection, the fascination, my curiosity, the euphoria, the satisfaction or fulfilment of this or that, is my belief in it. What connects me with negative emotions and expectations such as fear, loss of job, illness, sadness, lack of perspective, jealousy, loneliness, despondency, hatred, distrust, malice, pessimism, dissatisfaction, humiliation, despair, anger and rejection is my belief in it.

My behaviour arises out of this. I become aggressive, suspicious, malicious, hot tempered, demagogic, dogmatic, selfish, short fused, frustrated, underhand, deceitful, haughty, hysterical, ignorant, scheming, manipulative, phlegmatic, resigned, self-righteous, unscrupulous, immovable, anti-social, cynical and arbitrary. In a nutshell: quite an arsehole and a bitter old man. How should my fellow human beings react to someone who is like that?
Right, what goes around comes around. This unpleasant about turn would naturally shape my reality, because you don't trust someone like that. You don't give them a job. He is not invited and much more. The consequence is that all the things I have described in the previous section are intensified.

If I or you believe that your project, your plan, your products, your charity will make your little world a better or easier place and you give a good and at best positive meaning to your cause, then emotions such as joy, love, surprise, passion, gratitude, recognition, sympathy, trust, affection, curiosity, fascination, pride, euphoria, happiness, sociability, being carefree and contentment will arise. This results in behaviour. You become attentive, stand out, are exciting, extraordinary, impressive, inspiring, popular, enviable, perhaps even famous, admirable, charismatic, courageous, grateful, ambitious, honest, empathetic, committed, successful, fulfilled, capable, fascinating, peaceful, friendly, jolly, fearless, patient, winning, strengthened, credible, generous, cheerful, hearty, inspiring, interesting, powerful, motivating, beneficial, positive and much more.

Most of all you will be happy because all these emotions create a completely new behaviour, which leads to a new reality. How should people react to a person who is like that? How is such a person supposed to get a shitty job, not be successful or have bad luck all the time? It is not possible.

My belief forms my future and the world around me and is my salvation from all negativity. It's just hard for me to understand when I suddenly get hit again by something I never expected. All of us too often tend to believe the bad things in life and create a vision out of them instead of seeing the good and painting colourful and forward looking pictures.

I just have to believe, especially in myself. Belief in myself will always create what I need most.

Heaven and Hell

I once read a beautiful sentence. "Heaven and hell are only a belief apart." How true that statement is. For some of us, hell is as real as the chair we sit in. It belongs to the individual's reality, but the surroundings do not notice it and happily celebrate life.

I, like each of us, live in my own reality. Only through belief and perspective do I separate myself from other life bubbles. I am always where my worldview is and if it tells me not to worry, nothing will happen that will harm me. If I always believe that the worst is waiting just around the corner, sooner or later it is guaranteed to strike me down.

At the moment I have no reason to give a thought to the Corona virus. I also entirely rule out any other illness. I would find it downright bizarre if the universe lets me get away with my life after my suicide attempt, presents me with TREES of MEMORY, such an enormous task, as a new path, only to let me die halfway along of some crap. Sorry, but I would just not understand the humour. It is completely out of the question for me and that is why I will be 100 years old. If not, then burn the book.

I am always where my belief is and I live as it suggests. I constantly ask myself how things can get even better, and full of curiosity I call out to the great movement of life for what might be possible. I let myself be surprised every day, because I know that reality is created by my conviction and also the doubts. Both create emotions that determine behaviour. I give meaning to the whole because I am a feeling person. This is what creates my reality.

Perhaps the present Corona crisis is a good example of our individual reality. The view of some people is that the safety measures restrict our fundamental rights. Others see fanciful conspiracies and feel themselves prisoners of the system which is being turned into a dictatorship. For the time being, the individual is not responsible for this pandemic. Why it emerged, how long it will keep us in suspense or whether it has a deeper meaning, we will not fully know. It is a test for us all. It is a turning point and I feel as if Mother Earth is trying to tell us something. She has pulled the plug and shouted "stop" loudly.

It is up to us, it is up to me to find the right answer and learn from it if I don't want to go crazy. I am far from going crazy, on the contrary. I am more stable than ever. My depressions are therefore not coming back and suicidality, due to a diffuse fear of the future or existence, is not an issue for me. Other people who are affected are currently fighting for their lives. I feel as if I am seeing more reports of suicides every day.

What keeps me from illness and worry is my response to this crisis, the loss of jobs, existential fear and whatever else may play a role. Afshin will move out and that will put an end to our relationship. It seems as if everything and anything is against me. Others in my situation would cry out "Why me again? "The world has conspired. I will never get back on my feet. Life is so unfair." These would be plausible thoughts and there are not a few whose days and repetitive thoughts are fired with it. Not me. I lean back and relax because there is nothing I can lose. 'Having' is not what makes up my 'being'. The worst thing that can happen to me is that I have to apply for social welfare and end up at the lower end of the social benefit packages. I'm glad to live in Germany and not have to die on the streets because we have a well-functioning welfare state when things get tight. I have never made use of it before. The only thing I've ever received is unemployment benefit, which was two decades ago. Nothing happens to me. Our government even supports artists, freelancers and all kinds of single self-employed people with public funds. That does not happen in Italy, France or anywhere else in the world. So what should I be afraid of? Why not see the good instead of worshipping and dramatising the bad?

I wondered how I should react to this situation. The answer came promptly. "Sit down and write the book that has been forming in your mind for a long time." Right, now is the perfect time. There is nothing to do. I am not missing anything. I have all the time in the world. It's the perfect moment. If not now, then never.
Today is 8 th April, 2020, I have been writing every day for three weeks and rarely have my thoughts flowed so easily into the computer. I have resolved to hold my completed book in my hands by the end of the crisis, ready to be sold. Yesterday I received the book cover. The previous chapters are already being proof read and edited. Finished passages are coming back, while others are still being revised. I keep the accepted articles and tinker with the layout. Everything runs simultaneously, which is due to my latent impatience. I have always been like this. If I have a thought and a plan, it is best to put it into practice yesterday. I believe that I can do this, at least as an E-book. It may not be printed until a little later, because I can only control this to a limited extent.

When you read this, the book will be finished. Have a look at the publishing information to see when this edition was published. I hope that my plans worked out according to my belief and my wish. You hold the printed proof of my vision in your hands.

Refining perception

Our subconscious works as a filter and sorts out everything that could harm us or is not useful. This varies from person to person, depending on which character traits are in the foreground, which talents this person has or which perception has been sharpened by the job or a hobby. My brain is the world champion in filtering out information that is useless to me. When I read anything, I am so busy with the message and the content that my brain completely hides spelling mistakes or commas. Sometimes I can read through it 20 times and I can't see the mistakes. I tend to orientate myself more towards the speakability of the words, especially since I work as a funeral celebrant. However, through my work as a TV editor, I can see immediately what is wrong with a picture. In general, I am a visual person and can memorise pictures well, while names, dates, numbers immediately disappear into oblivion.

On the one hand this ability of the brain protects us. At the same time, however, it contributes to the further consolidation of negative beliefs, because potential possibilities and positive windows into another perspective are immediately closed before they reach our consciousness. If the belief system says "This will never work", it filters out any information that might help it to succeed.

This happens to me constantly in so-called IQ tests and I despair of it. There are tasks that are so logical when I hear the explanation, but I cannot see the solution in the situation itself. I am certainly not a stupid person, but a disastrous process is going on in my brain. It asks in the background why the hell am I doing this. It shouts out to me, "It's useless and your life doesn't need the answer to the question". So I go to work, knowing that I will never pass this test. When I see my result, I get really angry. How often have I tried the Lufthansa test for flight attendants and failed. This is so ridiculous. But this result kept telling me: "You can't work as a flight attendant." It's so absurd, but obviously serving tea or coffee, calming passengers down, supporting them and organising staff on the plane are not my thing. I could despair of this now, if I allow it. But I have decided to accept this stupid fact, even though such tests often miss the point with people and their hidden talents. I have other special talents that are more useful to me in life, that make me who I am and that are part of my personality.

This example shows that something can correspond to my will, but ultimately also fails because of my belief. If I were firmly convinced that I could never fall in love with a man again, then it would not happen, even if the man of my dreams were standing in front of me. If I am of the opinion that I am too stupid to go self employed, then you could put the perfectly worked out franchise system at my feet, which I would only have to follow step by step, and my being self employed would be in tatters.

One of my beliefs, which is deeply implanted, is that I can't sell anything which I'm not convinced of and even then it's hard for me. Whenever I try, I seem to fail. I can see that with TREES of MEMORY. If I could sell myself, I would have had sponsors and donations would be pouring in. But no matter how hard I work my arse off, it just doesn't work. This really makes me desperate, because I don't know how to change this want.

It's not possible for everyone to say how great my project is and that God and the world are deeply touched by it, but 99 percent of all people who meet me, send me away with praise and empty pockets, or click me away. I could console myself and gather all sorts of reasons for this: Too small a target group, no good arguments, presented in a stupid way, perhaps unbelievable, a curse is on me, a test of the universe, whatever. It cannot be ruled out that these arguments are justified. But as long as I have doubts deep inside of me, don't feel good and valuable enough and don't believe in myself, I will not change that, because it works against me. Could hypnosis therapy correct it?

The problem is that this belief can only be changed with positive experiences that prove me wrong. But they are not there. Or I do not see them. Or I talk my successes smaller than they are. With every further failure my energy and my will to try again dwindles. This creates a desperate vicious cycle. I also believe that there is another set of beliefs that clashes with my will and that leads to the fact that I have no sponsors or income from donations. The devil of all beliefs, my eternal hell: "I am not worth it. Why should anyone give me money? Why should anyone buy my product? Why should anyone give me the chance to carry my message to the world if I wasn't even worth that much to Jose for him to want go on living?"

I've come this far. I can explain so much. I notice more and more, and yet at the end of the day I am faced with the same realisation again and again, swinging back and forth over my head like a noose dangling from the ceiling, laughing loudly and shouting: "You are not worth it, give up!

Learning intuition

We have all heard about the so-called seventh sense. This expression does not exist for nothing, because intuition is a natural gift, which we have largely forgotten as an authentic occurence in the course of our lives, or we constantly ignore it. I think that most people do not even think about it at all, because they've never had to learn how to use it. At best, they wonder where the sensation in their stomach comes from or that great feeling before the contract is signed.

My gut feeling tells me what is right and wrong. Usually immediately. I can always trust this feeling. But sometimes I ignore it because I want to get my way. Like in 2007 in Ludwigsburg, when I signed an employment contract with Sonnenklar-TV. Immediately afterwards, I felt sick and my whole mind literally screamed that it was a mistake. That was to prove true. It was by far the worst job I have ever had in my life and apart from a few colleagues, especially in the management areas, they were a bunch of .... Hm, every word is a waste and an insult to the concept of collegiality and leadership experience. I am not saying anything.

Another example, which is not a nice one, was my marriage. On the day of my wedding I ignored the loud outcry from my intuition. My heart was racing so badly that I almost threw up. In the videos taken in the car, on the way to the registry office, you can see that I was about to hyperventilate. I well remember how I kept pushing away the thought that I shouldn't do it. I couldn't just leave the wedding party like in a horrible Hollywood film. If I could have vanished into thin air, or better, beamed myself far away, to another planet in a foreign universe, I would certainly have done so. Scotty, beam me far away. As cowardly as I was, I had to go throughwith it until the bitter end, the jinxed seventh year when not just one stone, but a whole rock cracked and fell into the abyss.
Thank God I also have positive examples. When I had the idea of writing a noodle salad cook book, it was immediately clear that it would work and that I could get a publisher interested. By chance at that time I had seen there were only two cook books for noodle salads. "I can do it better", I thought to myself. It worked and my books are still available for purchase on Amazon.

TREES of MEMORY is also a decision that was based on my intuition. As you can see, this decision was absolutely right.

Working as a funeral celebrant in winter was the last intuitive decision I made. It is now a permanent and successful part of my life.

Three days ago I followed my intuition and the many small signs again and started a training course. The result will be shown this year on www.trauerredner.berlin.

After Jose's death I started to listen to my intuition again. But not only that. I tried to relearn it so that I would not ignore it again. There is a connection between heart, soul and mind and I had to build it up again so that I could hear its voice. With the help of a reliable intuition I can make decisions with an inner security that feels light and leads to clear results. I have the feeling of being more relaxed in many situations in life because I can notice my body better and recognise warning signals. I can see which tasks are urgent and I do not let myself be pushed around so easily. This not only gives me more security, but also more energy, because I don't have to constantly worry about whether I have made a huge mistake. I can concentrate fully on my meaning-centred life and focus on the tasks I have ahead of me.

Unfortunately I am still far from "very good". If I were great at using my intuition like a tool, many things would go better.

Here are a few tips that have helped me to become better at listening to my intuition:
Learn the language of your intuition. It does not only speak, but works with images or feelings. In this way, spontaneous glimpses can appear before the mind's eye. With others, it is a powerful feeling, such as a tingling in the stomach. Acoustically, an inner voice can emerge.
Be attentive and see what speaks to you outside the norm. Be mindful of how it feels. Intuition uses the language that suits you best. Ask your heart and feel whether it feels light or heavy. You can practice this with anything and everything in any situation. Schnitzel or pasta? Cinema or bar? The woman or the man? Should I buy this one or that one? Does it feel light or heavy? Every easy decision is always the right one, no matter what the mind says. No matter what argument is put forward, trust the rumbling and the heaviness and as a consequence decide not do it. Really, try for one day to base every decision, no matter how unimportant, on a good or bad feeling.

Start with this in the supermarket and only put products in the trolley that create a positive gut feeling.

Meditate for at least 15 minutes every day. Learn to go into your silence. This heals the body and the mind. Meditation sharpens the senses. This is also not undemanding. I have been meditating for years and I still have problems finding peace and turning off my mind. But if it only works for a minute, it is a success. Once you have managed to be without thoughts for half an hour and just feel your body without thinking anything, you will discover that it feels like spending a day at the beach. A little tip to try out: The moment between inhaling and exhaling is characterised by absolute silence. For some reason you can't think at that moment, even if you try hard. This second can be extended. Try it. If you hold your breath, you will notice that. If you do not succeed, then go to YouTube and look for guided meditations there. There are countless of them. They all help you to get into a meditative state. There are also infinite apps. I use the app "Calm".

Another tip about intuition is to act spontaneously. Do not question which signal you are receiving. Just do it, don't think and discuss it to death and let the result of the decision surprise you.

Learn to trust and relax. Once you have made the first correct choices, your negative beliefs will be able to dissolve. The new experiences will positively influence your thinking and your actions.

There are many sites on the internet that deal with learning intuition. They show you how to practice intuitive writing. Ask yourself a question and write down what comes in to your mind. Don't see if it makes sense. Write it down and don't judge what you say. Take your time with it. After the first nonsense you will suddenly see a common thread and a theme develops. Write until you are mentally exhausted. I am not talking about 5 minutes, but about an hour or a day. That is how this book here is created. I wrote down keywords and now I am writing round them. The words guide me from one thought to the next.

If you are willing to expand your approach, then the facts and the possibilities of your life will expand automatically. You just have to have basic confidence and be courageous. Yes I know, that is difficult too. Let go!

See the signals

In addition to intuition, we all receive small signs and signals now and then, which we usually do not understand or misinterpret. Surprisingly, these experiences are made by people who walk the Way of St. James. It is a phenomenon that makes this walk so special and unique. I also received many small signals that always brought me back to the right place as I walked the Way of St. James, in 2010. Harpe Kerkeling has also written about this in his book "I'm off then".

You don't always have to get lost or experience some adventure from which the universe should save you. No, it's often the small everyday things and events that do it.
The best thing is to try it with an example: One Sunday, a few weeks ago in Dresden. I had spent the weekend there and it was time to go to the station. My rucksack was packed and I wanted to leave the hotel room. When I went out, a strap on my rucksack got caught on the door of the wardrobe and literally pulled me back. When I tried to free myself, I remembered that I had left my jumper in the wardrobe. I would have completely forgotten it without this signal. When I wanted to go out again, a rubber cord from the front of the rucksack got caught on the door handle and prevented me from closing the door, which could only be opened with a door code which had already expired just minutes earlier. Had I noticed in the corridor that I had forgotten something, I would not have been able to get back into the room. As I was tugging on the cord and trying to free myself, my gaze fell on the bed, where my belt and cable charger were still lying. What a scatterbrain ......

Believe it or not, but I no longer believe in coincidence. I keep having such experiences and know meanwhile that I have to pay attention to them. Very little in our lives happens for no reason.

As inside, so outside

Only when I know which of my monsters are to be found and eliminated in the labyrinth of the mind can I set out in search of the right weapon against them. I like to compare this with a computer game. I have to ask myself what blocks my view and which tool or argument opens my view.

Currently, my feelings about Afshin are blocking my view. I am biased because he is a small, lovable child at heart, who should be protected, especially from himself. We have fun together and I already miss the banter and his childish silliness. I am blinded by my wish to be back in that situation but the story is an illusion which cannot be. But I have learned from my story.

With hindsight I could have spared myself so much with Jose if I hadn't been so mercilessly in love and had brushed aside every factual argument and intuition. "We'll work it out", I said to myself. Although it was probably always more about me changing the man until he fitted in. We all know that this doesn't work and such statements are the malicious crux of the matter. I have a vision of a relationship and of a man which I want to see fulfilled. For this I bend over backwards and worse, I try to change my partner as well. In the end both are unhappy and then there's trouble. If I am honest, there was only one man I did not want to change. That was Rasmus. This is not a glorified and romanticised view of things, but a fact. That is what made our relationship unique. At least up to the point where we both changed and increasingly forgot each other, we could easily live side by side and love each other as we were. I am grateful that I was allowed to experience this at least once. I have not given up hope that this could happen again. I will see.

Back to the feeling of the obstructed view: I have to ask myself what could open my eyes. In the current situation, this is the past and my vow never again to get attached to a man who doesn't address his psychological problems and pretends that they can't harm him. I have tried to offer Afshin my help. He does not want it. I have to accept that. I have to draw conclusions from that. If I do not do it, the monster will spread out again in my inner dark labyrinth. It will feed me with fears. The fear would lead to panic attacks. My belief that I am not good enough would be fed again. With Afshin's statement that, despite

my work with TREES of MEMORY, he would not trust me because I am not a doctor, he brings it back to the point, "You are not good enough."
But I know Afshin. Even if I was a doctor, he would not trust me because he doesn't trust anyone on principle. In the meantime I manage to keep an emotional distance, because every romantic feeling has been brutally killed in the last months and I have said goodbye inwardly for a long time. That opens my eyes. At the same time it shows me how powerless I am when emotions block the line of vision. How many people told me to keep my hands off Jose? How many times have they shaken me and shouted at me to see with open eyes what he is doing to me. How many conversations did I have with my therapist, who at some point was helplessly rubbing his head.
I wish now I could be a smart arse and come up with the ultimate advice. But unfortunately I cannot do that. The only thing I know is that by hook or by crook you have to be able to open your own eyes. If that can only happen with the help of friends, then so be it. In such a case I have to trust people who mean well and swallow the bitter pill that they usually only see one of many view points. But what would be the alternative? Going to the dogs.

When a world looms inside of me and the feelings let me slide into the desolate heaviness of the dark being, in which there is no colour, no light and no joy anymore, then I let positive visions slip away, which otherwise could be materialised in full colour. In my dark time, when everything collapsed and then, just before my suicide, there was no light left to illuminate my darkness. What I touched automatically disintegrated into dust. My job was slowly disappearing into thin air because I was no longer able to meet the demands. I became a huge emotional burden for many friends and naturally they tried to reduce contact. But they were my companions and did not let me down completely. For this I thank you all with all my heart.
My exterior life was more and more aligned with my inner life. I was on a course of self-destruction without realising or suspecting that I could change course at any time. But even if I had known it, I am not sure that I could have done it. I am aware that there is a huge difference between 'wanting to' and 'being able to'. I am fully aware that there will be people who read this book, or watch my videos, and think "that's all well and good, but I can't". I can't even leave the house. If the 'can't any more' has become stronger than 'wanting to', then I don't believe that you can help a person if he or she rejects all help and doesn't want to be guided. If Jose had gone to the hospital for treatment, he would still be alive today. But he did not want to. I racked my brains a thousand times over whether he didn't want to or whether he couldn't anymore because the illness had limited his view of the essentials, and the consequences of his actions, to such an extent that he had become a weak willed puppet. I could not stop my suicide at the time either, although I

was aware that something was going completely wrong. There is no reason to think that it was not like that with him.

Our inner life is reflected on the outside. Our life is the reflection of the soul and reveals a lot about the emotions that determine our actions. All the riches of the world will not be able to hide your screaming loneliness. Afshin's eternally funny teasing of me is nothing more than a desperate plea to hold him, to love him and to protect him. His freaking out when offered help is the panic fear of losing someone again after he has let him into his heart. It is the panic of pain and loss.

My or your appearance shows the inner attitude and a glimpse of your own values. Empathic people are able to recognise quickly whether the head or the heart has its say with me. You can feel whether I am acting out of love or out of fear. My inner peace radiates, as does my pain. With TREES of MEMORY I have decided to be myself and to drop the mask placed on me by society's expectations . Acceptance is the first step in every phase of life, when we are supposed to feel good or have to cope with a situation.

Each of us must accept death. It is not negotiable. Those who do not accept the death of their own child or wife will never be able to break out of the spiral of grief and suffering. Never. If I want to have a life that takes in all my character traits and shapes itself in the way that is good for me, then I have to accept myself. I have to stop pretending to people. It is necessary to accept my helplessness, my pain, my not accepting, my suffering or my inner joy and let it out. My charisma will always betray me. Anyone with a little empathic knowledge of human nature will know whether I am real or not. The acceptance is the oil that keeps the engine running smoothly.

Mothers often mourn for years because they believe that grief is proof of their love. This is an illusion. Their maternal warmth lies paralysed in front of a grave and stares powerlessly into the past. The family dies, but the mothers don't see it. The remaining siblings are lost because they become second-class human beings. I have heard that mothers don't take their own lives just because of their pets, because without them the dog would be so helpless. But the dog doesn't give a damn who feeds it. After a few days of mourning, doggie just carries on. But the children who lose their mothers cannot go on. They can't make it when they lose their brother or sister. Fathers work their pain away. Many drink it away. They would like to go on, but what will happen to the mother? Fathers ignore their suffering and pain and bury it deep down. Their hearts sometimes turn to stone, because that is the only way they can survive and carry on. Why do mothers deny their husbands and other children the pain they would suffer if, after the sibling, the mother also takes her own life? Mothers have the pain of giving birth. This pain is nothing compared to the pain when their own child dies. The emotional death of the mother often only brings more suffering, grief, lingering illness and hopelessness to the outside world, i.e. the family. The sick inner, desperate world becomes an apocalyptic collapse of all that was the most important thing in the whole world before the suicide: the family.

As inside, so outside. If the mother does not accept death, farewell and suffering, and keeps herself in mourning in a toxic way as the language of love, the sun will no longer shine for anyone. Nor for those who need their mother, no matter how old they are. What if the family can't do it any longer and wants to live and so distances itself from their mother? Sometimes it seems that mothers force this deep into their subconscious. Then they might give in to their pain, follow the child and pass the blame on to the family. But nobody is responsible for everything that has happened.

I would like to give a warning to parents: Your other children need you more than ever because they have lost their sibling. Their brother or sister is your own flesh and blood. It hurts no less. Your children break because they lack your love and because they lack their sibling's. Your children are not nobody and are no less important than the child that has been lost. Now the burden lies on those who remain to overcome the grief and to start a new life together as a family, which can and is permitted to be accompanied by fulfilment, hope, joy, love and laughter. It is a life in which someone is missing - always and constantly, but it is again a life journey. It is an existence that you live together for your child and always have it with you in your heart. What you feel determines your life's story.

My inner belief in my vision, in TREES of MEMORY, or in the fact that I can bring something good to life with my eulogies, lets the world come into being. Trees of Memory is only a reflection of my character, my dreams, my suffering and my hope. Now, emotions and the reflection of myself are mutually dependent on each other, and are constantly building up to new happiness. As inside, so outside.

Accept death

We humans experience birth and death as a beginning and an end. In general, our perception is always limited to a beginning and an end, although infinity is right at our doorstep. If we look into the sky, we see the imperishability of the universe. We cannot comprehend this infinity and eternity. It is beyond all human imagination. I, for my part, always gasp when I try to imagine that something is infinite.

I do not believe that our death is the end of our being. The body is transitory, but my spirit, the energy behind it, cannot dissolve into nothing. I used to have an incredible fear of death. That was because I did not know what could come after. It was also my parents' fear, who said that there was nothing more. Or the fear of my God-fearing grandma, who told me about the devil. But actually it wasn't my fear.

My own short death took away my fear of death. I gave it a new meaning. When a very sick person dies, we all give death a meaning because we see it as a release. We often hear it said that death is the best thing that could have happened. It seems that it doesn't matter what comes after. Really? If there was a hell, then the death of a human being would be the best thing that could happen, the main thing being no more suffering, but possibly eternal purgatory? You're not serious, are you?

If a person commits suicide, then we are right to struggle with death. We cannot believe that the great unknown is supposed to be so much better than life here on earth. We don't want to believe that suicidality is an illness. A malignant defect that acts on its own authority and whose end is death. Suicide is the final symptom of various mental illnesses. No matter how and no matter what, many people see death more as a punishment that nobody deserves.

What do we know about death? Right, nothing. All we see or hear are theories. Even near-death experiences can be everything and nothing. Maybe everyone sees a tunnel of light when you cut off the oxygen to the brain. Presumably at this moment all memories spit out their fragments and it seems as if the hunch backed relatives are already waiting for us. It is not impossible that my father and my great-grandmother are waiting for me with a beaming smile. Who knows. I wish it for all of us.

We know nothing about death. We only know what it does to our bodies. Every person who pretends to know if and how an afterlife could be lives in his reality, in his illusion, he knows nothing, he even lies and we still have to accept his reality because the lie could be the truth. Two poles, one level, both exist. Everyone is right, everyone is wrong.

What if death, in whatever form it ends our life, is always a gift of this great movement in which our life is involved? What if death means that we have successfully mastered the most important task in this life? Would it be possible that in different lives we work off our karma and have goals that we consciously know nothing about? Could our life be structured like a computer game? We walk, run, jump and fight, collect points, beat opponents and when we have reached our goal, we die so that our soul can jump into a new body, or state, to live another round. What if we have to begin our existence and live it over and over again in every possible perspective? Would it be conceivable that the soul commits suicide because it is not up to the game in this life and does not have the right tools to cope with the tasks at hand? What if it has effectively pressed an emergency stop? Could it be that there is no purgatory and no punishing God at all, but only a divine omnipotence in which everything can and must be? A power in which everyone can and must be everything, in order to always get a little further with all their experiences. Towards a goal that we cannot comprehend, grasp or name with our limited human senses? Potentially there are really nine or twelve different dimensions and we here on earth live in the three-dimensional world, which we first have to see through and live through several times in order to be prepared for life in the fourth dimension. If necessary, we learn here in this dimension what we need in the future. Can the love for a human being be interrupted by death only for a short moment and we see each other again in the next life? Would it be possible that we are all connected from the beginning of time and that we all keep changing roles and grow through this experience?

I have sensed a feeling in my heart that tells me that I need not worry. Not about death, not about the salvation of Jose and all the other deceased. I feel that we are still connected and will never experience a separation. This feeling is good for me and has freed me from the burden of pain and grief. Primitive people live with their ancestors and know that they are still with them and have only gone before. They go so far that their bones, or their mummies, are worshipped and stay in the house because they are and remain part of the family.

Even with the subject of death, it is possible for me to get to the origin of my belief system. Who taught me that there is heaven and hell, that the Lord punishes or loves and that we are surrounded by guilt and therefore have to go through life suffering and God-fearing ìuntil we are redeemed from life to burn in hell or sing Hallelujah as angels? This was taught to me by my terrible grandmother, who was the first to run into the church after every church bell. The woman who, when I was 14 years old, stopped speaking to me after I announced that I would no longer go to confession because I could speak to God at home and had to lie to the priest in the confessional all the time because I had not committed any sins. I really did not want to go into the subject of masturbation in the confessional and I could not see any sin in it. As a result, my grandma did not speak a word to me again, right up to her death, 35 years later. She even crossed the street when she saw me coming. If there is a hell, then this woman is probably still barbecuing. But I think in the meantime she'll have her head in her hands and wondering how she could have been taken in so disastrously by the Holy Roman Catholic Church.

The faith of depraved people, churches and religions that frighten children is the last thing I need if I want to have a fulfilled life. You are not right. You are right. I am not right. I am right. God, the universe, or whoever, speaks or does not speak, to everyone or to noone.
I can always create a new idea for myself and give it a meaning that will carry me through life. This new idea transforms the previous mistaken illusion that my life is supposed to go exactly one way or the other. A reality arises from this. I become the creator of a new perspective, which I am allowed to live in a self-determined way, like all the other 9 billion people are allowed to live their perspective and illusion. Whoever has a God in his reality will meet him. Whoever calls him Allah will meet him. Whoever wants to believe in a Virgin Mary, will meet her and for everyone who needs it, Jesus or Buddha will be there. They all exist because we want them to and because we are their creators. Not to believe in them and not to create a being that controls the fate of all being is also as close to reality as Jesus. My belief in the universal laws described in Kybalion is also a reality. These principles of order are there and they work because they work on me every day in my life bubble and help me to let my life come into being.

Death is nothing for me to be afraid of. I will never agree to a terrible chemotherapy just because I stick to life like a fly to tape. For me a deadly

disease is merely the vehicle to the other world. I did everything I wanted to do and I had all the fun in the world.
I am ready to go. But I think it's pretty wicked and cool here and I would like to be allowed to stay a while longer. Life is beautiful. Death is a gift. When it comes for me, I am ready to go.

We are all right. We are all wrong. Every idea is reality. Every reality is an illusion.

View into infinity

When I set off to walk around the world, on 31st March, 2018, in Frankfurt, together with about 20 other people, I suddenly had a very strange feeling. Of course I was deeply touched because so many people had taken part, but there was something else. It felt as if I was allowed to take a look into infinity. Before me were all the possibilities of this world and I decided which of them I would take. What came over me was a completely detached view into the infinite future.

I had this feeling again many weeks later. I had said goodbye to Mathil, for whose brother Free I was allowed to plant a tree. A few minutes after my farewell I met Heike, who arrived by bus to walk with me to Cologne. At the former state guesthouse, in the mountains around Bonn, we suddenly stood on the highest point of the region and in the bright blue skies we had a view that felt like it only vanished on the horizon 1000 km further on. No more stupid low mountain range over which I had to walk. Only a plain as far as the eye could see. At this moment I realised that there is more out there than the stupid limits of my brain are willing to allow. I think that at that moment I felt that I was capable of almost anything. That was the moment that finally freed me from suffering and mourning for Jose, because in this feeling a universal truth was revealed on the stage of my life.

Suddenly everything was possible and the "either/or" disappeared from my mind. The separation that had run like a thread through my whole life was no longer there. Where before there was an "either good or bad", where the "either I'm unlucky or I'm lucky" determined the day, where I fought with people about the "either you believe me or you don't" or where I assumed that I hated or loved something, I arrived at the centre of myself. I am allowed to be "either" and I am allowed to be "or" without feeling bad or excluded. To be allowed to be both and to accept this became a relief. I am not forced to walk around the country as a saint and pretend that nothing can harm me. No, I still have many faults and points of view that do not suit everyone. I'm still allowed to hang out for 12 hours in a Berlin club and I'm allowed to laugh where others stifle their laughter. I am allowed to cry when others laugh themselves to death. Not having to decide any more makes it easy to stop judging. If I am good and bad myself, what right do I have to judge others? The fact that I no longer have to make or take decisions has taken a burden off me. Of course I still do it too often in my subconscious. But the little I have managed so far lets the sun shine daily and the night welcomes me in peace.

When I was able to tear down these limits for myself and perceived this feeling of infinity, new worlds and perspectives opened up where previously a barrier had divided my brain into left and right, good and bad, yes and no, up and down, right and wrong.

Wish and belief

What distinguishes me from all those who constantly, and unfortunately, still want to tell me that TREES of MEMORY will not work is my belief in it. I am firmly convinced that I will be able to do all this without any major problems. I also believe that one day I will be able to sit on a well-known talk show and tell millions of people about Trees of Memory. My wishes, past and present, have always been accompanied by the conviction that I can do it, even if I didn't know how.

Whenever I hit a brick wall, it was not because of my 'wish' that it had failed, but because of a lack of confidence. Empty wishes that are not driven by a convinced belief in them lead to madness. Imagine, I wished for nothing more than to climb an 8000 metre peak. Without believing that I could do it, I would die during training at 2000 meters altitude. An athlete who is asked by his coach all the time to reach a great goal without believing in it would go crazy. Psychologically, it is hell to have a goal in mind that is unattainable because you can't imagine getting that far. That's why the best trainers are not those who have every stupid technique for this or that. It is the coaches who ignite a fire that burns down all obstacles on the way and creates the visualisation of a goal that is pursued with unshakable certainty.

Unfortunately, I have often had wishes in my life that were without any hope because I never thought it likely that they would be fulfilled. I also had parents who trampled every belief to death, no matter how small. It is different with my dream since childhood, namely to become a policeman. I had this huge wish, insanely bad grades, and yet there was not a second when I believed I would not make it. Not only could I make it, no: "I can do it". Without any ifs and buts. And that's how it happened. In my training as a textile finisher I had enough A grades and so I could easily apply and managed to get the job without any problems. The only tragedy was that after one year I realised that the dream had become a nightmare and that I was not made for this job. My whole life's plan went up in smoke. Looking back, it was not a mistake to try and not give up my belief.

Today, I know that my belief in the future will have to beat my wish until I can't stand it any longer and then rush off to do what I want to do if I want it to succeed. But woe betide me if I doubt it just a little. Then it's a big flop, but so what.

Now, more than ever before, I feel that my thoughts, my will and my belief form a solid unit, because they are connected by a positive energy coming from within and work as a complete package. Out of this arises my present life, my new reality, my tomorrow.

The visions that I will tackle in the future need my emotions and thoughts, which, with my will and my unshakable conviction, merge into a solid unity if they are to be fulfilled. I must never forget this and I must always be aware of it.

Robbed of energy

When I walk through the forest for days on end and am woken up every morning by the loud chirping of birds, the day begins in the most beautiful way I can imagine. I lie there and listen. I am part of the forest. Nothing disturbs, separates or isolates. I simply belong to it. I look forward to the next forest, the same day, some time in the evening, somewhere 20 km away, where I can meet people who will enrich my life and who will surprise me. These days have a precious meaning. Waking up like this is the kick start and energy booster par excellence. I feel that I am on my way and that I am following the meaning of my life. What could be better?

For you, as my online companion in these hikes, this kick start might be different, because my meaning is not yours. If you wake up by my side in the morning and don't immediately sit on a firm toilet seat while coffee is simmering in the kitchen and eggs are frying in the pan, you are in your worst nightmare. You already know that before it happens. If you lack the security of your own four walls and can't look into familiar faces and don't know whether you'll be able to buy food next week or have to walk 20km to the nearest restaurant only to find yourself in a goddamn forest again, you know you've arrived in hell and will surely die soon. You wouldn't be the only one who would feel that way. Just the thought and the meaning of this vision robs you of all energy and leads you into panic mode. This would change if the meaning were different. If a TV channel had made an adventure out of it, you were a candidate and in the end you could win1 million Euros, then it wouldn't be half as bad, would it?

For me, the idea of standing on an assembly line all day sorting fish or making the same hand movement over and over again is a real nightmare. I can't imagine it and for my character it would be hell. I don't have situations like that and yet I have to do things that don't make me happy and burden me. These include, for example, compiling the tax returns. It's not fun, but I don't dwell on it emotionally. With every negative thought about it, I only make the situation worse.

I have learned that I can assign a meaning, which I decide, to every second of my life, every moment of my existence, every experience, every day and many of my thoughts and the people around me. If I give a meaning, that frightens and burdens me, to a situation or a person, it robs me of energy just by its very existence. But if I give it a meaning that advances me, then it gives me vitality. The job that I have to do to earn 1000 Euros burdens me perhapsfor three days in which I torment myself a little. But the money helps me to buy food for two to three months when I am on the road for TREES of MEMORY. Others would say that the 1000 Euros would not be of much use with their mountain of debt. A drop in the ocean. They give it a negative meaning. I would see it differently, because having 1000 Euros less debt is a big step. Ask how long a young hairdresser has to work until she has 1000 Euros in her hands. The meaning we give to our plans, visions, our lives and the people in them determines whether we feel good or whether the consumption of energy leads to the fact that our actions derived from it lead to a bad future.

Why and what

Most of us have closed the opaque curtain that screen us from the spectators of our life's stage and we rarely reveal the view.

If I get a glimpse of a person, I immediately judge them. With me it is quick. I am the world champion in pigeonholing. He/She is a joker, snob, egotist, liar, sensitive, criminal, nice, super sexy, extremely eloquent, absolutely moral ... whatever I may have seen and perceived.

When I push the curtain aside and enter the performance area, I get closer to this person and lift the divide between us. We are now both in the spotlight. The understanding for him or her becomes a different one.

Everything I see now can be traced back. Behind every "What" there is a "Why" - both separated by just a few or by many intermediate steps. When I think about it, it is clear that without the "why" there would be no "what". The "why" is always there and is like a fat root ball deep in the earth. It provides us with nutrients or it poisons us. As bad as it may sound, every offender is usually a victim of a "why". No one is born a monster. Every attack against me, against you, against your loved ones, has its origin in a "why", which we usually do not see, do not know about and never question. I have already sat down and asked myself why this or that person is the way he or she is. Sometimes I know the "why". Mostly I don't but tried to get to the bottom of it.

For example, the behaviour of my ex-husband Hubert. One day he simply stopped talking to me and didn't even tell me the reason why. He did that from time to time in our marriage. The "why" behind it is as simple as it is disloyal. His mother used 'not speaking' as a punishment. She didn't speak a word to the children for days when they were doing something silly. Such behaviour is hard to beat in psychological cruelty. She still does it today. When we both got married, his family stayed at home to make a point because she had a problem with it. When he was young, even the priest was set onto Hubert so that "it" could be prayed away. That's what you do in the Rhön. For more than two years there was silence between the family and Hubert. No hello, no phone call, no nothing. Although my ex suffered extremely as a child and as an adult, he continues this behaviour and finds it appropriate to do what his mother did to him. The "why" behind his not speaking is his mother's method of upbringing. The "what" today is to copy this method. He is therefore a mother and accepts what has been done to him. He legitimises the cruelty and carries it on. You can imagine that his behaviour causes nothing more than negative vibrations and emotions. I am lucky that I don't care and I don't mind anymore. But during our marriage it was hell, because language actually expresses love and affection. His "why" became his "what", from which a conflict arose, which further added to the reason why I separated from him.

Imagine if I were a father today and, as a result of my own "why", I beat my children. Hardly anyone would understand that. Psychologists would explain that it would be perfectly normal to act that way. We humans are like that, they say. Hubert would find the beatings and the monstrous violence abhorrent. But his silence is OK.

I don't care what psychologists say. People can be like that. I am not like that and for me, those who pass on their own suffering are despicable creatures who get no sympathy from me. They stand still mentally, they do not progress. Nothing good comes out of it. Mental toing anf froing, everyone can work on themselves and those who do not do so do not want to and their own ego is more important to them than the welfare of children or other people. Nevertheless, at some point in their lives there was a terrible "why" that turned an innocent child into a monster, a bad husband, a murderer, a thug or a very sick person.

Everyone deals with their "why" differently, but most of us are controlled by emotions and memories. My "why" for TREES of MEMORY is obvious: The suicide of Jose and the dramatic consequences.
My "What", TREES of MEMORY, is the answer and is meant to protect me and help change my circumstances. The violence that was done to me as a child was nothing more than pure helplessness, desperation or envy. The "why" gives me reasons, but it does not take away the responsibility for my actions. It takes away the guilt that was intended to be placed on me. Therefore the "why" behind a person can become forgiveness. I am able to do this. The old "why" becomes a new "why" that will one day produce a powerful "what".

There are some people I have had to forgive. With some I still have to. This is not easy. How can you forgive someone, or as in my case those, who made me suffer all their lives, when all the facts are known and an "apology" would be enough to satisfy us both. To do this, it would be important to know the "why" behind my mother's story. There is a part I know, but that cannot be the answer to the question why a mother so heartlessly abuses her own child. I still have a big task ahead of me. Either, without the answer, I will manage to let her "why" become forgiveness or we will never see each other again until the end of our days. I don't know if that would be bad, because at the moment I feel good about it and only occasionally does the anger overcome me.

The forgiveness towards my stepfather has given me a sigh of relief and has taken away all the negative beliefs he forced upon me. I became freer and happier.
But absolution also bothers the ego - I know that. It hurts for a moment and then suddenly everything is resolved. We can all forgive. Even I could.

Why x What = Illness & Life

None of us doubts that too much nicotine, alcohol, fat, drugs and whatever else there is can make us seriously ill. If we overdo it, one day we will have to pay for it. Nevertheless, it's like a lottery, because not everyone falls ill. Science knows the triggers, sometimes the processes, but nobody knows why one smoker gets lung cancer and another one turns 100 as a chain smoker. Doctors argue about whether the daily glass of wine makes us an alcoholic or whether a glass of red wine together with a few olives is good for our health. But no matter what, in the end we could die because it was not healthy for us despite all this.

When I first heard from my doctors that negative thoughts, emotions and trauma can cause depression, I was stunned. Even today I still lack understanding. I do not understand how this can be. How can persistent anxiety, bad feelings and hurts change the brain's chemistry? I have no answer. I only know from my own painful experience that this is the case. Whether my mother's smacks or my father's fist or the resulting fear flipped the switch, no one will ever be able to explain.

I have had conversations with my doctors about whether my experiments with drugs at a young age might have led to depression as well. The answers are as vague as all the studies on this subject: "It could be, it does not have to be. There is no evidence for it and no evidence against it". I decided for myself that it was probably not beneficial, although the fun remedies did help me out of my deepest holes.

Stress, including emotional stress, as a trigger for various illnesses is known to us all. I know the stress that is brought to me from outside and the stress that I create for myself. When I think about it more carefully, I come to the conclusion that there is no such thing as stress from outside. There is only one deed or action that is carried out by a third party against me. Or a condition, such as not having any money, leads to tension. The stress itself arises only within myself. I stress myself because I often act and exist in limited beliefs. I still allow negative emotions in because I am easily annoyed and don't rise above them. Like in the last few weeks, when the stupid and irresponsible behaviour of potential flatmates was extremely stressful for me, because they didn't give a damn about anything and they put themselves first. Not one had the decency to keep or cancel an appointment. I am stressed by the expectations of our society, which I also have in reverse. Both are nasty stress factors that do not have to be.

In my life there are a whole range of "whys" that affect me. My "what" has expressed itself in depressions, fears and suicidal thoughts. When I started to find the orginal building blocks for this and that, and expanded my thinking and the resulting possibilities, I was able to release the stress and be heal. This was no hocus-pocus and no esoteric wishy-washy. To give and example, the mental stress I had with my stepfather was released by forgiveness.

There are many tools that can help. But they only work if I broaden my perspective and my belief. My will is the strongest force and the best remedy. Depression is perhaps the loudest and clearest message of all illnesses, telling us: Your body needs to rest, your belief should be different and your basic thinking processes need to change so that your mind can heal.

Your job is medicine

At this point I must be grateful, because I almost always had the luxury of having a job I loved. I did an apprenticeship as a textile finisher, which surprisingly I enjoyed. I couldn't believe that I could be so good in chemistry and physics or that I would be able to recognise the colour composition of a colour sample by just looking at it.

Directly after my successful training I managed to start working for the police. It soon turned out that this was going to be the worst job ever for me. I was looking for recognition and what did I get? A job in which you are a hated idiot for most people. You can't blame Joe Public. After all, as a policeman you usually only turn up to bring bad news. Either you pull people up in traffic, hand out traffic tickets or you come to their home to tell them that their child was killed on the road. If you're unlucky, like two of my colleagues from the Biberach site, you'll be shot while you're still in training. No, that wasn't my life and with my resignation my whole life's plan went down the drain.

The next bad decision was to train as a hotel professional and at the same time to do a course in business administration for tourism. That was no less shitty overall. I was constantly dealing with image neurotics and nobody thanked me for these three years, during which I worked my arse off seven days a week. I really like waiting on. In a bar behind the counter with cool people, I think that's really great. I'd love to do it again for one day a week. But cleaning up hotel rooms and serving people in the hotel restaurant as an invisible servant and then letting them take my tips were not my thing. I went through with it anyway. But I really couldn't grow old in these jobs. What was even worse, I went to work every day for three years and hated it even before the alarm clock went off in the early morning.

One day a friend of mine, a cameraman at the Berlin station IA Berlin, now TV Berlin, said that they had an apprenticeship going with them. If I felt like it, I should call in. Well, the weather was rubbish anyway and being on a TV editorial office for a fortnight would certainly be exciting. I would never have imagined that after only 5 hours I would be in the broadcast of Fire and Flames. Not only that, I also had no idea that I had a particular talent for making films. There was a position for a trainee, but first I had to prove myself.

The other guy with the same goal had been there a few days longer and was supposed to show me the broadcaster on the second day. He shook my hand and greeted me with the sentence: "Hello, my name is Jens. I'm going to show you all the departments. But who knows, maybe you'll take away my apprenticeship".
At that moment I thought: "Arsehole! You don't have that position any more...". I thought that was so outrageous.

Two weeks later I got the six-month unpaid placement, where I had to prove myself worthy of a trainee position. That was such a great time. After about two months, I was supposed to film a background story with my colleague Torsten at Berlin Airport. Well, he was supposed to film it and I was the general dogsbody. The next day we were supposed to meet the team at the airport one hour before the first interview appointment. Well, everyone was there, except Torsten. He was also not there when the management stood in front of me to give the interview. He wasn't there 30 minutes later either. His mobile phone was switched off and was lying on the bedside table next to a drunken Torsten who was still in a deep sleep. I didn't know what to do. My cameraman just looked at me and said: "I'll help you. Grit your teeth and get on with it." Since I had helped prepare the film, I knew what we wanted, but I had no interview questions, nothing. I made it up out of thin air. Then we ran around the area for five hours and I just pointed my finger at something I wanted to film. To make matters worse the report was supposed to run that same evening and so I had to edit it myself. I still remember how the chain-smoking Paula came out of the editorial office, where she looked at the final result. She just grinned and gave me a thumbs up. The next day I got my volunteer contract. I am still grateful for Torsten's drunken stupor.
I must say that this was the most awesome job of all to date because we were such a great bunch of colleagues. I would have loved to work with Thilo, Ralf, Susanne, Andrea, Horst and some others for the next 30 years.

After the station went bankrupt, I went to the TV station SAT1, to breakfast television and the news programme at 17:30. Later I went to a production company that worked mainly for Stern TV. Many years later I ended up in Los Angeles. When I came back from the USA, I went to Frankfurt and Wiesbaden until I packed in my TV career in 2007. I was done with it, burnt out, I didn't want to go on. After that I went into business for myself with my small PR agency and then out of the blue got a teaching position. I have been teaching until now, April 2020 and I loved my various teaching jobs just as much as I loved my everyday life as a TV editor.

In between I was overcome by depression, a suicide attempt and all the drama that was to follow. As time went by I felt that the subject I was teaching had increasingly exhausted itself . It no longer suited my inner self, for whatever reason.

For decades I was able to do jobs that corresponded 100% to my inner being. I usually changed professions when my personality changed. The jobs I found terrible did not reflect my character and soul. They contradicted my values and my feelings. This automatically created a resistance that became stress. Colleagues or superiors, to whom career was more important than human interaction, contributed their share.
Having to experience inner stress is almost more strenuous for me than anything else, because I am constantly asking myself how I could avoid the strain. This causes me to slip even deeper into the stress trap, because my questions and the search for a way out are energetically as negatively charged as all the circumstances that led me into the situation.

Now, with my work as a funeral celebrant and with TREES of MEMORY, I have brought my inner life and my outer life into harmony. I have turned my inner consciousness, my values, wishes and desires to the outside and I live what I feel. This no longer requires energy and therefore no longer creates stress. I no longer wake up in the morning with stomach ache and worry because I have to go to work. I don't start to be annoyed by colleagues or students just because they are part of what is stressing me. I no longer have to put up with disappointments because colleagues or superiors are unable to look beyond their own noses and ask what's going on. My job feels like a hobby again, and it doesn't matter whether I work 8 or 16 hours on the trot. I no longer feel any strain, even with tasks I don't like such as book keeping. I am myself again and authentic. Now I can once again achieve top performance with the least amount of energy. The result is a life that is fast, that feels good, for which it is worth getting up early for and going to bed late every day.

We all know a professional life that goes hand in hand with wishes and demands. We want more pay, a better job, a cool boss, nice colleagues and great career opportunities. We want to be someone who has achieved something. I wanted that too. I didn't get what I wanted, although I already had the dream jobs. We all have goals, but our inner life does not go along with them. We often don't have the talent for this or that and of course we are not perfect in everything. So it doesn't come easily. Against this reality we build up a resistance over time. We become angry, disappointed, grumpy, bitter, sad and desperate. This resistance triggers our stress. This state of mind increases in intensity and from this an unhappiness arises, which leads to depression. This is caused by our subconscious running a programme to protect us. Therefore we withdraw or a certain form of sadness overcomes us because we cannot be what we want to be.

At such times you must learn to recognise and define the resistance within yourself. Only then can I let go of the resistance. As a result you let go of your ego, which is a basic prerequisite for negative emotions, and the associated stress, to disappear. It is always in our inner self where the muddle is created. It is our thoughts and feelings that both trigger and relieve our stress. If this is clear and understood, then the way we act, and especially the way we think, changes automatically. From this a new reality is formed, in which we feel relieved and better. A much healthier and happier future follows.

No matter what form of stress we have, whether in our relationship, at work, in money matters, in our identity and whatever else, the solution of all problems and the liberation from the cycle of depression and suicidal tendencies begins with the removal of all the reasons that cause us stress.

We share nothing

I can understand and sometimes relate to the many different life bubbles around me. This is not always successful because, like all of us, I only know a fraction of the life story of the other person. I have to remind myself of this lack of knowledge again and again, especially when I judge or evaluate someone. We, and here I include myself, are always quick to pigeonhole someone. We only see the drunkard, but not the reasons why he drinks. I see the bottle collector and I don't worry about the fact that she has toiled hard for 50 years and that her pension is no longer sufficient today. I see the prostitutes at the roadside and don't know the dramas that drove them into this job and have no idea that they may be disgusted with themselves but have three small children at home who need to have a future.

I am quick to make a distinction between them and other life styles. Maybe this is a very natural act, because I don't share my life, my personal history and my beliefs with anyone. We all share one earth and space, but that's about it. As a couple, you share a life but not 100 per cent. We do not connect our individual realities. At most we have intersections. Sometimes more and sometimes less. When things are going well, I dream with my partner of various ideas about how our time together should go. The personal significance of this lifetime is unique, especially when it comes to emotions. You have to be very lucky if you meet someone with whom you share your own wishes, ideas, longings and on top the meaning of all this. Such a person may be your soul mate. With such a person you might create 60 happy years of marriage. I still dream about that. I have not yet given up the desire to find someone with whom I share more than just the bed. I still dream of the Silver Wedding and I am still young enough to be able to do that. But I see that time is getting shorter. The meaning of my relationship is different for me than for the average partner who has had a childhood where he or she experienced love. For me, a beautiful relationship means not only being loved, but having a value. More than just being good enough, but being the one who brings a little happiness into life. In this common ground I can share the multiple possibilities of life.

But this is exactly why relationships often fail. It is not the multiple possibilities that are shared, but the limits that prevent our possibilities. This is especially alarming when one person sees plenty of potential and approaches his or her visions optimistically and the partner gets stuck in the limitations of his or herself and does not dare to break new ground.

I experienced such a drifting apart with Afshin. The past years and experiences have made a new person out of me, who deals with questions of life. I can't put that on anyone. Either you have reached that point yourself or not. The more these thoughts separated us, the more often the feelings of unhappiness appeared. That changed the reality I felt. From this reality new thoughts and emotions arose, which led to changed actions and statements. Faster than we thought, both of our life bubbles separated until they docked again on another bubble. Imagine it like soap bubbles meeting in the air. Some stick together and yet are separated. Others meet and become one big bubble. Others are splashing together and drifting off in new directions. Still others collide and burst immediately.

Eliminate problems

It may be old hat, but we all, including myself, make a huge mistake when it comes to eliminating problems. Depending on how much I am burdened by the situation, the focus is on the problem rather than on the solution.

A typical inconvenience for us freelancers is the situation when we sometimes don't get enough bookings in. Even right now, the situation sucks because Corona has robbed me and thousands of others of all bookings. I don't get any reduced hours compensation or anything like that. I sit here and have to watch how my money saved for TREES of MEMORY, which I need for this year's hike, disappears. Every day I am getting more tight fisted while shopping, every day the worries over money are spreading more and more. If I now make the mistake of panicking and focusing on the impact, I would send a lot of energy to this problem which would only help it increase. With every image that appears in my mind as I open the letterbox and I am threatened with the worst, it is more likely that this very image will materialise. I have experienced this so often. Even if patients who panic know that something will never be as bad as you imagine it to be, to focus on the problem will make it happen just the same. This also applies to fears that build up, for example, about travelling. If I just think that I will get diarrhoea and all sorts of diseases, or that there is such a high risk of becoming the victim of a robbery, then not only will every lousy jungle worm attack and contaminate me with its plague, but also every tramp in town will be lying in wait for me.

I've really travelled a lot in my life and I've spent weeks in the slums of Nigeria's capital Laos, for example, or crossed half of Madagascar barefoot and nothing ever happened to me. Why? Because it simply never happened in my imagination. That is why I am sure that nothing disastrous will happen during my hike around the world.

The more intensively I deal with a problem, the bigger and more unsolvable it becomes. Also problem solving lacks the energy it needs to become reality. Problems create feelings and the more painful my thoughts and emotions become, the more unattainable the solution becomes. That is why it is important to understand the facts, to outline them and, if necessary, to write them down. After that, it is important to focus every single thought on the goal and on the steps I have to take to eliminate the problem.

At the moment, I can't help it if Corona is taking all our jobs away. I have to accept that. No one is to blame. There is no bad guy. Acceptance is the first necessary step. So how can I get orders?

For example, I make an offer that is appropriate for the present time. I offer to record the funeral service on video free of charge and send it to the relatives who could not attend. Or I put the offer "Ghostwriter" on my website. I write the speech and the relatives can read it out themselves. I am thinking about whether I should broaden my offers for doing a speech. I might as well speak at weddings or establish myself as a keynote speaker. I have set my advert placements to zero for the time being, so that no additional costs arise for as long as large funeral ceremonies are suspended.

In fact, I am using the time to write this book and I am grateful to Corona. Without the lockdown, without the lack of jobs, I would never have had the time and peace of mind to write down all the things that go through my mind. Even if it doesn't make any money, the end product is better than having done nothing at all.

Of course I too hope that it will be better in a few weeks. Our Chancellor Merkel has now extended the time of *stay@home* by four weeks. I don't know yet whether the relaxation will affect funerals. I am reflecting on the now. This is the only way I can organise tomorrow.

In my problem solving scenarios, I sometimes don't really cope with the flood of tasks. I want to do everything at once. I want to take as many steps as possible all at once. That does not work. I cannot do justice to everything. I have to take every single step with care and full concentration. When I have listed many different approaches, I direct my thoughts, energies and effort to the most promising approach. Imagine that you have a certain amount of electricity and 50 light bulbs that you want to light up. If you divide up the energy and send a little of it to each bulb, not a single bulb may light up. Therefore it is necessary to solve one task at a time.

When I am desperately looking for a solution, I sometimes fall into the trap of the past. I remember situations that were equally as bad and where nothing worked. Immediately negative emotions arise. "Oh God, it will be like back then. What, if, again........?". I am immediately ruled by the emotion of fear, which then makes a decision. Even the unfamiliar, the new and the less known are filled with fear. If I ask myself whether this can go well, or express other doubts, and remain like a rabbit in headlights, because it seems comfortable and safe, then nothing good will come of it. What sort of action would come out of a negative memory and a bad feeling? Of course none that is positive.

I always pay a high price for such behaviour. I sacrifice the many possibilities I now have, because my past determines my present actions. These actions become the future. Bad past + terrible decision in the present = a bad future without a happy ending. So I have given up the prospect even before it has started. There is a nice saying that describes this matter well: 'Nothing can come out of an old coal bag but soot'.

If things went great in the past, if I was able to solve the problem and the memory of it is full of positive emotions, then this helps me extremely well in the present. It motivates me. If the signs are the same, there is no reason why this should not end happily again.

What does that mean for me in these Corona times? Fuck Corona. I've really experienced crappier times which were much more modest. I survived it and found a solution. It's not going to change now. Why should it?

Let the sun shine

Everything I have experienced has influenced my life. The love, jobs, travelling, friends, people I met, of course my family and everything that has to do with TREES of MEMORY. In the meantime I have learned that I can determine how these influences affect my life. They can influence me positively or negatively.
The significance of my stepfather should no longer have an effect on me. That is why I had all the therapy. I also no longer want depression to ruin my life. That is why I have studied my life, philosophy, Buddhism, Kybalion and some other writings. All this has helped me to get a new perspective. After reading this book the reader will undertand its influence. In this way I decide for myself about the meaning I give to my ideas, visions and memories. I was able to free myself from the victim role and change into a creator mode. Of course, I can't help all the dramas and catastrophies that have rocked my life and almost destroyed me. But I am responsible for every single answer I give. It is my response that will create my reality in the future. Nothing else. It is not the event that effects me in the present, it is only my reaction to it.
My former best friend Brutus, with whom I was a close friend for 20 years and who never contacted me again after Jose's death, will not negatively affect my life, although I have struggled with it for a long time. It is the meaning I give to this event and my actions resulting from it that will take me forward. If I were to burden myself emotionally with it day and night, I could not allow friendships to develop. If I were to place an inherited guilt and a basic suspicion on all my friends, my life would change dramatically. I was able to decide for myself that everything has its time and that some friendships are not forever after all. For twenty years it was great. I didn't notice at what point it changed so unfavourably. What is important are the people who stayed and not those who cleared off, even though the pain caused by those who left dominated at first. You feel the hurt and it often hurts more than all the things that should please you. I think this is a poor trait in human nature. Or maybe it's just me who is made that way. I don't know.

I don't think we do ourselves any good by constantly waiting for experiences and events in order to fill them with feelings, meanings and actions. Do I always need a setting to be able or allowed to be happy? Am I only allowed to feel joy when the opportunity for it has come into my life? To put it clearly: it is

not necessary to wait for an event to happen. It works without. You can feel joy, happiness, love and many other emotions without any event. If I do that, suddenly the weirdest and most positive life events that you could ever wish for happen.
This leads to new courses of action and I start a cycle that can only be interrupted by my own very negative reactions and actions. Do I want that? Of course not.

 Do the others want that? It is so derogatory when people talk about the "sun shining out of their arses". The envy and resentment that resonate in these words are unbearable to me. Is it so terrible to see other people happy? I believe that people who have had bad things happen to them have a special right to be happy again. Yes, even the mother who has lost her son may one day burst with happiness. This is not a betrayal of the child. It merely shows how deeply, intimately and indelibly there is a love that has never been doubted and that forgave long ago.

Control your reality

The most effective way to change my present, my future, my life and reality is to reorient myself. It does not take much to do this. I just have to dismantle my underlying beliefs and follow my heart. I have managed this before.
What I struggle hard with is that I can only change the other person in a positive way by repositioning myself accordingly. It applies here that constant dripping wears away the stone. If my work colleague or supervisor were an obnoxious arsehole, the only way I can cope with it is by consistently treating him the way I would wish to be treated if the roles were reversed. But now, unfortunately, I'm very emotional, sometimes sensitive, touchy now and then, and sometimes an Italian hot blooded male. I don'tlike it when people treat me like a piece of dirt. In my thoughts I give them one slap after the other and of course I don't succeed in showing positively what decency means. If I did, sooner or later I would be a cause to which the other person would have to react with a change of behaviour of his own, if he is not a sadist and enjoys hurting others.

At the same time I have to live with the fact that there are always people who disagree with me or who do not see the point of certain activities, do not like my tone or get grumpy because I roll my eyes if I am asked the same question five times within ten minutes instead of just listening. Such groups of people then have nothing better to do other than to act out their ego, for example further education participants, or students, who write an anonymous bad evaluation or those who are not on the same wave length make up for it with bad tempered comments . But that shouldn't bother me — and it doesn't. Being at peace with yourself is a kind of protective wall. If I were to lose my job because of slander, I know that the boss is no better than the spiteful slanderers.

In a situation like this, it all depends on what importance I give to an evaluation, a dismissal or a situation. With every job I lost, or gave up for whatever reason, a better door opened and I never had to take a step back. Never. In my mind everything happens at the right time, even if I don't see it at first. After many years of such experiences I can safely and unconditionally trust in this.

I see it this way: The end of a job is always as the effect of a cause. Inwardly, I had sometimes long since given up and thus unconsciously lived the change that I had wished for. The hoped for effect came about. Mostly unexpectedly. The brief moment of shock and anger usually disappeared quickly.

Another important reason why my world changed was forgiveness. Forgiving my stepfather, or Jose, gave me space for new thoughts and actions, where I could create change. I immediately felt the positive energy that came from it. Forgiveness means that you allow the other person to be right in his reality. "Therefore I forgive you. Therefore I understand you. I take responsibility at this point." But this does not mean that this person is actually right in my life bubble and reality. My stepfather was not right when he said that I would never get anywhere and that I was as worthless as the mud on his shoes.
I will never accept that a person does not know better than to pass their own experience of suffering on to the weakest. The old geezer was as pitiful and despicable as my mother. But in both their realities they were trapped in their helplessness, in their anger, in their envy and in their rage at life. Two pitiful monsters who became victims of their minds and who did not have the intellect to realise how wrong their behaviour was. They not only ruined my life to some extent, but also their own. There are no Merry Christmases or birthdays in the family. There is no reunion. There is the pain of loss on both sides. There is pride, which is stronger than love, which makes you ill and which will suffocate you. Such people have no idea that they will take all this with them when one day the great journey into the universe begins. This unresolved task will continue to occupy us all. Until we are able to solve it. Whether forgiveness alone will transform it, I don't know. I am afraid that I will have a strange father thing going on in a future life and if I can't get it sorted with my mother, that will continue as well. If only I knew what the real task was. But that is a different matter.

On the other hand if I blame the other person I hand them a powerful negative weapon with which he or she can determine my reality. I would disempower myself if I were to off load the guilt for my feelings and thoughts on to my mother. By doing this I would give her an imaginary carpet beater in her hand again, with which she could once again beat me. At the same time, this does not mean that I absolve her of responsibility. No, together with my stepfather, she laid the roots of my depression and suicide. That is as sure as eggs is eggs. They were the cause and the effect at the same time and my resulting negative actions shovelled a lot of rubbish on top of it and became new negative causes and effects. To give her sole responsibility is right.

At the same time it would be possible to forgive her because she herself was a victim of herself and her parents. However, her behaviour today does not allow anything positive to develop from it and I want to forgive her. Since she refuses to acknowledge my feelings and gets lost in the excuse that she cannot remember anything, she has to live with half of my wordless forgiveness, without having the chance to resolve it for herself and find her peace. If her own child is not important to her, then I accept that, because in the 50 years that I could not understand and accept it, I was broken by it.

After I made a decision and reserved the next 50 years for myself, I was able to take back the power over my mental well-being. Since then I have been on the road to an unprecedented recovery. I can only warn you not to feel guilty because you believe that family ties mean responsibilities that you cannot get rid of. No, blood is not thicker than water and my German family proves that they don't give a damn about each other. They have not learned to care because there has never been a loving grandmother or mother who has passed on care, motherliness, warmth, compassion and kindness. These are values they do not know. But I am very surprised, because my great-grandmother was a loving great-grandmother full of warmth and joy. But who knows what the war has done to her and how the hatred of foreigners has torn her soul apart. Now the old woman has had to bury one child after another for many years and I don't feel that at any point there was any form of remorse or that she has forgiven her children. On the contrary, she even smacked her son, my uncle, when he was already over fifty.

It is not difficult to be destroyed by such a family situation. Rather, better to free yourself from them. To accept such a gang and to go in peace unilaterally is a real tour de force. One that is worthwhile if you want to have a carefree life again, one that looks towards a happy future.

Be yourself

My mother is an unpleasant example of the fact that what I see in her is a bit of myself. Something that can be seen in me. In this case it makes sense because it is to do with mother and son. I am as stubborn as she is and I respond with her arrogant pride, which leads to nothing but frustration. Sometimes I do it on purpose, sometimes it happens unconsciously. But what about non-family members? Actually, this truth applies equally to strangers you are dealing with. Things that I get super upset about, that really disgust me, are sometimes a part of myself. Often coupled with fears and inadequacies. Some things disgust me, which is why I find it even more repugnant in others. It's completely gaga and unfair, but that's the way we humans tick. There are many examples of this. How often do I read about the worst homophobes who, armed with the Bible and the cross, would like to see us gays dead. One day I read about these very people who were caught with a rent boy in a hotel room, trying to live out what they would like to murder others for. At this point I will deliberately refrain from writing a personal example to illustrate this. I should be allowed to keep a few secrets.

We all know the saying "He who cries out loudest will be heard, but he is seldom right". In such cases you are allowed to do a double take and question whether someone should really be demonised or whether it is not only about the ego. Now that I write it down, I remember the statement of my married uncle Holger. Many years ago I talked about my old geezer and let it be known what was going on at home. He was totally bewildered and couldn't understand it at all. He told me about an evening when the two of them were sitting together and my old geezer is said to have told him that he admired and envied me. He really said that? Do you express your admiration by beating your adopted child throughout his childhood? Or is it anger at his own life because it took away the opportunity to become what he always wanted to be? He had always had to work in the fields and he often told me that the bedrooms were so cold that his eyes were frozen shut. His dreams were denied him and taken from him. Was my rebellion to get a self-determined life reason enough to beat me up for daring to do what he was afraid to do? In my eyes he was a coward and a poor sod who had chosen his own fate . If I had not forgiven him, it would have been a clear sign that I had not forgiven myself for something. Imagine if he had broken me and today if I was an unskilled labourer, I would have made no progess. I would have a lot of hate in me. Even more than before. The present reality that surrounds me is a mirror of my inner being and that includes all the people around me. "Birds of a feather flock together", we say or "opposites attract". "Show me your friends and I will tell you who you are" is also a saying that points to our inner reflection in the outside world. If I call someone stupid, naive or dull, I express my fear of being seen like that, because I feel that I have all these things inside me as well.

Our behaviour is always projected directly from the inside to the outside. If I experience a mental and psychological disorder, then my flat will also look like that. If I am dealing with a nit picker, then I can be sure that his flat is as sterile as a doctor's surgery. This behaviour will spread and anyone who does not match up to their own standard will be judged and denigrated.
It is irrelevant whether the other person lives with clutter or not. It is his life and not mine. To be a messy hoarder does not mean he is a bad person. In truth, we do not say that either. When we insult someone as a dirty bastard, we are simply venting our fear of that very part of ourselves that we are trying to suppress by force. Perhaps everyone carries this little "dirty bastard" inside them, which had been forbidden during childhood to come to the surface, under threat of punishment. So today that person, as a victim of his false way of thinking, is therefore rude to others in order to feel better.

The changes that have been associated with my present life have reflected my innermost being. The decision to earn money as a funeral celebrant during winter time is a reflection of my emotions. I had to go into my own grief in order to find a way out of it, so that with this grief, which is still within me, I was enabled do what has now become my life's task: to support the bereaved.

What I realised one day is that every negative judgement I allow myself and every upset builds unpleasant feelings and resistance within me, which lead to stress. Troubles that take away my energy to do something positive. Strength, which I need in order to live a fulfilled life, is therefore missing.

In the end, perhaps to say this much: "Tit for tat" does not always have to mean something negative. With TREES of MEMORY I heal the wounds of those concerned. At the same time I heal my own hurts. It is an automatic giving and taking. But no matter what happens or how it may appear from the outside, my actions only work from the inside out and not the other way round. Every detail of my life is a window into my consciousness. If I forget this and I behave according to what is expected of me, I can set the clock accordingly and watch how I fall ill again. I would predict terminally ill one day.

"Be yourself and change the world", says Dain Heer, author of the book of the same name. He is damn right, because wanting to be someone you are not will only cause damage, inside and out.

Take responsibility

When we structure our lives, plan a future and act in the here and now, we must take responsibility for it. That is not always easy.
After Jose's death I felt like a victim. My whole life was against me, the man I loved was dead and a few people I trusted turned out to be scoundrels, villains and monsters. It was easy now and then to put the responsibility on my childhood,on my parents for beatening me, my depressions, lack of help, the devil and the dear God as well as the universe. When I did this, I wallowed especially in self-pity and appreciated that there were some people who could not see the tragedy and who, thank God, supported me with their friendship and love. Nevertheless I felt worse every day and no helping hand could reach me. No matter what I read, it fell flat. Every cry to the Almighty just disappeared into thin air. I was getting scruffier and death as a solution was within reach again. It could not get any better, because by giving up responsibility I had given up all the possibilities for my life's reality. Therefore I could no longer be the creator and developer of my life. For better or worse I was at the mercy of circumstances that could not improve, because well-intentioned compassion does not bring positive energy with it, but has a destructive effect on me with negative energies. I had dried up and instead of being the source of my life I was not even a trickle anymore.

Blaming everything on José's death gave Jose power over me. Assigning everything to fate made fate the authority that seized power. It doesn't matter what faith and ideas carry us through life. They do not come from the outside, but arise exclusively within ourselves. Sure, we read something now and then and think "great". But still we have to accept it ourselves, want to manifest it and at the end of the day to live it and implement it. No matter what we believe. Faith will move mountains and give us the life we always dream of. This is just a symbol for the fact that noone is stronger than ourselves. We give this strength away when we transfer the responsibility for our life on to other people.

Of course we cannot take responsibility for the dramas in our lives. I cannot be responsible for Jose's refusal to start treatment. I cannot be held responsible for a drunk and violent stepfather. I cannot be blamed for my mother beating me, she was underage at the time. But I alone decide what meaning I give to all these things. In this way I take responsibility. This is how I am able to recreate my life. When I realise that responsibility means power, the most hopeless situations become our most valuable guides. They lead us far beyond our limits, overcoming every limitation.

2016 was the year with the deepest and deadliest pain that my life has ever inflicted on me. This made it the source of my happiness today.

Problems become opportunities

We believe that procreation and birth are the beginning of life and death is the absolute end. Therefore, for us humans there must always be a beginning and an end. These are the rules of the game, without which we cannot be. Everything has a beginning and everything has an end, except God, whatever it may be, which has always been there and always will be.

Although our brain is extremely well developed, compared to all other living beings, our perceptions without exception are three-dimensional. Length, width and height are all that most people can imagine. We can accept time as the fourth dimension. We can manage this notion. When physicists and mathematicians talk about space-time, most people stop. That is no better for me. If I listen to people who talk about higher dimensions, into which our souls are taken up and are constantly given new tasks, my maltreated brain takes a gasp and can no longer follow it. Eleven or twelve further dimensions are said to exist and we human children find ourselves in the third, say people who pretend to be able to penetrate into certain areas, such as the Akashic Chronicles. When we travel in our dimension, we need a vehicle with which we can move through space, or dash along the road. In other dimensions, as some multidimensionalists say, we travel with the help of time.

This little explanation shows that there are indeed infinite possibilities that could help us to make a difference in the larger picture. However, since we cannot imagine infinity, we limit the space and life in which we find ourselves. Of course, in the here and now, no vision of this world, no matter how great my belief, lets me travel from A to B with the help of time. At least not with the current state of technology. But it cannot be ruled out that we have not yet found the trick.

We know that every truth has two sides but refuse to accept that each side has infinitely multiple truths. We only see day or night. We never see day and night, even though we know that neither exists without the other. We continue these divisions and do not stop at ourselves. We divide into: This is me, this is not me, this is you, this is not you, this is what you have, this is what you don't have, this is what you want, this is what you don't want, this is what you need, this is what you don't need, this is what you have to do, this is what you don't have to do, this is what you're allowed to do, this is what you're not allowed to do, this is what you can do, this is what you can't do. These separations divide us and exclude the possibility that both are present and can work simultaneously. It is the worst and most blocking separation of all our possibilities.

I don't know why it was so difficult for me to let go of opposites and understand that they are identical in essence. Affection and hate may sound like two opposites, but in fact they are in essence the same and are just two states that carry sometimes more and sometimes less love.

I only moved one step further and somehow felt complete, when I turned "I can do that" and "I can't do that" into a neutral value of "Can". This was achieved by moving to the middle and not hitting myself on one side or the other any more. With the lifting of this separation, stupid thoughts and painful experiences, resistances and pain dissolved in me. I cannot remove all the things that harm me by pretending that duality is all that exists. I do not have to take sides and be for one and against the other. It is only through combining both that I feel better.

This conclusion is confirmed by my work with funerals. My life did not improve when I tried to banish pain, loss and grief from my life which was full of mental violence. I wanted to put the happiness, the beauty of my life and everything that was good for me into the foreground, so that it could outshine the dark emotions forever. What a fallacy. Only when I accepted the grief and made it part of my love for Jose and thus an equal part of my life, did it change back into what it originally was: love. Today the grief is gone and what remained was this chamber in my heart, which is filled with Jose's energy for the rest of my life and which no one can take away from me.

Perhaps you think this is good. Others may think it is bad. Wouldn't this be an occasion to try to understand what it feels like when you move towards the centre and acknowledge that it is both and have a reassuring neutral feeling? In the middle you can see both and I can sympathise with any condition. This is important to be able to perform empathic actions. The equal distance to each pole no longer separates me, but creates a connection. No side can attract me. No side can disadvantage me any more. From this new thoughts, feelings, meanings, actions arise which become the cause. Causes that have no value and create a new reality with their positive energies.

Here is an example that may help you to understand this way of thinking, which I have experienced many times, especially in the gay scene. We all know that we wake up one day and suddenly we are a sexual human being who feels a desire. None of us can explain why we like thin, thick, blonde or redheads and some like small or large breasts or why we like a short or long penis. It is simply the way it is. Well, I too woke up one day with a hard on and found that stuff turned me on. Unfortunately, I soon realised that in our society, people were not happy with the fact that a boy goes for other boys. This forced me to live a "normal sexuality" which was rated "good" in the world around me. But for me it was quite bad and very stressful. Physically I had to assign myself to the "good pole" and emotionally I was completely at the "bad pole". That didn't do me any good and as the years passed I suffered more. It was only when I looked for the middle and allowed myself a man every now and then that I felt better and was able to breathe again.

Now this example is only good up to this point, because one day I wanted to take one side completely. But as a gay man, I don't run around saying that heterosexual sex would be bad and evil, like many of the heteros do. I have experienced it and I am in the middle of it, even if I only live one side. But being in the middle of myself creates my peace with myself and allows me to be above the derogatory opinion of others. In other areas this leads to new opportunities. A problem may at first feel terrible and stand like an obstacle in the middle of the way. If I climb up and look at the other side, I see opportunities for which my view had remained blocked until this moment.

The principle of correspondence

The principle of correspondence is known as the second hermetic law and is best described by the sentences "As above, so below" or "As in small things, so in great things". What is meant by this is that every form of existence, every process and every condition has a correspondence on every level of being.

The basis is that every existence is represented several times in itself. Thus large forms always consist of identical smaller forms. Some people know this under the term fractals. This analogy can be shown by means of a triangle. In the following example you see a large triangle. This geometric form contains 19 triangles.

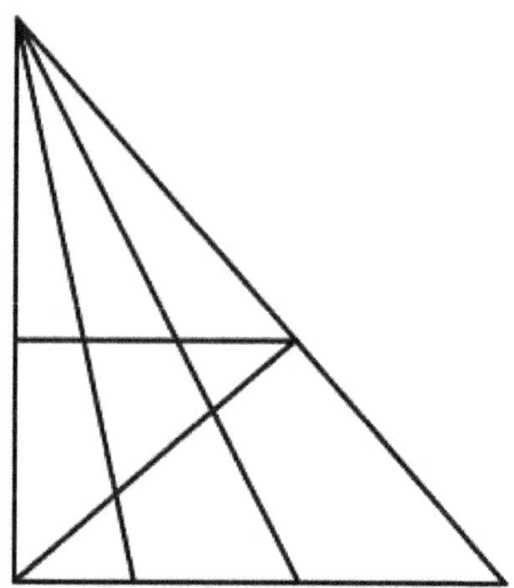

If we add a line, new triangles would result. There are infinite possibilities for further triangles and we cannot see most of them because they are too small for the human eye and all units of measurement known to us. In reverse, I can duplicate this triangle on every side, making it bigger and bigger. And I could keep doing this endlessly.

Another example of "As in small, so in large" is evident in our universe and in the smallest of all particles, the atom. For example, the earth is orbited by a moon and the force of attraction prevents it from drifting apart. We also find this construct in a hydrogen atom, where the electron orbits the proton and is also held together only by the force of gravity.

"As inside, so also outside" can be represented in the same way with atoms. A look at the periodic table shows, for example, that the element boron consists of five protons, which are orbited by five electrons. Similarly, identical physical properties can be found in atoms, as can be observed in the interaction of the planets. Thus the lighter electrons always orbit the heavier protons. The light one always orbits around the heavy one. All galaxies and all known solar systems have a constant heavy centre. In our galaxy, the massive centre is our Sun, which is orbited by the lighter planets Earth, Mars, Jupiter, Mercury, Venus, Saturn, Uranus and Neptune. Around our earth the moon orbits, which is smaller and lighter than our home planet.

Even the complex biological structure of a human or an animal corresponds to the less complex living being of a single-celled organism, from which everything originated billions of years ago. It only becomes difficult now if we want to enlarge man, the blue whale or the elephant as a biological system. I can't think of an equivalent, but there is the so-called Gaia hypothesis according to James Lovelock and Lynn Margulis, which says that the earth, with all the trimmings, is a living being. OK, it is a thesis and for most people it is difficult to imagine. But we could try, because the existence of something is not suspended by the fact that man has such a limited knowledge and his bird brain cannot understand everything. Who knows what is waiting for us out there in space? Who knows whether the bacteria in our intestines, or any viruses in our bodies, do not also think that they live on a planet that is travelling in a bubbling galaxy? By our standards they do not think, I know. Are you sure?
In any case, it can be said that the earth, as well as mankind, represents a self-organising circulatory system, by and within which we live. In whatever form it may take, it doesn't matter for the time being.

And what does all this have to do with me now? A lot. If I imagine that I am a small being that is able to grow up and act in the same way inside and outside, this opens up completely new perspectives for me.

Let me try it with an example: I started to crochet hats and scarves for homeless people out of leftover wool and to distribute them in shelters for the homeless. As a result in 2013 I founded the "Winter-Knitters". A group of people who knit and crochet winter clothes for homeless people from their leftover wool. In the last four years this group has grown to almost 2000 people, without me having to advertise it. At least five new groups have emerged from it, one even in Vienna. Also the project "Helfen Wollen" in Berlin is now huge and is a direct reaction to the "Winter Knitters" and was founded after people talked to me and asked if they could take over my idea. For four years thousands of hats and scarves have been knitted and the homeless shelters meanwhile ask directly for new things every winter. So the group, the number of helpers and the need grows from year to year. As in small, so in large. It started with a pile of leftover wool and a cap and my vague idea.

TREES of MEMORY is growing and is still in its early stages. People from nine countries have joined in with this idea and have ordered their tree and more than 30 000 people are following what I do and how the project develops. The first newspaper article was followed by others, then came the radio and now the requests from TV companies are becoming more numerous. The number of members has almost doubled every year and the amount of donations is increasing year by year to such an extent that the association can finally put into action many ideas and plans. I have even received an enquiry from India. The local suicide prevention organisation SARA has launched a project there and would like to plant an avenue over 300 km long with trees in remembrance. If everything works out, I will contribute some trees myself. As in small things, so in large. As above, so below.

It is we ourselves who can set something in motion by a single act or thought. Many of us do it all the time without thinking about it or being aware of the consequences. No matter whether it is the "Winter Knitters" or TREES of MEMORY, both were initially just a thought, from which a crazy idea was born, which was often sneered at. Even the homeless shelters were not convinced and were totally surprised by the success of the project among the homeless. Their reasoning was that homeless people wanted to remain inconspicuous and would not accept colourful caps. A super gross misjudgement, as it turned out. For my part, I never doubted it and found every reason absurd, even if it sometimes seemed logical to me.

It was just the same with me with Trees of Memory. I knew what I was feeling and what emotional stress I was exposed to. If this is how I feel, then there must be other people with similar feelings and experiences. I am convinced of this. None of us is the only one. There is always someone among the almost nine billion citizens who shares the same problem. These people must be found. How many letters have I received in the meantime, describing how people are excluded, abandoned and blamed by friends and acquaintances. How many e-mails testify to the powerlessness of trying to counter suicidal thoughts. How many bereaved vegetate and only function because they are no longer able to live and their hearts and souls are falling apart day by day? I want to find and reach these people and that is why I am writing this book. What has helped me will also help someone else and even if it is only one person. This is the one to find.

I have never thought about what I have already initiated in my life. Some things remained small, others became big and may be many things went unnoticed. I never gave it a thought because I thought I was lucky or it was nothing but coincidence.

In practice I can consciously trigger some correspondence. For better or for worse. If I want to support somebody on the internet, I only have to post it often enough and soon I will get a Like and find people who support my goals and form a group that will become bigger and more successful in their actions, despite all the wrong criticism. That is the reason why Trolls also have their followers. We should be aware, however, that there are always more people who support something good than those who are only interested in harming others. If you have a great project, you don't have to wait long for people who are interested, journalists or people who are affected, to get in touch and a small wheel starts to set a big gear in motion.

I can achieve a lot. Finding people who want to plant a tree in remembrance is just one of many possibilities. To sensitise my fellow human beings not to take lightly depression and suicidal thoughts and to support those affected is also one of my goals. All suicide prevention campaigns and organisations work at this and their educational work follows the principle of correspondence. I am convinced that good ideas and projects can be reproduced on a small and large scale. I believe that the success of hate messages and campaigns and the incitement of people to hatred and resentment, on the basis of lies and lack of insight, will not have lasting success. On a small scale, as on a large scale.

In October 2016 I received an email from a friend of Jose's in which he called me a murderer and hoped that I could live with my guilt. Between the lines you could read that he wished his own imminent death onto me. The paradox is that it was he who told me: "Go to Berlin, switch off your mobile phone and I'll take care of Jose. Don't worry". I am sure that he will not gather around him 30,000 people who will carry his ill-considered, blind hatred and despair and the outwardly projected guilt feelings into the wider world, no matter what he does. I hope that he finds a way and a life based on compassion rather than on blind hatred, so that he can find people who appreciate and like him.

Just consider what you have already given for the bone of contention. Whether good or bad, big or small, important or unimportant, contemporary or long ago. I am sure you will find something and who knows, maybe there is something in it that could show you a new way of life. Here are a few questions that might help you to identify it:

What was the last idea that friends of yours, family or another group thought was great and put into practice?

What projects or what behaviour is there in your life that has its origin in an idea, a TV report, a book or something similar?

Which values connect you with a certain group of people?

Which rumour have you ever successfully put into the world?

Who have you been able to help or harm because of your actions that inspire other people?

Why do your children pass on the values you have taught them to their children?

What ideas and ideals did your late partner or wife, child or friends have that were never expressed and implemented? Can you pass on his or her spirit?

The law of dichotomy

The law of dichotomy, or polarity, as it is most often called, has taken on a self-evidence in our lives that we never think about at any time. That is why I would like to consider it here.

The law of polarity indicates that there is always a pair based on opposites. High and low, hot and cold, dry and wet, positive and negative, inhale and exhale, seeing and blind, good and bad, far and near, big and small, South Pole and North Pole, sick and healthy, love and hate, sweet and sour, day and night, light and dark and many thousands more pairings. There is no aspect of our existence and our actions that cannot be seen in opposites or that can be turned into the opposite. Think about how close love and hate can be or how quickly life is followed by death.

It is important to understand that no opposite can be better or worse than one part of the pairing. Of course life is more beautiful than death and of course it is definitely better to be healthy and rich than poor and sick. But the good cannot exist without the bad and how would I know that the water is cold if there was no hot water? Imagine that every drop of water, whether in the sea, in dew, in rain, in the condensation of your breath, no matter where, was always 25 degrees. Then there would be no words to classify this state. Hot, warm, cold or freezing cold would be useless.

Poles are dependent on each other, inseparably connected. You can compare them to a sausage. Two ends that are connected to each other. This example shows how much sense it makes not to judge. Both ends are the same. And yet there are people who do not eat the first slice or the end and butchers do not sell the ends without being asked.

What is considered evil in our culture is just the other end of the sausage in another culture. But, whether it is this way or that, there is an opposite pole to everything we think, what we do and what we are. Always be aware of this.

This cosmic law has been given special attention in many philosophies and religions. The Asian Yin and Yang for example. If one part of the mating pair were to cease to exist, the other would become extinct. This is a bit abstract to imagine, because it would be great if the evil would die out. But then there would be no more good. It could be that evil exists so that good can come into being and people know what has to be done.

But back to the subject. Polarity is a universal law. In science it is proven and everything we know, see, feel and do is based on this law. Therefore there can be no exclusively male God. It would be illogical if the Almighty created everything in His own image and likeness and then suddenly came around the corner with something feminine. If there is a God, there is also a goddess. If the Creator unites everything in Himself, He is neutral and neither one nor the other. Polarity can only have arisen from "his" (we don't even have a mixed-gender and neutral word for it) existence, from neutrality, so to speak. To enslave, abuse and treat in an inferior way women, disabled, gays, lesbians, transgender, people of different colour is in my opinion a crime against the divine, no matter how it may look. Everything that exists is a variation. Sometimes with more, sometimes with less, but always equal.

Where there is light, there is always darkness. We should never forget this aspect. Therefore it would be fair not to judge or condemn people one-sidedly. We are not only good or evil. We are only less good now and then.

The fact that our mind can act very contrary to the awoken consciousness leads me to the thesis that the mind and the brain also represent two poles of our being and nature.

The law of vibration

The law of vibration is quickly explained: Everything in the universe vibrates. Every object, every plant, man, our brain, radio waves, microwaves, simply everything. Everything has its own natural vibration with its own frequency. This can be scientifically proven and measured. It is measured in hertz and even the planets have a definable vibration.

Wilfried Otto Schumann discovered the so-called Schumann resonance frequency. This is the frequency of the planet Earth, which is 8 hertz, 7.83 hertz to be exact. It is known as the fundamental resonance frequency, which vibrates up to and including 100 km in our biosphere. It will be exciting to see whether people resonate in this range. And indeed they do. An electro-encephalograph has been used to measure the electromagnetic brain waves of people. They are in the range of 1 to 40 hertz, depending on the activity, and are divided into the following four states of consciousness:

Delta waves (1-3 Hertz)
Deep sleep and comatose states

Theta - waves (4-7 Hertz)
Dream sleep.

Alpha waves (8-12 Hertz)
Relaxed waking state, meditation or just before falling asleep or immediately after awakening

Beta waves (13-40 Hertz)
Normal waking state

The Schumann frequency forms the boundary between theta and alpha range and you don't have to be a professor to see from the numbers alone that this is an extremely pleasant state. Meditation is much more than switching off all thoughts. With meditation you simply resonate with the earth at the same frequency.

During my time in the hospital, daily meditation exercises were an obligatory session. This daily hour was extremely good. But it did not always work, especially at the beginning.

The whole room was quiet, everyone focussed on their breathing and in my head a wild and loud war was raging, which I could not switch off. You have to learn to do that that and unfortunately I still have extreme difficulty with it. But if I succeed, I feel a noticeable improvement immediately. With every hertz that the brain shuts down, I feel a greater sense of calm and wellbeing. In the hospital I knew nothing about the earth's vibration and at the beginning I often thought to myself: "Now you have to do that guru nonsense again". But I quickly learned that this is not rubbish and now, with all my new knowledge, it is so logical and more than just therapy for depression. To be at-one and find the centre will be difficult to put into practice if you do not take the time to pause mentally and physically to feel the pulse of the earth.

Finding this point is not only desirable, but absolutely necessary if we, like animals, want to stay healthy, as Professor Persinger from NASA, Professor Wever and the biophysicist Dr. Ludwig have discovered. The absence of this vibration can cause disorders in general health. The result can be headaches, drowsiness, changes in pulse and breathing if the so-called "biological normal" does not occur.

The limbic system in particular reacts to the Schumann frequency. This is where feelings are located. The amygdala, which is located in the brain area of the hippocampus, seems to respond to vibrations because it is responsible for the perception of emotionally significant stimuli.

These findings are used in psychotherapeutic treatment, the so-called brain scanner therapy. During the session, a mixture of frequencies from the alpha wave range, which comes from the patient's subconscious, is detected by the brain scanner and returned to the patient with a slight delay. This results in a harmonisation of the vibrations in the conscious and subconscious, which is triggered by the biofeedback mechanism. The treatment ensures that problems and tensions are no longer perceived as such and a deep, inner equilibrium is created. Treatments include anxiety, depression, various addictions, neuroses, pain and psycho-vegetative disorders. There is no dependence on therapy and the effect is lasting.

My tip - I do nothing else:
Buy a meditation CD and read about the basic principles of meditation on the internet. You do not have to make a science out of it. Take a deep breath, feel your breath and exhale deeply. That is all you need to do. Consciousness and concentration are enough. Follow the speaker's guidance and don't despair if

your thoughts drift off. It happens to me almost always and daily. When you notice that your mental activity has started again you just have to find your way back to your breathing. You will notice that it improves from week to week. You don't have to sacrifice an hour every day, because 15 to 30 minutes have a beneficial effect. It will do you good, I promise.

Another advice to go into a good meditation is to count backwards from 100 to 0. This will bring you down and if you do that for 10 days, every day one or two times, you will feel the effect very soon. After a month, you can start to reduce the counting to 50 to 0. After some months you will be able to count from 20 to 0 and finding yourself in a state of deep relaxation. Try it!

The law of attraction

No, you won't find out here how you can materialise your wish for a million Euros or get a load of money from the universe as often as you like.
Forget it! Why should something like that work? Books like "Wishes to the Universe" and "The Secret" are only half the truth and their basis is unfortunately quite secular and materialistic. Of course, the so-called hermetic laws show their effect, which I will talk about later, distinct from each other. But first you should try to understand the connections and to put them into practice for yourself. Since I put it to the test and tried it, many things have become easier for me.

There have been periods in my life that have felt good and right. But most of the time it hasn't been like that and the less pleasant events have been accumulating more and more. I never knew what was happening to me and could not find any explanation for different events.
I am not a bad person. At least that's what I think. But what about the time before, in another life? I personally believe in reincarnation. Did I lay the foundations for my present life there, based on cause and effect? I do not know for sure. I suppose so.

The Law of Attraction closes the circle of all principles and laws that keep our universe running and influence our existence. All the threads come together in this principle of order and make it clear how complex life as a whole is, and therefore the way we should behave. We all know the saying "Like attracts like". That is the theme of this chapter. Put simply, you will reap what you sow by observing and implementing each and every universal law.

Do you know the saying "As inside so also outside?" We have all heard it with different variations. The actual meaning is explained relatively simply. The origin of all our life situations is within ourselves. We reflect in to the outside what we are inside. An unstructured chaos that is turned in on itself will usually not lead an orderly life. The adventurer will not be happy behind a desk in the long run and a romantic woman will not feel very comfortable at the side of a man to whom candlelight and red roses mean nothing.

What will your depressions and all those nasty, unjust thoughts reflect in your real life? Yes, exactly! The battle you are fighting in your life, in your reality, is a battle against yourself, which you direct deep inside yourself. The present is the projection of this battle.

When Dain Heer, in his book of the same name, asks you to "change the world and be yourself", he is getting at much more than just the fact that you have to find yourself again. By concentrating on your true self, by being yourself, by acting in such a way that you always find the universal centre and accumulate positive karma, your life's reality will automatically change and you will change the world, i.e. your world. Positive and sustainable.

Mahatma Gandhi sums it all up with his statement "You must be the change you want to see in the world". How am I supposed to get other people to give meaning to their lives again, or to pay attention to whether their friends and acquaintances are doing well, or to make them more receptive to the concerns of those left behind after a suicide, if I do not align my own world accordingly? Trees of Memory would not work. My work as a funeral celebrant would be a non starter. I can even feel that something is going down the drain at the moment, because I don't focus my life accordingly any more. My teaching job is getting increasingly difficult and my client is getting more bitchy. We constantly rattle each other. I can feel that they are looking for a new lecturer and it is only a matter of time before they find one. For me this job suits me because I know it inside out and therefore have time to take care of Trees of Memory. But if they want to get rid of me, then it's OK, because then I'll devote myself 100 percent to funeral services. This is a profession that touches people and helps them.

With my hike around the world I have taken on the huge task of pointing out the many possibilities and opportunities that exist despite suicidal tendencies and depression. I want to be a spokesperson for those who are affected by suicide or have thoughts of suicide themselves. I want to help to break the stigma and the taboo. This is why I am on the road and why I communicate with people all over the world. This will make a difference sooner or later. Whoever thinks that this is just a drop in the ocean and not worth talking about, or the effort, has not understood anything.

The actions I take and my thoughts about them have created my new life and changed my world. I can already see how Trees of Memory has changed the world of other people and families for the better. This is not my success. Nothing I can claim.It is the effect of the causes which I started with a belief in myself and the project.

The hermetic law of spirituality and the principle of polarity work well together, as seen in my example. I had an idea, a subtle thought. Nothing you could grasp, nothing you could look at. On the other hand, there is matter and everything that can be touched. It was only a matter of time until both sought to balance in the middle and the idea became something solid. I had it easy. Trees of Memory is something you can imagine, something that produces images in your mind. Many people think that it is crazy and possibly doesn't work, but everyone can imagine it in reality. How do you think Einstein did with the theory of relativity? Space that you can bend? Time that can be travelled using wormholes? How are you supposed to believe this and how are you supposed to imagine it metaphorically? How did they deal with the first man who claimed that the earth was round and not flat? And who could believe in atoms that could not be seen? How did the idea of photographs spread? And didn't the first attempts at flight fail because nobody wanted to believe in them? Everything that surrounds us began with a thought that became matter and is now taken for granted in life. Everything that surrounds us today is the result of a personal belief.

You only have this one idea. You are the only one who sees the idea as a vision and firmly believes in it. You can literally feel it. That is how I felt. You start talking to people who can help you. You need someone who can make it happen. You have to convince everyone. Step by step something like this comes into being and with every small success your own belief in it grows. Your conviction, your daydreams and your thoughts expand your vision, which has been on shaky ground so far. Suddenly it becomes a big and powerful reality.

Think of all the fixed ideas, such as developing a network for the university. Marc Zuckerberg thought to himself, if only something small was practical. His vision of Facebook became a breathtaking craze that changed the lives of around two billion people.

Believe me, your thoughts are power. They contain the building blocks and the cement to create what you believe in. According to the law of attraction "Like attracts like", your thoughts will materialise on this level. I consciously do not write "can". No, they will when you see and feel your vision. I have experienced this with all my dreams. OK, it doesn't work if I imagine that pile of money, but where will it come from if I don't do anything about it? Logical, right? And quite honestly, if I found a money box behind a bush with a million euros in it, I wouldn't have a moment's peace. I couldn't just deposit the money in the bank, I can't get on a plane with it, it would be risky driving across the border in a car and when I came to spend the money, I'd always be afraid it'll be marked or something. There was also no note on the suitcase:

"This is for you, Mario, what you've always wished for. Love, your universe." So I would assume that this million belongs to a criminal who would be extremely angry because the suitcase is no longer there. Do I want that?

There is the possibility of winning the lottery. I'd think it's a great gift from the universe or karma or an assignment handed to the winners with great excitement. We know that so much money can also become a curse if I don't think about how to invest it. I would be happy about it and I would put it to good use. But have I earned it? Or is there a reason why I have to earn everything myself? It is not impossible that I was already stinking rich in a previous life. Now I have to get to know the other side. It is also possible that one day I will be born destitute in Africa to have a new experience and learn something.

I prefer to think about what I can achieve in this reality now: To send my depressions to the eternal hunting grounds, to murder suicidal thoughts the way they tried to get rid of me, to let Trees of Memory grow strong, to lay the foundation for good karma. Even if there is no more life to come, I will die knowing that I have been a reasonably good guy.

I also advise you to think of things that are big, crazy and unbelievable, but can be done in theory. Make yourself aware again and again: "You are not the victim of your fate, but the creator of your life". And as for your depressions, I can tell you that you will never get rid of them if you sit in the corner always crying, telling those around you about how miserable you are.

In all the books of the great religions it is written in various ways that the soul has something divine and is the creator of its own destiny. It says in the Talmud: "Pay attention to your thoughts, for they become words. Pay attention to your words, for they become actions. Pay attention to your actions, for they become habits. Pay attention to your habits, for they become your character. Watch your character, for it will become your destiny". Count Leo Tolstoy said: "Thought is the beginning of everything." Therefore, the most important thing is to work on your thoughts. There are many quotations on this subject and numerous scientific studies are devoted to the power of thoughts. In the end, they all come down to a common denominator: "You are what you think". This results in the mirror image, i.e. the projection from your inner being, which is your life at this moment.

It is this knowledge which shows me the difference between me and my old geezer. When I built my mental castles in the air, he got upset about the useless fantasies. While he wondered all the time why I had such nonsense in my head, the question "Why not?" was of much greater importance to me.

I have always done the opposite of what was expected of me. When someone says to me "You can't" or "That's not possible", not only does an incredible amount of defiance come up inside me, but also the huge cloud in which is written "Why not? Immediately, all the gears in my brain start to work to prove the contrary. Just because some complete idiot thinks it is not possible, should the rest of the universe think it is not possible? If you think so, then you will not get rid of your fears and depressions - I promise. You will never climb the top of a mountain if you cannot see yourself on the mountain.

Only last night I had another conversation about Trees of Memory and my partner expressed concern about what could happen to me and that it was impossible to say that I will be able to carry it out. I could die, be eaten by a tiger, lose my legs in an accident or fall in love with a great guy and hook up with him. Yes, it could be anything, but there is one thing that proves that none of this will stop me from carrying out my plan. I see myself arriving in Frankfurt and holding the first tree I planted for David. This vision is so clear and distinct and that is why I can hardly wait until I can hike without having to take winter breaks. By visualising how my brain will be and completely excluding certain things, I mentally anticipate the achievement of the goal and thus materialise the vision. If we go through our dreams, wishes and goals again and again and keep visualising them, we make sure that the energies necessary for this are put on the right track. Albert Einstein left a beautiful quote for this: "Imagination is everything. It is the preview of the future attraction of life". And which of you does not know the saying: "Faith moves mountains."

The law of attraction is accommpanied by the law of resonance. Everything in our universe vibrates and these vibrations send out waves. Our bodies and our thoughts are also vibrating. If there is something out there vibrating at the same frequency, it will resonate with us. That is one of the reasons why we make friends with other people or fall in love with them. We vibrate on the same frequency. We say, "We are on the same wavelength." Like attracts like. A greek proverb says, "Show me your friends and I will tell you who you are". In fact, we only need to look at the vibrations of our friends to understand how the other person ticks. That is why I always advise you to look at the friends of a new love. If they have a screw lose, you should be careful with your chosen one.

I should have taken immediate action when I met Jose's so-called friends. I didn't, and to my detriment I got involved with them. Many of them have even more severe social shortcomings than Jose had. During those two years, I was always concerned with the question of how it can be that someone cannot have one really good friend who is characterised by understanding and respect. One who will drop everything when asked for help. Today I know why and quite honestly: If I meet someone again who has no friends for no comprehensible reason, I will be gone.

When I think about it, I feel again how grateful I am to be blessed with many very good friends. Friends who have been by my side for decades, no matter what has happened over the years. Friendships clearly prove that everything we find in our lives has been attracted exclusively by ourselves. Why does the pretty woman or the nice guy smile at us? Because we smile too, the vibration is there, everything is in harmony and we have similar vibes.

Unfortunately the law of attraction also applies to everything negative in life. If our thoughts concentrate on the many bills that might drift into the house, then they will be attracted. If we are afraid of the bailiff day and night, one day he will surely be at the door. If we sit in the underground and are afraid of being punched by the five bald men who have just got on the train bellowing loudly, we will surely get a good thrashing. If I walk through the city on holiday and focus my energy on possible muggings, I will be robbed. And if I were now constantly worried about what diseases I could catch on my hike around the world, I would certainly never reach my destination and die of cholera on the way. Oh no ... at the moment Covid-19.

The principle is comprehensible. In our lives we will constantly be confronted with our own deep-rooted fears. Sometimes they are so present and dominant that we think about them constantly. We direct our thoughts and our energy exclusively towards the threatening and imaginary misfortune.

There is the beautiful word "target focus". I have an example that proves what it is all about. I am a paraglider pilot and the very first flights, at a height of 20 or 30 metres, led from a small slope into a flat valley. Somewhere in the field there were huge bales of hay. So big that you certainly couldn't miss them when you steered towards them. But on the right and left of them there were 200 metres of space before the next bale of hay. No bushes, no trees, no electricity pylons, nothing that could get in the way of the beginner. Dead sure terrain, in other words. When the instructor told us not to swoop into such a hay bale, almost every one of us directly hit a bale of straw. I was hanging in the air and could think of nothing else but not hitting the bale of hay: "Just don't hit the bale of hay ... Oh man, it's coming towards me... What am I doing? Come on, more to the right. Ouch!" My hands could have pulled the sail just an inch or two to the right or left and everything would have been fine. But I was like paralysed and focused on the bale of straw instead of the beautiful piece of meadow just behind it.

It is curious that all of us usually focus our attention on the things that frighten us instead of turning to the beautiful things, letting our dreams come true and imagining what it would be like to experience, to have or to discover the greatest this or that. The most difficult part of all this is not discovering that we can attract everything we want into our lives, but to deal with the difficulties of everyday life and to get rid of all the rubbish that blocks our view and forces us to look at the crap and the arseholes that make our lives difficult.

That is the big challenge, also for me. I've never managed to get through a whole day thinking positively and with joy and ease in my heart, because there is always something going on that gets on my nerves and activates all my Italian drama freak-out genes at once. In the evening I ask myself again why I can't manage to look away from the incident with a smile. To cope well with life is a state of mind and a learning process that rewards us by life treating us well.

Everything we wish for in life, what we think about, what we are afraid of, will enter into our existence as an experience and so from this there can be no coincidences. I think that they really do not exist. Perhaps only in the form that it is coincidence whether a white or a blue bird craps on our head. Don't you think so? Then think very intensively about the fact that bird crap will soon be delivered on to your head. Ready? OK, come on...

For these reasons, I disagree with many religions that want to tell me that life and everything that happens in it is predetermined and that the dear God has sealed the fate of every human being even before they are born. Sorry, I think this is complete nonsense and has nothing to do with a loving God. That is why this idea does not exist in my life bubble. In your bubble it can be an option. For me the idea that life follows laws that we can influence ourselves and that we have the possibility to influence our near future and our coming lives in a positive way is a logical thought. If our life trajectory were based only on coincidences that promote chaos and if we were exposed to the arbitrariness of a god, I would find myself in a hell. I think that we ourselves bear the responsibility, even if we cannot see the causes of what happened. Because there is no good or evil in the universe, but always only polarities that come to light with a little too much of that and too little of this as the effect of a cause, it is all the more important to remember regularly to pay attention to what I want, what is good for me, and not to the impending disaster.

What do you think? How will your depression feel when you think about not taking any more pills at the end of next year? In comparison, what would happen if you had to take ever stronger pills for the next five years and did not get well at all? In such a case, your energy is focused on the fact that you will never get well again.

My decision to stop taking pills, to get rid of my depression, was not made through a book or by the remarks I write in this book. No, I thought at an extremely difficult point in my life that if it doesn't stop now and get better, I'm going to follow Jose and die miserably in a corner somewhere. It had to end. From that moment on I no longer concentrated on my depression and grief, but on my life. I used to take four different medicines a day. That went on for almost four years. Now I only take one pill. I used to take 45 mg of it. Now I half the lowest dose of 7mg and only take 3.5mg. That is almost nothing any more.

Now that I am writing all these things down, I sometimes see how everything has developed in accordance with the universal laws, and still turns and twists, and I get dizzy. Sometimes it is still difficult, because my entrenched thoughts tell me how I should behave.

If attitude and action are one day anchored in my mind and come from the heart without having to think, then everything will be fulfilled as it is predestined: as a logical sequence and reaction and not as the script of an old man in heaven. Actually you can say that life is predetermined because there is a logical consequence to everything.

I wish I had known about all these things when I was 12 years old. I would never have made the mistake of being afraid of a grade five in chemistry or going to a class test knowing I couldn't do it. No, I would have concentrated on the fact that I could do it and not been afraid of it. I would have concentrated on writing a grade 1 and got a 3. All good. But I was so afraid that I couldn't write, learn, make or do anything else because I visualised in my mind's eye the fear of getting another thrashing. I would have been spared a lot.

Unfortunately, the law of attraction also presents us with a great dilemma, which becomes a problem for those of us who, like me, are extremely impatient. We put our thoughts into the ethereal world, create our castles in the air in daydreams, work on the realisation of our wishes, but the materialisation of our thoughts takes time. I think to myself that I have now done everything possible to approach potential sponsors. But they are still not there. That's why doubt and fear gnaw at me and I start to direct my thoughts and energy to the question: "What happens if I don't find sponsors? What happens then? Increasingly I concentrate on not finding sponsors, instead of not attaching any importance to time and being sure that they will come, sometime. I find it hard to believe and visualise. What vibration do I have to develop to draw them into my life? As you can see, all this is not easy. Nevertheless, I am not giving up.

Please, do not give up either.

Don't give a damn

At the very front, in the first row, amongst those who should not interest you, are the people who don't give a damn about you. The people who don't care if you have gone through hell or not. There are those who have looked away all their lives but never missed an opportunity to give their verdict loudly, those who have discredited you and with their consistent silence support all those who want to harm you. There are all the uninvolved onlookers who do not want to notice anyone. There are all the people who mean well in any way, with all their advice and judgements based on their own lives. Their life story is not comparable to yours. Even depression, suicidal tendencies and the loss of a family member cannot be lumped together. There is everyone who does NOT say: "I believe in you."

It has taken time for me to understand that it is all about my life and my future, which does not have to be lived by anyone else, but by me. I am the one who wants to get up in the morning with a smile and be over the moon when things work out. I am the one who can't sleep for nights on end, because my thoughts go round and round and deprive me of sleep. I am the one who, driven by a sick mind, has tried to take my own life. I decide whether a hammock is more important to me than a BMW. Only I can feel what money does to me and what money without vision and belief does to me. Only I can appreciate the hugs and tears that are shed when the right word has been said or the best cause for new effects inside and outside has been created. No one will ever create my future, fulfill my dreams, have my fears and die from my worries. I am the only one who can decide whether the path leads me into darkness or into light.

Why should I, why should you listen to someone if he or she cannot feel what moves and guides you?

The wrong responses I have given are understandable. Because I was ignorant and blind. Because I wanted to be loved which is the worst killer of motivation for any change and for any success, however that is defined. Because I was helpless. Because I bathed myself in self-pity.

Likewise I am not interested in the right moment. There is never the right moment to break up, to fall in love again, to change jobs or to have a go at your dreams. Every moment is right and every second can be wrong. The right time is a fairy tale, an illusion, a myth. It does not exist. I have often kidded myself by waiting for the right moment. With this I sabotaged myself before I started.

The right moment is now, right now, this evening, tomorrow morning, in two days, next month, Christmas or next year. It is always when you feel that now is the right moment. It is your decision, not someone else's. Sometimes dark forces come from nowhere and give a stupid devious reason, because we don't want to hear the word "Now" and we ignore it.

Inspiration and Motivation are also two causes that I am not interested in. What or who inspires me is irrelevant. Sure, that can be a push in the right direction. But not having motivation and not being inspired and not even looking for it is a sign that I am not yet scruffy enough and that my level of suffering is not high enough. The only thing that gets me any further is to do it. I am a doer and not a waiter. I do not want to discuss everything to death and do not want to plan myself into ruin. The result is more important to me than perfection. Anyone who hangs on to the fact that I have a wrong comma here and there, is floating in a bubble that has nothing to do with my existence. Whoever holds onto such trivialities has no problems and believes he can make up for his own imperfection by insulting others, burdening them, being spiteful. Such people take a position that is not theirs to take. They are trolls who do not deserve any attention.

Do you know the sentence: "Just look what he or she has achieved. I'm nothing without a Rolex, a great career, a great house, a huge car, crazy guys at my side and certainly not impressive with this potbelly. I am poor, a have-not." Honestly, there will always be bigger, smaller, richer, poorer, better or worse people than me. Someone will come one day, pass me and snatch my crown away. If I were to follow the constant gaze upwards, I would have fallen into a bottomless pit long ago. Why do I have to watch TikTok. A million followers, my walk-in fridge, my shoe collection, my abs, yawn. The only correct answer to displaying "I'm the greatest" is a hearty but determined "Fuck you!" If I want to sing and succeed so that I can make a living out of it, I don't need to fill a stadium, because I can do what my desire is calling for: singing. My happiness lies in the street and I only have to bend down to it. I know that there are always pennies lying around, sometimes one or two euros. In rare cases there is even a note. But why should I make life difficult for myself and desperately hope that there is a suitcase with a million just waiting for me to find it. What if I do? Well, if I do, then I'm happy because at some point in this or another life I've done something right and I'm now getting my reward. This is how I see it and I feel more comfortable with it than with all the thoughts born of greed, envy and the expectations of those who are not involved. I will not be destroyed by the inaccessibility of stupid dreams, because I am happy with what I have and that is nothing. An extraordinarily liberating feeling. I can only recommend this.

I was one of the people taken in by the craze of positive thinking. "You just have to think positive, then everything will be fine. Think positively and you will draw wealth into your life. You have to think positively and look ahead, then everything will be fine again". Oh man, what a load of rubbish is being preached in this context. The one who has brought us this fairy tale should have to slave away for a lifetime in a quarry on just bread and water.
Seriously, why should I believe and accept for just a moment that positive thinking makes the world around me better? To consciously put positive vibrations into the world in order to change it is more than just an "all shall be well" thought and is not to be counted under positive thinking. If I can't get off my arse and don't actively take care of my life, even the most positive thought will not be able to protect me from bad times. The only thing that positive thinking changes is my condidtion. It would be more miserable because of assuming that positive thinking could save me. No, good thoughts, well-intentioned sent to another person for strength, can arrive and help in a supportive way. But they do not help me to write this book, to hike around the world or to make bearable the suffering of those who suffer from suicide. I must do it and not think!

We should all be allowed to be ourselves and follow our visions, then this strange positive construct is not needed. I know many who were allowed to dream, who were supported and in pitfalls were caught with love, and they are the lucky ones today. They are my heroes who do their thing and have themselves found the greatest fulfilment. Those who have always been different from the others have made it to be something. They have found their centre and live their own riches. If they are lucky, they are even rewarded and get what seems so important in our society. Not that this is particularly desirable, but it makes life easier. Sure, wealth would open up other opportunities. When I imagine that I could make a TV spot for TREES of MEMORY, my heart stops in excitement. At such moments I smile and when I open my eyes, I am speechless and I can hardly catch my breath for sheer amazement, because, look what has happened so far, without any wealth: I hike, I plant trees, there is an association, television reports, people know me from the internet, you bought my book and complete strangers send me emails that make my heart bleed and fill my eyes with tears. Others open the

front door and take me in their arms like the prodigal son and sigh: "At last you are here. I have waited so long for you."
I don't think this has ever happened to a baker who has toiled away to become a millionaire.

Can it get any more fulfilling? It doesn't matter what anyone else says. In the subject of happiness, you must only listen to yourself. This is possible without harming the world around you and being an arsehole.

Let go

Being able to let go is not exactly my strength right now. I've always been stuck in relationships that haven't been anything to write home about. I was stuck in jobs where I was exploited but had fun. I found it hard to part with material things because they held memories and because they defined me. Mostly I could not let go because fear played a big role. It took a while before I could accept that I would always carry fears around with me, both large and small. Most of them are completely insignificant and it's part of it that not everything you set out to do works out. Of course I misjudge my abilities from time to time. Sometimes I mess up a plan because I missed something important. And I get turned down often enough because there is always someone taller, smaller, dumber, slimmer, fatter, richer, poorer, older, younger or just blonde.

It is part of my life to have to live with disappointments as long as I am not aware that I am carrying within me the attainment of whole universes. Nothing will happen if I wait for the key to success to be delivered from the outside. There will always be things and desires in life that are not meant to be. God alone knows why.

What I have learned is that everything has its reason and that the explanation will be delivered at some point. I can show this with a small example.
One day it was on the agenda that Jose and I could move in together. That failed because of our completely different ideas. I wanted the open kitchen and he wanted one separate from the living room. I wanted to live on the 10th floor with a view and he hated it when he couldn't see people on the street. And so it went on and on, until I gave up, exasperated and decided to rent my own flat. I found a flat that I liked in Bad Vibel. The disadvantage was that there was only a limited timetable for the bus connection to Frankfurt. The advantage was that there were only three stops to Jose's flat. The estate agent assumed that I would get the flat because I was the perfect applicant. I made plans and knew how I would furnish it. Then the call came with a rejection that nobody could justify. I was disappointed. I started looking again and found my little dream flat in Offenbach, which was much better than the one in Bad Vilbel.

Three weeks before I could move, Jose took his own life. It would have been terrible to live in Bad Vilbel and to have to drive past his flat every day for the next few years. I am not saying that there is an omniscient prediction that influences events. But I have had the experience that everything has a meaning, with the exception of Jose's suicide. Letting go is now easier for me with this knowledge and the experiences associated with it.

Letting go means accepting. Whoever accepts something automatically lets go. It is important to accept what I cannot change anyway. Everyone has strengths, everyone has weaknesses, humanity can get along without me, there will always be someone who needs me and others who don't and much more. All this is not negotiable, just like death. Dying is part of life and some of us have to leave early, others are as old as the hills. Illness is part of life, even if you have different opinions philosophically, spiritually and scientifically about their origin.

With TREES of MEMORY I have learned to let go. I have given away all my possessions and had to sell them at traumatically low prices. I had to learn that most people don't care if I spent a fortune on individual items or not. It doesn't matter a damn whether I use the proceeds to become the most charitable person on earth or to buy myself a bicycle. I was ripped off and almost only my friends bought things from me at a fair price. Of course, it mattered that the classic Ebayer or classified ads customer thought I was pulling their leg. "Yes, yes ... hike around the world..." Items that I wanted to give away from the outset I was supposed to deliver to their front door. Whoever accepts a gift has high expectations.
In retrospect, I would have been better off finding a cellar and storing everything. I could still have thrown it away. I took 14 suitcases and rubbish bags full of clothes to the homeless shelter. More than 60 pairs of trousers, 85 shirts, 120 T-shirts, 24 jackets and 30 pairs of shoes changed hands. I received a heartfelt thank you, also because I was known there through my project, the Winter Knitters. I divided my art and travel souvenirs among my friends. Everybody was allowed to take something with them. It should be a memory of me and should I have a permanent residence again, then I will get the things back. I only have what I can fit on my hiking cart, plus a few boxes of winter clothes and stuff for my study that I need in winter. During the winter months I take a room or get an invitation to stay somewhere and I work day and night. I don't miss any of the things I used to own. In the beginning there were moments when I cried my eyes out and couldn't believe what was happening to me. I had lost Jose and lost my life, and now I was supposed to give away everything that was dear to me? What was unbelievably difficult at the beginning became easier every time and at a certain point I just wanted to get

rid of everything. In the end I put everything out on the street and watched them suddenly fighting amongst themselves over some stupid picture frames and taking away metal cabinets from the 50s which nobody wanted before.

Letting go turned out to be a great relief. Minimalist life, Back to the Roots and Tiny House Movements used to make me smile. Now I am a fervent supporter of them and would love to teach 'letting go' in seminars. I would like to have no more possessions. Not carrying property around with me brings freedom and creates opportunities I have only ever dreamed of. For me it is perfect and the right thing. For many others it would be perfect too, but fear makes you cling to the possessions that you don't need. They believe that 'having' is the definition of their being. Others die thinking that they no longer have their own home and would have to make do with 10 T-shirts.
In America there is even a movement called the "333 Project". Wealthy businesswomen reduce their wardrobe to exactly 33 pieces, which they wear for three months. In the videos they suddenly notice that nobody notices that they are always walking around in the same clothes. Some of them have turned their entire lives upside down and reduced everything, not just the contents of their wardrobe. The most radical representatives, mostly the digital nomads who dream of life on the beach, where they earn money with their laptops, have reduced their entire possessions to backpack size. No matter where they go, they have everything they care about with them. If each one of us knew how little we get by with and how happy we are without all the crap that we are being talked into getting every day, the world would be a different place.

I still have too much on my hiking cart. There are things there that I have never touched in two years. My water filter or the heavy roll of tape. I should part with it, but if I ever need it, it could save me. In a few weeks' time I will take matters in hand and weigh up whether I want to continue carrying it around with me.

I had to let people go. So-called best friends, who sneaked out of my life with the death of Jose. Casual acquaintances, with whom I could usually go for a drink and who suddenly made themselves a judge over me. Most of my German relatives, who didn't even have enough decency to express their condolences to me. And last but not least I let go of my mother, who was never there when I needed her during my whole existence. After Jose's death she continued to drive around Germany to visit zoos but didn't find the time to stop in Frankfurt and give me a hug.
I have separated from her and from my German family and I should have taken this step decades ago. I have forgiven her for beating me because I know she

has her story too and is a psycho victim. But I don't have to understand why she didn't see the need to stand by her son during the worst days of his life. I accept all that. This is her. This is the woman who doesn't love me as I would like her to love me or, as I would define it, as mother love.

I accept that my sister pinched her home for her four children, knowingly with my stepfather, shamefully depriving our mother of her possessions. I accept her vested interest, which is worth more than a few phone calls every anniversary. I accept her statement that after my stepfather's death she had a detective search for me who was obviously too stupid to find my website and couldn't find the only Mario Dieringer of the two that exist in the world. Therefore it was impossible for her to inform me about the death of my stepfather or aunt.

I accepted it and that's how I was able to let it go, even if the anger is still there when I think about it. The acceptance and letting go helped me not to fall apart over it. This separation has given me emotional freedom and health.

I no longer see the need to understand their actions over the past 50 years. Blood is not thicker than water. Being a mother, sister, father, uncle or grandmother does not confer any rights and obviously does not imply any moral obligations. Love and home are where the heart is and where there are people who care and love you. We can always create a family of our choice.

My letting go not only brought freedom, but a tremendous amount of love that I found in people all over the world. Since I have been on the road, my family has been growing, because TREES of MEMORY creates new and emotional connections with depth. It has created friendships that are worth more than any family bond.

Letting go became the most important building block of my mental well-being and new beginning.

The power of hope

In many cases all hope dies following the ending of something.Tomorrow is full of uncertainty and today is smothered in painful emotions of all kinds. We have the feeling especially after a death that there can be no more hope. How could there be, when the dearest person, your own child or your parents have been taken from you far too soon. What is there to hope for when it is clear that this person will be gone from our lives forever?

On days like Christmas, Easter, birthdays or when an anniversary is coming up, the hopelessness is felt twice as strongly because someone is missing, a place is empty and the sadness competes with your own melancholy.
Losing your livelihood, your business or your current job can also be accompanied by great hopelessness. This is something I sense in many people in recent months, due to the Corona pandemic. If we are bankrupt we Germans land softly onto the state's social support and we will never starve on the street, yet people do take their own lives because their whole being is anchored in having and having seems more important than their own lives and the subsequent lives of their children, parents or siblings.

Those who have lost their job or their own company find themselves on the worst possible thought carousel. Immediately, thoughts are found that destroy any chance of finding a new job. I am too old. I am not good enough. I can no longer reorient myself. I no longer have the strength to take the step into self-employment again. I have no money. These are all examples of hope fading until it is lost altogether because we have talked ourselves to death. Especially those of us who are used to holding the reins, the so-called doers, fall into a deep hole because they believe that hope is unrealistic unless you take the matter into your own hands. They see the uncertainty as a danger, even as an enemy. But what if the uncertainty of hope is seem as an infinite space full of possibilities?

I often experience how my hiking companions send me a list even before the start of the tour, with all the things they cannot do. Never hike more than 15 km. Just don't sleep in the forest. Heat is not an option. I could make a long list. And what do I do? When asked how far we've hiked, I always lengthen or shorten the details in my answer, depending on the terrain we've covered, so that in the end we've actually hiked at least five kilometres more than "by no means more than 15 kilometres". Three days later we are doing 25 kilometres. The best way to regain hope is to leave your own comfort zone. Only then will you find out what you are capable of. That's why I advise you, for example, to plan your hiking route a bit longer rather than too short. Or a steep tour up the mountain instead of a leisurely one along the river. The same applies in all other areas: leaving your comfort zone creates new space for surprising possibilities that give rise to hope.

If you learn, despite everything that has happened, that you can have hope again and that it is inexhaustible, you will become yourself again. If you are 100% yourself, there will be no more limits for you and hope will carry you to success. I see this every day in myself and in friends. Those who rarely deal with themselves, who don't meditate, who question everything and have never learned to trust in the great unknown, suffer greatly from the pandemic and all that it brings with it, and suffer psychological damage. The others, including me, shrug their shoulders, find it less fun and annoying, but none of us is shaken to the core. My life in particular has not changed. I sit in front of the computer and write. I make myself active, do Trees of Memory, and I focus on problem solving and not on the problem.

All of us have heard the story of Icarus, who wanted to fly and was laughed at and failed again and again to rise up into the air like a bird. For many millennia, it was impossible for humans to soar through the air. Everyone agreed: you can't fly without wings and feathers. That was the perceived truth until someone said: "Of course man can fly, just differently". Every failed attempt was met with nationwide ridicule and the visionaries were laughed at and not infrequently humiliated. And today? I am a paraglider and, if I catch a good thermal, I can circle in the air for many hours. Sometimes together with birds of prey that show me the way to unimagined heights. I feel like a bird and can lead the way. I never know if the flying day will be a good one. What sustains me is hope and since I am not a professional, hope is worth more than my flying skills.

When I made it public that I would be hiking around the world with TREES of MEMORY to plant trees in remembrance of suicide victims, many laughed at me. I even got emails saying that they had never heard such nonsense and that such a plan could never be implemented. The reasoning was often that I couldn't walk on water. It seemed to me that I was the only one who thought my vision was possible. But over time, people from all over Germany became infected with my perceived visions. Today, more than four years later, I have hiked many thousands of kilometres. An idea became an international project. From 11 visionary people, who found each other through me, a European non-profit association has grown with members from two countries. Dozens of trees in remembrance have already been planted all over Germany and there are invitations from 13 countries where trees are to be planted.

I am devoted to my idea and abandoned all pragmatic conventional thinking. What seemed impossible in the first few weeks is now a lived reality. This reality has become a vast space of infinite possibilities in which hope is inexhaustible. I don't have to let that be ruined by those who say: "You're not hiking around the world, you're still in Germany". Would you tell a marathon runner that he's not running a marathon just because he's on his first 5 kilometres? Do you see what I'm getting at?

One day you will have a vision that others don't feel. You will walk towards a goal whose great whole will remain hidden from the spectators at the side of the track. Yes, even your competitors will reject new points of view and look straight ahead from their corner, unaware that you are looking around the corner where great things are opening up. It doesn't matter what others see. It is your project, your dream, your vision, your goal and most importantly: your life. A life that, beyond all drama, sadness and misfortunes, will still deliver many great moments. Just because you don't feel and see them yet, doesn't mean they are not there.

It may be time for you to question your limiting of your actions to what feels safe. You wanted and still want to control the unknown by imposing your stance on it. Have you not learned that you are at this difficult point in your life today because you have no control over the unknown and the great movement in which our lives are involved?

Be willing to live in the now of reality and allow yourself a new perspective full of openness. Don't close yourself off any longer and take notice when something encouraging happens outside your comfort zone. Take a step back from old behaviours. Be mindful, watch out if you are replaying an old pattern or telling your friends and acquaintances the same story for the umpteenth time. Don't refer to old habits, because they only reflect your careless thinking and acting.

When you become aware of what you are doing and try a new way within the framework of self-knowledge, then - but only then - change happens. If you let yourself go and allow hope to present a good result without wanting to control it, you will not be disappointed. But beware of sending a worked out wish list to the universe like a little child. It is not necessary to wish for a light blue

Lamborghini when you desperately need a car. You can always trust that the images of your goal sent to the universe as visionary hope will lead you to the best outcome. Trust it, even if you don't know what the result will be and how you will get to the goal of your wishes.

For years I have had no idea how to achieve this or that, even in the context of my hiking around the world. Of course, I often think to myself: "Lord, let me win the lottery, then everything would be easier". But would it be good for me and all that is yet to come if I were to hike around the world with millions in my pocket? Then I would no longer be able to hike as an encouraging role model if I could simply afford all that and have my tired bones soothed by a nice masseur in the Hilton Hotel and in the evening to end the day with a juicy steak and a little champagne. In such a case, everyone would say: "Easy for him to say". Even without a million, or precisely because of it, TREES of MEMORY became much bigger than I ever imagined or dreamed. Isn't that worth much more than everything else and my thoughts of luxury?

As a child I often dreamed of becoming a famous author and I still look with envy at stories like Harry Potter or authors like Ken Follett, whom I have had the pleasure of interviewing. By the time you read these lines, I will have published my third book and no one will know me. Maybe it's better not to be famous. But I am doing what I have always dreamed of. I always wanted to see the world and become an author. Now I hike around the world and write a book now and then. I am living my dreams, having paid a high price and only through that have I been able to do so. Perhaps you must first give in order to receive?

The path of hope and your own fulfilment is and remains a mystery and always unpredictable, just as, praise God, we cannot foresee misfortunes either. That does not make the feeling of having hope any less trustworthy. On the contrary, I find it extremely exciting and incredibly beautiful. But I don't have to hold the reins in my hand, I allow the horse to carry me where it is good for me, even if I don't recognise that at first glance.

When you go for a walk today, and your thoughts are circling madly and wandering away from everyday life, bring them back under control by saying to yourself again and again, aloud or silently:
I have all the hope in the world.
Use it like a mantra. It will calm your mind. Take ten steps and say "I have all the hope in the world". Ten steps ...
When times are difficult you could dedicate the hours to the theme of hope and help yourself to let go of control. To do this, it is important that you learn

to trust in the unknown, even in the completely alien. Experience how your consciousness contains an infinite source of creativity in which you can place your trust. Be yourself and feel how the hope which comes will give you strength and courage for every step you take.

Don't let fate, pandemics, stupid employers and people who don't care about you and those who only see their own little hopeless bubble, rob you of your dreams, abilities, desires and hope.
Tell yourself every day when you wake up in the morning: "I have all the hope in the world" and let yourself fall into the emptiness of the infinite space full of possibilities. You are worth it.

Come with us on your own journey

I began my journey to happiness as a child. The shortcomings of my parents' terrrible parenting methods could not stop me from dreaming. My failed relationships could not make an embittered contemporary out of me. When I am invited by people, I don't think they mean me any harm. When I travel the world, I cannot imagine that I could be attacked. I have always oriented myself towards the good. I am convinced that this was partly the reason why any bad people avoided the crossroads where we could have met. I can only hope that it will continue to be so.

I already know that I can still be disappointed and hurt. It has happened before. Well, these people, for whatever reason, have chosen to do the not so positive. That doesn't mean that the good around me was not there. It was just not used. It is pointless to think about why that was the case. I can accept everything and it makes me grateful for all the wonderful things I was allowed to experience because I trusted. This has brought me here into the present and shown me my place in the future. It is the place where I would like to be in the coming decades, or from where I will take the further journey of my development.

Even though I constantly believe in the good, I do not deny there's evil. I need the light if I want to illuminate the darkness. I use the darkness of the deep when I want to experience the joy of light. By combining seemingly separate things, such as day and night, lie or truth, love or hate, and seeing them as one, many a wish disappears and makes room for the realities of my life, of which there are still many to discover. I will continue to try and separate myself from the meanings that have caused sadness, pain, anger, disappointment, helplessness or hatred in me. I will exchange them through the opposing positive values so that I can continue to find my centre and my inner conflicts can be resolved.

In doing this I can stand by others who are affected and help them to explore new perspectives. Every weakness has strengths and every mistake has its justness. Every windowless room has its openings and all problems, that show up in the future, will offer a big colourful basket of various solutions,

possibilities and great chances. When I die, it will not be the end, but rather the beginning of the journey, of that I am convinced.

If pain and suffering come to haunt me once again, I will take away their time so that they no longer continue. Without time, suffering cannot arise and pain cannot expand. Both pass away together with the past at the moment of their creation and have no possibility to escape into my present to ruin my future from here on.
I no longer like to compare the causes of the past with the motives and effects of my present, because my brain would get an idea of how horrible the future could look and make it look as terrible as it has been for years in my past.

In the last four years I have experienced many positive impetus and their effects. I see no reason why I should travel further back in time to build my tomorrow with my tears from that time. I do not allow the past to release energies that can destructively damage my present and my future and ruin my health again. If I do, I want to remember the love, the happiness and the joy, so that the laughter on my lips and the joy in my heart will release a fire of positive meltdown, from which new being will arise.

Why should suffering and lack always be nearer to me than happiness? I do not want your pity and I do not want envy. I want the speechless encounter that fills all spaces of this time with our appreciation, our compassion, our esteem and our respect. I want "to be able to be" and "to let be". I want to paint colourful pictures and not create futuristic models from the emotional ashes of death, grief or hate.

Of course I cannot counteract a future full of suffering by blanking out the past. Life is past and present. The future is my vision and at the same time nothing more than an illusion, until in one and the same second it reveals itself in the here and now as my reality and vanishes again in the blink of an eye. I need the effects of the past because they allow my belief to arise out of experience and strengthen it until it is unshakeable and the last negative belief on the pyre of history becomes of no importance. Without my hopes and the belief in myself and my reality, tomorrow would not exist anymore. A strong belief is the foundation of a happy future for each of us. Only then will I be someone who will not be restricted by what was yesterday. The unlimited possibilities show me the values of my goals. They are at the same time my status and possessions, looking back and building on a series of successes and failures.

I want to create my reality and my life and not be the product of circumstances or be created by demands, expectations, society or anyone else. If I did not do that, I would live in resistance. A very negative energetic state that attracts nothing but other adverse circumstances, which would lead me to further adverse actions. Nothing good can come out of this.

With my positive thoughts I want to light a fire in which I can continue to forge and shape my iron will. Only in this way will my thoughts become a real hopeful being that leads into my future-oriented life. I do not want to focus my attention on shortcomings any more. I want to see my inner reality, which is full of dreams, visions, goals, love, nonsense, laughter and fun, become an exact copy on the outside. I live out my strong belief and crazy images of the future, with TREES of MEMORY and much more, that defines me. From this, further dreams arise, which as a sign of my fulfillment start each time I breathe. I just have to decide what they mean to me.

The reality of dreams has always existed because I lived them in my imagination and even as a child I travelled through Africa, making discoveries, dreaming of hopping about on the Titanic and creating memorable and emotional times with people of all nations and races, arm in arm. I never wanted to become president, a multimillionaire or a homeowner. I only ever wanted to be me and I became ill when that was taken away from me. I still adore Pippi Longstocking, who created a world as she wanted it. I did the same and had my own Taka Tuka Land. The power of my imagination is the endless possibility of my future manifesting itself in the present moment.

The other day I had a big discussion in which the statement was made that love proves itself through our deeds. For some partners you are either for one or against one. To love and yet not agree seems to be unimaginable for everyone. Self-love is often declared to be destructive narcissism. But those who say this just can't cope with the fact that the other person doesn't want to caress their ego all the time. "I love you to the moon and back" is not possible if I do not carry the same amount of self-love within me. It has to get out and does not want to find its way always and exclusively into a strange heart. As unknown as love is in its essence, it is a powerful affirmation. Love is not, and never is, what we do. Love is exclusively what we are.

No matter what causes I create in the name of love today or tomorrow, they will continue to work until the end of time, while their origin, in the present moment and action, becomes the past, which you will soon hardly remember. I learn from my frailty every single day of my life. This helps me to draw from the fullness of life in the present time, so that my visions will guide me into the future and connect me with the people who touch my heart.

Would you like to join in and go your own way?

- the end & the beginning -

Non-profit association
Trees of Memory e.V.

Mario Dieringer's plan to hike around the world and plant trees in remembrance of suicide victims made many people curious. Quite independently of each other and unknown to each other, eleven people found it useful to support him as an association. I was one of them.

My son committed suicide on 23rd March, 2015. The day on which my world came to a standstill, tore me apart inside and destroyed many things in me. On this day a period began in which I merely "existed" in my mind, but could no longer really participate in life. It was a balancing act between the desire to die and the hope of finding myself amidst the grief and inner chaos, even though in the meantime I had inevitably changed so that I was simply a complete stranger to myself. I stumbled by chance upon Mario's idea and something began to change. The idea of being able to plant a tree in remembrance of my late son, as well as the emerging desire to have something alive, something growing as a counterbalance to my infinitely deep grief, gave me hope and confidence to start my life afresh, despite the grief. Above all, the whole thing sounded so crazy that it could only be right.
The death of your own child by suicide is extreme, distorts your view of the world and questions your own life. So why not see if this unconventional idea can put something in a different light? This was the reason for contacting Mario, Trees of Memory was not yet being talked about and he still called his project "Footpath of Life".

At the same time as contacting Mario, I offered to support him in the background, if this was desired. I was not the only one having this thought. Other people also offered to help him. And so it happened that in November, 2017, eleven people met for the first time, in Offenbach, to found the association TREES of MEMORY e.V. From the outset, the members are not only themselves victims of loss through suicide but they also include people who want to support Mario's project out of sympathy and only came into contact with the subject of suicide as an aside. Martin Georgi supported us with words and deeds as an outsider when we founded the association. He has already helped several associations as an advisor, a fundraiser and was himself a board member of "Aktion Mensch" for several years.

The most important thing for us as an associtation was the support we could give Mario, so that he could carry out and live his vision more safely. And also to make visible on our website the different ways of helping relatives after a suicide, as well as for people with mental illness. The website was created by a great team at the same time as the one for Mario. We are grateful to Jana, Miriam and Arne, former students of Mario, from "Freundeskollektiv" for the design, the structure and the good introduction, so that we can now maintain and update the website on our own. As members of the association we do not live centrally at the same place, but are spread all over Germany and so we are always faced with challenges concerning communication or working jointly. At the same time, this opens up new and different possibilities and ways for us, so that events can be planned and implemented in the most diverse locations.

The distance challenged the board of directors, consisting of three people, of which I am a member. Board meetings are held via video conferencing, which for some was uncharted territory. The technology also pushes some people to their limits ... at least me. My technology freak, my son, who was responsible for teaching his old mother how to use a mobile phone and other technical things, was no longer here. To do all this on my own was new and actually everything in me blocked against it at first. I didn't want to learn if my son couldn't teach me. Suddenly others had to help me or I had to get through it myself. I was challenged unexpectedly to get a grip on my life despite all my grief.

For me personally Trees of Memory e.V. has become something extremely valuable. I stumbled upon Mario's idea when I was in a total standstill. My life could only continue for the sake of my husband and my daughter. My existence was a daily "endurance", but had hardly any prospects. The grief for my son, missing him and the many agonising questions made everything more difficult and robbed me of all strength and energy. Through the work in the association something was opened up for me which made sense to keep on fighting, to take life back with small steps. At the same time a different confrontation with my grief and my fate began. I could no longer stand still, there were people out there in the world to whom I could offer help through my involvement. It was steered in a positive direction. Even though I always reached my limits, because I lived through my own grief and this work was related to my own situation. Suddenly there was this spark of hope that somehow it was worth fighting for.

Even before Mario's "hike around the world" began, the association members met for their first meeting in Coburg after the association was founded. Mario was also invited. The idea of an interdenominational memorial service came from our member there and she organised it and helped put it together. It was touching to see that there were also people involved in this organisation, who actually had nothing to do with the subject of suicide and yet were willing to get involved. It showed that others noticed us. It was a successful start. The first public presence. That weekend we got three new members. Three weeks before that, our first new member joined. For me personally it was another step back into life, as I spent a complete weekend among several people, although I had withdrawn myself more and more for almost two years.

Many of us got together for the first tree planting in Frankfurt. The first Tree of Memory, planted for the deceased partner of our then second board member Sven König. It was a moving moment. Mario's hike then set off until the first overnight stop, accompanied by 26 people, including me.

Our association processes the requests for tree planting, contacts the necesary authorities and the tree nurseries. We start the planning together with the people who wish to have a Tree of Memory, support the call for a fundraising campaign if necessary, so that the tree planting can be financed. Often this can take months, as the date of planting is based on the route of Mario's hike. Sometimes it is not easy to get the authorities to approve the tree planting. But we know how important and valuable the Trees of Memory are for the bereaved, so we try our best and fight for the approval with patience and reason.

Another personal concern for me was to be able to give a little more support to the bereaved after a loss through suicide. An idea came of how to bridge this gap. From my own experience I knew how important it is to exchange information with other people who have been affected. And how big the gap can be at the beginning, between mourners and their own circle of acquaintances. Many feel alone with this fate, misunderstood and completely overwhelmed. At first I also knew almost no one who had experienced a similar situation. There wasn't anyone to listen, no way of being allowed to express your own feelings and thoughts. To be understood through and through. And that is so immensely important. My own circle were often helpless and silent, because nobody wanted to do anything wrong or was overwhelmed by the situation, both inside and outside the family.
Nobody thinks about where to get help in advance in case of a suicide in the family. Why should they? You push this thought as far away as possible. So you

don't know where you can find somone to listen when a suicide has suddenly happened and the ground disappears from under your feet. Many of those affected do not know that there are self-help groups. They are afraid, they do not find the strength to start looking for help. For more than half a year, I didn't know that there were different groups for this on Facebook and I only found them by chance. For half a year I felt completely alone with my fate. My own family was affected by it, so that you never wanted to overburden them but inevitably often did so anyway. A friend stood by my side from the very beginning, for which I will be eternally grateful. Being able to talk personally to someone, who was affected by it himself and who was not as close as the family, was missing. It was not possible for me to go to a support group, as the distance was too great and the time unsuitable. Moreover, I did not dare go among strangers. That would have killed me. I think it is important at the beginning of the mourning to have the necessary space to talk about what happened. To be completely in focus. Not everyone is able to do this in a group at the beginning, because you might feel overwhelmed by the other deaths at first. You first have to understand yourself and your own situation. At least that is how I felt. I had missed the one-to-one conversation with the bereaved. Many of those affected, with whom I was in contact in the meantime, had also seen this as an option that was missing at the beginning of their grief.

Everyone I asked what would have helped them shortly after their loss, what was missing, had the same answer: "Someone who listened, someone who understood". And so the "first point of contact" was born. It is still "my baby" because it is a matter close to my heart. Some asociation members, including new members who found their way to us because of this, set up an area around their place of residence where they could act as "Sponsors". Depending on your own availabilities or the locality, this area is between 20 km and 50 km. It is sufficient to send an e-mail to info@treesofmemory-ev.de, and the sponsor responsibile for that region will react promptly and contact the person who made the request. Whether it should be an exchange of e-mails, a telephone call or a personal meeting is decided by the person who has sought contact with us. The districts are chosen by the sponsors themselves because we can "accommodate" the bereaved. This means that no matter whether the conversation takes place in a café or in their own living room, the sponsors will come to a place where those seeking help can feel safe and comfortable. Each sponsor offers to listen, to have a conversation and offer understanding which is so important.
We have put together further regional offers of help, which we can pass on as information. Be it the contact address of the nearest self-help group or addresses of therapists and counselling centres that can offer professional support. We can help you to get in touch with them if you wish. We would like

to accompany the first steps of a mourner until further help is found and taken, which is appropriate for each individual and their personal needs. We are not therapists and with the exception of two of our sponsors we are not bereavement counsellors. We ourselves are affected. We draw from our own experiences in order to spare others from some of their experiences or to better prepare them for the future and to show them that they are not alone with their misfortune. We can also encourage and show that there is help and there are contacts. It goes without saying that every conversation is treated confidentially. Not only does it help those who take advantage of our offer, it also helps us, because we feel that we can make a difference despite the gravity of our own situation. We can offer a bridge between powerlessness, because of what has happened, and help. We can help people in this way.

At first we were able to offer this support in eight regions, but now there are thirteen in Germany, in the north, west and south. We haven't any sponsors yet in eastern Germany.

At the same time as the "first contact points" we started outreach to the the wider world. Since it is important to make it known regionally that this support exists, we contacted the most diverse agencies and explained what we can offer. It is important to us to create a good network between all those who can offer help in any form. The more the various agencies and associations know about each other, and are in contact with each other, the greater the level of help and support for those who are affected. This also meant "becoming brave" for me again, because I had to make contact with people unknown to me, to open myself up more. Together our members worked out a presentation which we used to personally present our work in hospitals, counselling centres and other institutions.

Our public relations work is becoming increasingly diverse. Appearances at trade fairs help to make us visible and establish contacts with other bodies. We try to organise events in the different regions especially around the 10th of September, the International Day of Suicide Prevention. Besides the charity run, "Every kilometre counts", which can be held anywhere and by anyone, there are memorial services, lectures by medical specialists or a reading by an author, as well as an information stand where anyone interested can talk to us. Every single event requires energy. But it gives back much more.

All this would not be possible for us without our great and committed members, who contribute with their ideas and energy. People who see our work as important and valuable help us by getting involved in the organisation and the events. Without this help from outside, many things would not be possible. I am grateful with all my heart to every single person, whether a member or not, because it shows us that what we do is right. Through all our activities we try to break the taboo by bringing to the public's attention the subjects of depression, suicide and loss through suicide and giving a voice to those who are too powerless to speak for themselves.

In Germany almost 10,000 people every year commit suicide and about one in five people suffer from depression at least once in their lives and this is sufficient reason for making the public aware and reducing marginalisation.

In addition to helping those affected, we are now beginning to get more involved in suicide prevention. A big taboo still exists when it comes to depression, suicidal behaviour or suicide. We want to take away some of the fear people have of talking about it and show the possibilities for dealing with each other sensitively. Therefore we are currently working on lectures, or a teaching unit, which we want to offer especially to students. After that we are planning a workshop which can be offered especially to the police and emergency services. All this is time consuming and is made more difficult by the often large distances between us, so that we act within the bounds of what is possible and it sometimes takes a while before a project is complete and can be offered to the public.

Due to the circumstances of our lives, which are partly marked by the loss of a loved one, our own mental well-being is the main focus of attention. Not everyone always feels as strong or strong enough to get involved at the same time as someone else. Therefore, the following applies: Each person to do only what is possible for them, according to their own state of mind and their own resources. Tees of Memory e.V. offers me a good training ground, as I tend to push myself forward and overtax myself.

What I have learnt, or am still learning from working with the association, is to be careful in dealing with myself. Some things just take time. And may need it. Whether with myself, or in working out the many ideas that arise in the association. The association has personally helped me to find a meaning in my life again. And at the same time I have met many valuable people who enrich my life. The work has made me courageous and has let me grow. I am grateful for that. Despite the energy that I and all of us invest, it is not just giving. We receive something in return. Encouragement, support, input and gratitude. Sometimes even rejection, which is painful, but I am aware that this comes from fear of an unpleasant and unfamiliar subject, which many people do not want to think about or deal with. The big taboo...

What defines us is our diversity. Meanwhile Trees of Memory e.V. consists of 42 people. Every single one of them, as different as we are, is valuable because of the knowledge and skills of each person. Whether making suggestions, doing research in the background, making contacts, planning, presenting or as a member, which encourages and supports us through the membership fee, each individual counts and helps us to grow and prosper. I can only speak for myself, but some of us certainly feel the same way as I do, even if perhaps not with the same intensity.

Trees of Memory e.V. is something for me to grow with. Something worth fighting for and spending time and energy. A second family, in which I have found a place.

The suicide of a loved one makes grief very difficult. Besides the misery itself, feelings of guilt, a thousand questions about why and self-doubt arise. The way out of this is long, sometimes eternal. This makes it all the more important to find something for yourself that can give meaning to your own life again. Whether this is working with children, senior citizens, with animals or anything else fulfilling. It needs something you feel comfortable with. For me it is Trees of Memory e.V.

My son is never coming back. It hurts and will forever remain a terrible pain in my heart. It will always move me into a deep valley of tears. In the meantime there is this "but, still...". Nevertheless I can and may live on, changed as I am now. I can pass on what I have learned since then. A reader can find himself in our BLOG, in our thoughts and feelings. In spite of all that is broken in me, I can be a helping hand and confront my own powerlessness.

Since we finance ourselves only through membership fees and donations, and since we would like to continue to offer lectures and readings free of charge, even though our association incurs costs, we will continue to depend on the willingness of many to donate. Each one of us contributes voluntarily, invests time and sometimes our own financial means, which we let benefit the association. Incoming donations not only finance the tree planting of Mario's project. All our public relations work, whether flyers, maintenance of the website, purchase of necessary materials, fees, honoraria for readings, training for the sponsors of the first contact points and much more - all this is only possible with donations. We can only do what we have the financial means for. We would also like to produce a video, or a small film, that shows the problems of depressive, suicidal people and bereaved dependents. This has to be done professionally, so that we have to hope for the support of outsiders and donations in order to be able to finance it. This is a vision of the future that we keep in mind and hopefully will be able to fulfill one day.

The tree for my son Kevin, for Sandra and for my work colleague "Perle" was planted on Easter Saturday, 2019. The walnut tree is a community tree in remembrance of three wonderful young people whose strength was no longer sufficient to continue living. To watch the tree grow, to see the first leaves sprouting in spring and to visit it again and again gives me some peace inside. It makes me smile and shows me that many things can grow again. Not only the tree, but also the memories, happy moments from the past buried by grief. And I am growing.

Mario's project TREES of MEMORY (www.treesofmemory.com) and Trees of Memory e.V. (www.treesofmemory-ev.com) are both independent. They are interwoven and work together in parallel. Just as his project, his vision has grown in the meantime, so has our association. From a delicate plant to a small tree. We will all continue to grow.

No matter whether someone wants to become a silent member or wants to be active, we are always happy to grow and can use all the help we can get. Individuals, or companies, who would like to support us financially on a one-off or ongoing basis can help us to continue to implement our projects and to keep on generating new ideas. Every donation, no matter how small, helps, is important and valuable. Our association's activities can be followed via our website www.treesofmemory-ev.com as well as on Facebook on the page run jointly with Mario and his project.

Iris Pfister
Board Member and Treasurer of the Association

I need help

If you want to support my hike around the world, planting the trees and all the associated projects for suicide prevention, you have several options, all of which help me:

1. Monetary Donations via PayPal
Send a donation via PayPal, my virtual tip hat.
 Please use this link for this:
https://paypal.me/pools/c/8nBrpp8ytE

2. Usual Bank Transfer
If you would like to support TREES of MEMORY with a few Euros by bank transfer, the following bank account is available:
ING DiBa
Mario Dieringer
BIC: INGDDEFF
IBAN: EN63500105170831619540

3. Sponsorship
I am looking for compatible sponsors who not only see suicide in my project, but rather the message for life and the immense social and emotional support that all those who are involved in the project and in the association, can give to the numerous people who are affected.
I am happy to carry your brand message around the world on foot, in videos, in texts and on my website. Let's put our heads together and see what makes the most sense for us. Over the years I have generated millions of media contacts. That will not change in the future.

Of course I am also open to material sponsorship. For example, hiking boots are always needed.

4. Invitations

On my way around the world I am very grateful for every place to sleep, a hot soup, a warm shower or a little food for my dog Tyrion, who would also be a grateful sponsoring partner, by the way. Look on the website in the menu "Stations" to see if I am approaching your area. If so, send an e-mail to info@treesofmemory.com. I will get back to you as soon as possible or include your invitation on my route.

5. Create Awareness of this Book and of TREES of MEMORY

Without publicity, no one will know that the association exists, that this project exists and that there is a possibility to plant a tree in remembrance of a deceased person.

Without PR nobody would know about this book, the proceeds of which will go to TREES of MEMORY. Therefore I would be pleased if you would mention both in your social networks, post a photo of the book cover with a link to my website www.treesofmemory.com and tell your friends about it. Reviews on the online portals, where this book is available, are also a great help.

I and the association lack the financial means to employ marketing agencies. We implement every idea and task ourselves. Often to the limits of our time and physical capacities. Therefore we are grateful for every "good word" that is spread.

6. Help as a Social Media, PR or Sponsoring Specialist

If you are a social media marketing manager, PR consultant or a sponsoriong specialist.....

then its time to get to work ..... write an e-mail to info@treesofmemory.com and I will get back to you as soon as possible.

Social Networks

I would be very happy if you would connect with me via the social networks and accompany me virtually on my hike around the world.

Your Likes and your friendship will help people and companies who are considering the project Trees of Memory, to see it as relevant and we may get the chance of sponsorship. And even more importantly: those who are affected will find the project and can find new courage.

Facebook:
https://www.facebook.com/mario.dieringer

https://www.facebook.com/TreesofMemory/

Instagram
https://www.instagram.com/treesofmemory/

YouTube – daily videos from the hike in German and in English
https://www.youtube.com/channel/UCvM_KH22HGab73HeRmUKgxA

Polarsteps – follow my route
https://www.polarsteps.com/MarioDieringer/1557283-trees-of-memory-2018

Twitter
https://twitter.com/FootpathofLife

TikTok
https://www.tiktok.com/@treesofmemory

LinkedIn
https://www.linkedin.com/in/mariodieringer/

Rautie is a comic artist and painter. He is the creator of some timeless stick figures. His excellent comics have won many prestigious prizes. His paintings and illustrations are on tour in various exhibitions. He lives and works with his family in Hanau. Rautie is one of the most sought-after creative people with his recognisable style. He breathes new life into the traffic light figures which he created and turns facades into art objects.

In 2016 his son Valentin took his own life at the age of 14. His life has changed like a flipped light switch since then. There is a before and a now. In his paintings and comics the artist tries to process his grief. He describes his current, non-commercial works as communication with himself and as therapeutic confrontation.

Why did Rautie support this book?
"Mario has planted a tree of remembrance in Hanau for my son Valentin. We are united by the pain of suicide. That is why I immediately promised him my support for this book. Its chapters provide enough material to create a completely sketched novel. Therefore it was not difficult for me to find the right pictures to illustrate his inner dialogues."

www.rautie.de

Acknowledgements

At this point I would like to thank above all my friends Robert, Peter, Bernd, Davide, Marco, Hans, Thomas, Jordan, Luis, Glenn, Tasos, as well as my ex-husband Hubert, without whom I would not have got through the time after Jose's death and in all probability would not have survived. You were with me from that first moment, day and night, and helped me whenever you could. You made sure that I did not lose belief and found the strength to live again. Even if our lives have separated in two or three cases, you can be sure that you are always in my thoughts and that there is no thank you big enough to express what you have done for me. I love you all and I am grateful that you have been an unconditional part of my life for years and decades and that I don't have to phone or write every day because every time we see each other it will always be like yesterday.

A big thank you goes to the founding members of Trees of Memory e.V., Jutta Opiela, Iris Pfister, Sigrid Abel, Katja Heußel, Birgit Klaiß, Gunter Huhn, Vitus Irrgang, Walter Kohl, Robert Schmidt, Peter Scherer, Christian Kuschel, Alex Detig. Above all, I would like to thank Vitus, who was largely responsible for turning his proposal into an idea, from which a now successful non-profit organisation has emerged.
All your initiatives have honoured, touched and inspired me. In the meantime, you have all spoken to many people. You have helped many of those affected and bereaved dependants to survive the pain that suicide causes. You have given them a new perspective. Due to its members, the association has become a European association and is constantly growing. This is thanks to all of you.

The extremely hard work and the very constructive cooperation with many positive outcomes are the result of the board members Gunter Huhn, Mario Kelter and Iris Pfister. Vitus Irrgang and Sven König, who were both on the board, have also left their valuable marks and have touched and shaped all those involved with their own misfortune.
I am aware of how much work, thought and time you invest in this association almost daily. You sometimes go to your limits and far beyond. Sometimes it doesn't last forever and there are personal consequences. This is

understandable, it must be so and will certainly happen from time to time. I pay you my utmost respect, combined with my great thanks for your responsible attitude,. For all this there is hardly a thank you that would be fair to the cause. Look at the successes that you have achieved with nothing, without having had the possibility of a big financial investment. The present outcome is the result of your passion, your compassion and your will to make a difference.

I would also like to express my greatest and sincere thanks because you believed in me, even though none of you knew me before and you often wondered how this and that would work. My standard answer has often given you sleepless nights, that the universe will present me with a solution. You had no choice but to trust. You still trust and that is why you have an eternal place in my heart.

A very big thank you to the comic artist Rautie, without whose illustrations and cover the whole book would not have had as much spirit. All this was not drawn in five minutes and yet you immediately agreed and made it far more possible for me than I would ever have dared to dream. I thank you very much for that.

I don't have any money and I don't want to go begging to publishers, the horror scenario of editors who mean well and with whose help this book would surely be even a bit better, but all these people need time and have their own agenda and they would slow me down. I can't write lots of letters and requests and wait for months to be offered a book contract with many conditions attached to it. Any rejection would do me more psychological harm than it would help me.

I would also like to thank Fritz Bude, a passionate tinkerer, who works day and night on all kinds of equipment. He made a dream come true for me with the hiking cart he developed and built, which I had not even thought of as a realistic possibility. Without this hiking cart I would be lost and it enables me to be seen. For weeks you have been working on it to perfect it. My thanks will accompany you on every metre that we both travel and I hope very much that one day you will enjoy seeing your hiking cart in front of an exotic backdrop. Thank you very much. You are a great guy... And another thing: Without the hiking cart Tyrion would not exist. Without Tyrion I would be in a bad way. I'd be very bad.

Speaking of Tyrion: To all Facebook friends who were involved in getting and giving me the fur love of my life: You have enriched my life so much and made me incredibly happy with this little guy. I thank you.

A big thank you to the few who were allowed to read one or other chapter and gave me a few tips and supported me with their favourable opinion. That was important and helpful. Anita, of course you will get the well worn handkerchief packs back.

There are so many people on Facebook, Instagram, Twitter and Tiktok who have accompanied me since the beginning of Trees of Memory. People who read along and encourage me again and again. I thank you from the bottom of my heart for all your words, smilies, views and the encouraging words when I am down. Many thanks to all of you.

What would Trees of Memory be without those who are affected and the bereaved, for whose loved ones I was, and still am, allowed to plant a tree. I have accompanied many of you for days. We shared our grief and I hope that I could somehow give you courage. Sometimes I succeeded, sometimes unfortunately not yet. Everything takes time and I will always be there for you when you turn to me. Give yourself all the time in the world. Be brave to take the first step. Without your faith that I would actually come, I would not have come so far today. Even this book would not exist. Our exchange, your thoughts, your wisdom became a part of my belief and my new path. I thank you with all my heart for your trust in me.

I would also like to thank my family, Sabrina Mauro, Giulia Decuppertini, Beppe Decuppertini and Angela Debiagi. You are all I have and I am very grateful that you exist and that life, albeit late, has brought us together. If Papa hadn't died in an accident, I would certainly be living with you today in my beloved Bologna. But what is not, can still be. I will be very happy if in a year or two I can set out to hike to Bologna and from there explore metre by metre the most beautiful country in the world.

Last but not least, I would like to thank the wonderful Geoff Holingsworth for taking on the work of translating this book. It is truly a pleasure to work with you. We had a lot of fun, especially translating directly sayings that we use in German that don't make sense in English. „Fart dry - I think my pig is whistling - I only understand train station - my ass is on ground ice" are just a few examples. We laughed a lot. Thank you from the bottom of my heart, Geoff!

Finally, dear readers, I would like to thank you. By buying this book you have supported my project Trees of Memory and make sure that I can hike a few metres more. If you liked the book and if you could take something from it for yourself, then I would be very happy about a rating or feedback on Amazon, the social networks or personal at Info@treesofmemory.com.

If you feel like it and would like to hike with me for a few days, you are always welcome. I am happy to have companions and it is conceivable that we will discover new perspectives and possibilities together on our journeys through life, especially if you lost someone in the past.

Website mentalhealthbook

A few days ago I bought the url www.mental-health-book.com
On this platform, I would like soon to address and answer questions and videos on the topics of depression and suicidality.

Please take from time to time a look at the site and help me to make it an informative place for those affected and interested.

Thank you very much and all the best to you.
Take good care of yourself and stay healthy.

Yours
Mario Dieringer

Jai Sat Chit Anand

Awareness of Eternity is Bliss